"ANNOUNCING A NEW SCHOOL . . ."

"ANNOUNCING A NEW SCHOOL . . ."

A Personal Account of the Beginnings of The Sudbury Valley School

Daniel Greenberg

The Sudbury Valley School Press

PREFACE

I was involved with The Sudbury Valley School from the beginning. In the late Spring of 1969 I set down, in rough draft form, my recollections of the history of the school up to that time. Now, I have recast the earlier draft into its final form.

This book, though necessarily presenting my personal views on the matters discussed, does not deal with personal matters except in the few instances where they are essential to understanding institutional issues. My main concern is with the problems that confronted the people who set out to establish an educational institution as radically new as The Sudbury Valley School.

Those who would like to learn more about the educational philosophy of the school, or the detailed day to day workings of the school, should consult the various publications of The Sudbury Valley School Press. Those who would like to find out more about my personal philosophy of life, of nature, and of history, should turn to my book *Outline of a New Philosophy* (SVS Press, 1973). Those who would like to read about the early history of The Sudbury Valley School should proceed to the following pages.

Daniel Greenberg

Sudbury, Massachusetts
October 1972

Contents

To M. S. and T. E.

"ANNOUNCING A NEW SCHOOL . . ."

First Thoughts

It was clear just as soon as our first son, Michael, had been born (in December 1961) that eventually we were going to have to face the question of educating him and whatever other children we might have, and that we weren't going to be able to do it in the usual context of the schools that we were acquainted with. But the time seemed safely far off and we didn't give the matter serious thought during the first few years of Michael's life. It was during the period of 1963-65, when I had resigned from Columbia University's Physics Department and was freelancing – when we were in a state of flux and trying to redefine our whole attitude towards life – that we began to give a little more attention to the question of schooling for Michael, even though this was still several years off. Michael would become six years old in December of 1967, which didn't make the matter exactly a burning issue. We had absolutely no intention of sending him to any kind of a nursery school or kindergarten, because we weren't about to hasten the day when we'd have to make some kind of choice *vis-à-vis* his education.

Throughout these two years we were thinking and talking and looking around for schools. I remember having heard about O____'s school, and going down and visiting. It made quite an impression on me. I think it was in its first year of operation. I managed to get in to see O____ for a few minutes. It was sort of a disorganized outfit, located in lower Manhattan in a brownstone. One was struck immediately by the atmosphere of vivacious, happy children. There was no question about it. They were alert and alive and you felt it the second that you entered the building. I was so strongly impressed that I decided to offer my services, to volunteer to be a teacher at the school for no salary, just so that I could get to know first hand what this kind of an educational experience was like. I made it clear that I was ready to work in any capacity and do any kind of work, and that I wouldn't be asking for any pay. But he turned me down. He didn't answer for a long time, and then he turned me down because, as he put it, I didn't have any experience in elementary school education, and I didn't have a degree from a teachers' college. He added that if I was really interested in teaching little children, I should get a degree from a teachers' college and then come back and apply.

That was quite a shock to me. This was my first introduction the progressive-liberal-Summerhill-type school movement. And it came as a terrific shock. I didn't really fully understand the implications of this reception at the time; to what degree it showed that in these schools we were still dealing with an ordinary liberal-type establishment. At any rate, that plan for my future didn't work out, but somewhere in the back of our minds we thought that if we were still in New York we still might consider this a school for Michael. And another alternative that we toyed with all along was the possibility of keeping Michael home, which we didn't like from a social point of view, but we felt would be far preferable to paying the price of "socializing" him an ordinary school context.

Then we moved to Framingham, and started looking into all the schools listed by the Summerhill Society. We were still not at all wise to what was going on in these schools. We had had it in New York, and we dropped everything and moved out to Framingham, to a converted barn which we rented. It was a real find, a very lovely country-like cove hidden away amidst all sorts of building developments, off Route 9, not far from the Turnpike, quite accessible to Boston and to Cambridge, something like a forty-minute commute for Hanna to her work at MIT. There were six acres of land, lots of places for me to wander around. Of course by contrast to New York it was an absolutely unbelievable heaven. We knew nothing about the neighborhood, nothing about the town. As a matter of fact, when we decided to move into the town we had been warned away from it by the friends who had helped us find the house, because by contrast to Wayland where they lived, which was a "good" community, Framingham had a reputation for being terribly industrial and having an awful lot of working people… As it turned out, this was quite true, though hardly grounds for avoiding the town. Framingham has a remarkable cross section of all classes, religions and races.

The religious composition is about 65% Catholic, and 20% Jewish, and 15% Protestant, which you really wouldn't expect in a New England town and is certainly vastly different from the population distribution in other towns around it. When we moved I isolated myself completely. My total income was from free-lance writing and editing, and from commuting to New York during the first year to teach history of science at Columbia. Hanna worked every day, full time. That was the first year that we knew Mrs. Parra. She helped us raise Michael and Talya, and she very rapidly became an additional member of our family, which she has remained. The very intimate relationship between us had a lot to do with future developments, because her background was so different from ours, her training and outlook so different in so many ways, and yet the fact that she shared our basic philosophy of education and so much of our philosophy of life was a source of great reassurance to us. She was a pillar of strength through the years of forming the school, and ultimately became completely involved in the school as a staff member. It was enormously important for us to see somebody so different from us who could accept and embrace the same views on education. That was a great experience. It made raising Michael and Talya much easier of course, and it made our task much easier because it gave us a certain faith that what we were doing made sense.

For me, it was sort of "retirement" at the time. It was a turning inward, and there was much thought given at the time to the schooling of our children. We were only renting the house. We didn't have any feelings of permanency and we certainly didn't have any feelings of belonging to Framingham or Massachusetts at the time. I wrote away to many schools, got an incredible variety of answers; was surprised and shocked at H____, who wouldn't welcome us as prospective parents to visit his school even for one day of operation. Later on we visited the C____ School, which turned out to be just a sanctuary for pathetically lost children. More and more we despaired of ever finding a school for Michael and then later Talya. We were quite convinced at the time that if we found the right place, we wouldn't hesitate moving out there and either joining the school or making a living somehow and sending our children to the school. We had no hesitation in deciding that, but we couldn't find anything that sounded right. They all sounded so affected, so one-sided. They didn't sound anything like the kind of school for a democratically based society that we were interested in. And we began to wonder and worry about the future.

At that time the choice between isolation and turning inward and rearing the children ourselves, and between doing something more active, perhaps even starting a school – at that time this choice began presenting itself. This was given some impetus by a visit from my father during the fall of 1965. By then my parents were quite aware of the different views we had on education, the different way we were raising our children, which they quite disapproved of in principle. They liked the kids, and they thought they were coming out all right, despite our terrible ideas, but they certainly weren't very happy about the way we were doing it. And added to that, they had to put up with my constant criticism of the educational system and my constant pushing for more freedom of choice.

During the visit, I took a long walk with my father and I was expounding these things to him. He was listening and actually fighting me every inch of the way, when suddenly he said, "Why are you telling me this? Write it down. Don't just complain, write it down and see if you can get somebody to buy it. See if you can get somebody to act on it." This turned out to be a crucial challenge. I realized that he was right. That was the occasion for my writing down the very first outline of what such a school might look like. Appendix 1 reproduces this outline verbatim. I must admit that although I started at that time to think that perhaps writing down this outline might imply that I was going to have something to do with implementing it, I felt it was more by way of publicizing what I thought education ought to be, and that somebody else would surely pick it up and do it for me. The motive behind writing that paper was not primarily to draw a blueprint for a school that I was going to be involved in founding. The possibility was there, and it helped me think about it in a more immediate way, but the outline was still more of the nature of an abstract exercise.

The ambiguity I felt about my role, and yet at the same time the strength of my feeling and the degree of clarity of my conception, can be gauged from the following excerpt from a letter I wrote on December 21, 1965: "My main preoccupation is ever and again my (highly unoriginal, but still somewhat different from the others') conception of education, and of the 'ideal' type of school for this generation. So much seems to me to be wrong with our way of educating and the remedy seems so close at hand. I had an almost mystic experience a while ago – a 'revelation,' vivid and pictorial and detailed, of a great education center embodying all the principles so dear to me. I *saw* it, and still *see* it, complete to the last detail, people and all. And I am gradually converting this vision, or dream, to a practical written account. It will take some years to do well, but when it is done, the dream *will come true* – I know this."

And a little later, on April 15, 1966, I wrote: "As for me and education, which has become my central interest and will probably remain so: the reason I am not rolling up my sleeves and getting to work, as you suggest ('*Do* something! *Do* something!') is that I am convinced (1) that that would be *very* easy to do but (2) that it would not have the desired outcome. Let me explain. The era of the quick, amateur, enthusiastic, personally charismatic free school is coming to an end (even though such schools continue to be set up). Such institutions have served their very important purpose by calling serious attention to the problem and showing that one can take real steps to lick it. But we are now ready for the next step – one in which the educational system is based on carefully thought out philosophical principles that are *arguable* (not simply shoutable), testable, demonstratable, and suitable as the basis for a dialogue with the rest of the rational – but unconvinced – world. Careful groundwork is now for the first time possible, and the fruits of such groundwork will be a school which *has a chance* to affect (and interact with) the mainstream of education. Nothing is easier than setting up an esoteric retreat in the woods. The time has come to leave the woods and *communicate* with others, so that the benefits of a broad base can be realized.

"For this reason I personally am spending the next few years *thinking*, reading, and writing, and slowly gathering the insight, information, and strength for the major assault that *will be* made in due time. I can only hope that others will add their insight and wisdom to a truly cooperative effort. The results can be very exciting, and the liberated minds (or rather, the unfettered minds) of the students will be ample reward."

It was during that year of commuting to New York to teach history of science at Columbia that I met Sandy Rabison, who was taking the course. He had an extraordinarily sharp mind, a keen ability to analyze, and a great deal of charm. At the time he was also interested in reforming education. He would often talk about hoping to be part of a new school. He came to our home and became very close to the family; this close relationship continued into the next spring. Knowing him was a considerable influence on us toward getting involved in a school. We would have very long conversations on education, and these conversations helped clarify a lot of points. He was somebody to talk to at length, somebody who reacted. At the time, the most important thing was to get the ideas clear and to get up the resolve to go ahead and do it, and he was a tremendous help in getting the ideas clear. Not so much because he would introduce me to new ideas, but because he would subject my first formulations to a severe criticism and make me sharpen them and resharpen them until I was satisfied with them, and, usually, he was too.

It was during that spring that the possibility of actually starting a school came more and more to the surface of my consciousness. Knowing a person like Sandy now made it seem as if there might be people who might actually lend a hand in this enterprise. And when we talked about it, although still very gingerly, he was quite definite about being interested in helping.

It was during that spring that Sandy forced me into a major step forward in my own thinking. All along, I had been talking about education, and about the kind of school I thought one ought to have. But this talk was really out of context. I hadn't given that much thought to explaining why such a school would be appropriate in America, why it would be more appropriate than the kinds of schools we already have. I really had no answer for people who said, "Look, the schools on the whole work pretty well as far as society is concerned. How come you want to change them? Why are you running to replace something tried and tested?" I hadn't really formulated the role of the school in society.

And I also hadn't answered another question, one that Sandy pressed on me over and over again – namely, if this kind of school was right, why hadn't it come about? How had the wrong schools come about? He kept challenging me on this point. I would say, "I don't have to write a history of education. I don't have to figure out why the mistakes are here. All I'm interested in is trying to find the right thing." And he would keep coming back and saying, "You can't do that. You've got to come up with a theory that explains how the present state of affairs came about in order to make sense out of history and to explain why yours makes sense in the context of history. Because there must have been some set of causes that brought about this school system, and unless you know them and can show that they're no longer operative, you can't make a case for your system." He forced this objection on me more and more until I resolved to collect my scattered thoughts and start creating a historical system and a philosophical system, in which the school and these ideas on education and on life would make sense. It was a direct result of these conversations that I decided to draft a manuscript on education which would piece things together for the first time.

During the summer of 1966, *Education in Transition* was written. I worked very intensely on it and was able to produce something that was a theory of history, a theory of education, and a philosophy of education, as well as a blueprint for the school. The latter part of the manuscript, the blueprint, is Appendix 2. The manuscript as a whole was very consciously drawn up as a first draft. I did not expect ever to make a second draft in the normal sense of the term. I knew that this was my first attempt at putting together a coherent system of thought, and that I was going to do a great deal more thinking about it, until I would come up with a different and more integrated philosophy later on that would supersede the early draft. For this reason, I never had any doubt that I would not publish that manuscript, because I was not satisfied with it. Unfortunately, there is no mechanism for making public work in progress that you're really not satisfied with. So what I ended up doing was a halfway measure. I dittoed it – I must have made fifty or sixty copies of it – and distributed it to friends and acquaintances for reactions and critiques.

Now at least I had something to work with, some system to work with, something that made sense. I was able to see that I was on the way. The reactions that I received were very interesting. What the manuscript did was make it clear to everybody that I was really on the way to doing something different with my life. Until then people weren't convinced. My circulation of that manuscript finally convinced them. It had the effect of being the first instance where I started losing several of my old friends, when they came to their senses and realized that I really meant to do something different with my life. I remember several of my friends being terribly disturbed by it. Some of them suggested that I go immediately into psychoanalysis before I do anything. On the other hand, the reaction of other people was that here at last was a program that could serve as a basis for some kind of action.

The Decision to Act

The summer of 1966 was spent in writing the manuscript, and now we were in the fall of 1966. Michael was approaching his sixth birthday, and the whole question of his schooling began to take on a much more serious aspect. It also added to our increased tempo of thinking about our future that Hanna was having second thoughts about continuing to work at the laboratory, which largely had to do with her dissatisfaction with the kind of work that laboratory research was; so that she was seriously thinking of doing something different. I continued to be a completely free agent. Thus we were faced with the problem of a school for Michael and Talya, and the problem of our own future.

We had leased our house on an indefinite renewal basis, and at the time we leased it, it seemed we might be able to stay there as long as we wished. As it turned out, the owner decided to come back to the Framingham area. We were given notice of this intention in the fall of '66. Since the lease was automatically renewable on a annual basis, this meant that 1966-1967 would be our last year in the house. So we knew that we'd have to make a move during that year. Things really began getting hot for us.

For a long time we hadn't known anybody on our street. The day we first arrived – in September of 1965 – our next door neighbor Mal Stalker brought us a big basket of fresh vegetables from his garden, and that was our welcome to Framingham. It was really very touching. But we were very much inclined to keep to ourselves. We were there to get away from everything. I had a great fear of the suburban social set-up. I'd been brought up in that set-up as a child, and I just didn't want any part of it. I wanted to be alone. I wanted to be alone in the country. So we carefully avoided contact with our neighbors. We had very few contacts with other people there, except for occasional visitors from New York. I would commute to New York regularly, and Hanna would work regularly, so that there also wasn't that much time. I would walk a lot n the neighborhood, as part of my "retirement". People noticed that I was a "man of leisure". They were fascinated by that aspect of my existence. But basically we didn't get to any of our neighbors when we first came, and it was only after being there for months, during the spring of '66, that we began to get to open up to people in the neighborhood. For example, one neighbor had invited Hanna several times for tea, but I think it was not until the spring of 1966 that Hanna finally went.

Slowly we got to know the neighbors, and they got to know us. We got to know the Hiltons: Fred Hilton was at the time the Town Moderator of Framingham, by profession a lawyer with a Boston firm. We got to know the Ammermans: Harvey Ammerman was the pastor of the local Congregational Church, and his wife Timmy worked in the Veterans' Administration Hospital. We got to know the Johnsons: Dr. Bob Johnson, who became our family physician, and Dr. Lorna Johnson, his wife, who was also an M.D. and who did medical research. We also got to know their children, all of whom were of school age, although quite a bit older than Michael and Talya. And there were others.

I guess the first ones we came to know were the Stalkers. During the winter of 1965, Bonnie Stalker, who at the time was thirteen, was having trouble with algebra in school. Earlier, probably one of the few times that I would stop and talk a bit with a neighbor, I must have exchanged a few words with Mal Stalker, who would often be working out in his garden, and he found out that I was teaching at Columbia, and that I was a physicist. After that I was always "the professor" in the neighborhood. That winter, he asked me whether I would agree to tutor Bonnie in algebra. I decided that I would, and I don't know how much she learned, but she certainly managed to get through her algebra one way or another. In addition, her overall studies improved. I don't know how much time we spent talking about algebra. But we would chat about all sorts of things, and I think that having the ability to chat with somebody who took a more relaxed attitude towards the whole educational scene probably helped to relax her attitude towards school, made it a little easier for her to get through. The direct result of all this was that through Mal people got to know that I was an educator and that I was a "good teacher".

Another thing that made an impression was that I had lectured at Concord Academy the year before we moved up. The lecture was a roaring success; any good show was bound to be a roaring success with a hundred-odd caged-up adolescent girls. And word of that had gotten back to our neighbors. The point is that a little bit filtered back from here and there. The obvious fact that Columbia flew me back and forth from New York made an impression, my credential also made an impression, the fact that I was "successful" with Bonnie made an impression – it all was grist for the mill.

All these things contributed slowly to creating some sort of an image of us, in particular as educators. Gradually, we met many people through our neighbors. It was Molly Stalker who introduced us to Carolyn Low, a friend who taught school in a nearby town, and through Carolyn, to Priscilla Parris, who later became very much involved in founding the school. Through Molly and Carolyn, Hanna and then later I met Alan White, who at the time was Carolyn's principle at the Lilja elementary school in Natick, and who subsequently moved over to Acton to become Assistant Superintendent of Schools. He was quite open-minded about our views on education, and he entered into what we were doing at a fairly early stage of the game.

In general, conversations on education took place more and more as we got closer to people in the neighborhood. I remember talking to Harvey Ammerman about education at some length, and his telling us how his son David had been such a marvelous artist when he was a little child and how, when he was six years old, he was told by his teacher to fill in some print outline with certain colors, and he never picked up a crayon or a paintbrush since.

It turned out that Lorna Johnson was well acquainted with the Columbia Teachers' College progressive education bit, and we would often argue about the merits of the educational system. And the Hiltons were knowledgeable about problems of fitting all children into one uniform school system.

And then there was this fateful day, as all this was happening and as we were beginning to think about either going off to the woods and isolating ourselves or again making another desperate attempt to find some school somewhere in the world that would be satisfactory for our children, or perhaps trying to do something on our own – as all this was going on, there occurred a fateful conversation. It was in the fall of '66, and it took place in Lorna Johnson's breakfast room one afternoon when Hanna and I were there, along with Fred Hilton and Lorna. We were chatting about education, and Fred said, "You talk so much about these things – why don't you do something – start a school?"

And the idea was picked up with great enthusiasm by Lorna, who thought it would be a wonderful idea. I think she welcomed the opportunity of having such an experiment happen where she could see it and know the people who did it and somehow be associated with it. Not too long before, Lorna had bought the house next door to hers. So she had this big, empty house on her hands, and here we were talking about founding a school, and in her enthusiasm she said, "You can set up the school in the house." There was a tremendous surge of enthusiasm: we're going to found a school! In no time at all Fred was on the phone, speaking with the building inspector, asking him whether we could use the big house for a school. The inspector said yes, though there had to be some modifications made. We had to have a fireproof boiler room and enclosed staircases and so forth. So here we had a house offered, we had a plan, and all of a sudden everything fell into place. That's what we were going to do. We were going to start a school in Framingham.

Thus the die was cast, at least in one respect. The suggestion had come from Framingham people, not from us. It wasn't a foreign implant that we were bringing in. It had come from them. We were doing them and the community a service as well as ourselves a service for our own children and for our own ideas. And it was apparent right away that we would have the support of some other people in town. This included another neighbor, who was a good friend of Fred's and who we came to know fairly well: Bill Randall, a lawyer and a State Senator representing this district in the Commonwealth's Senate.

It was clear that the entire idea of starting a school could become a reality in Framingham, because we had the backing of members of the Framingham community. This is a terrifically important point. You just cannot start a school that's in any way different from the ongoing establishment unless you've got the backing within the community. You can't just walk in and start something – if you do, you'll be ridden out on the next rail. You've got to have somebody in the community behind you, and really behind you. If you have that, you've got the most important single factor you need in order to get started. We knew that and it was from that moment on that the idea of starting a school made sense. Before then, it was just senseless for us to go out and start a school in Framingham out of the blue; we wouldn't have gotten to first base. But to do it with the support of these neighbors – that made sense. And here we were, with an offer of a physical plant as well – it was just a miraculous occurrence that happened all of a sudden.

We immediately started thinking: who would be the people involved in the school? Where would we get a staff so that we could really announce that we'd got something, and start looking for students? After some thought, we realized that the following people were interested: the two of us, Margaret Parra, and Priscilla Parris. Then there was a very good likelihood that Sandy Robinson would come, since he was graduating at the end of the academic year and would be free to join, and he had often expressed eagerness to be part of a school. That made five people. And then at that time Steve Cooper came back from Guinea, after spending a year and a quarter in the Peace Corps. He wanted to go to Princeton, to study history of science. At the time, in the fall, he expressed his interest in the school, and his sympathy with our aims and the kind of institution we wanted. He realized that there might be a problem in light of the residence requirements for the degree at Princeton, but he talked a good deal about being at the school, and it seemed like we had a sixth prospect as a staff member.

It was really quite exciting. We already had, in the fall of '66, backing, a plant, and six probable staff members. The thing looked like it might actually happen.

Second Thoughts

It very soon developed that Lorna's house just wasn't going to work out. The balloon burst immediately, just like that. Now you see it, now you don't. That started us on an agonizing journey that was to last through a full year of terrible alternation and crises, during which we would be seeking for a way to have the school happen, seeking for a way to have a physical plant, seeking for a way to make it financially, and at the same time, in the course of encountering one disappointment after another, we'd be looking for ways to isolate ourselves in the woods somewhere, to run away and be left alone to live and raise our children our own way; terrific, intense alternation between going ahead and leaving it all.

That was a year of great inner turmoil for us. It's very difficult to describe how our hopes would be raised over and over again, and how they'd be dashed over and over again; how, each time, we had to go through the entire decision process again. Were we going to try and set up the school? Why don't we just give it up? Over and over again, what kept us going – and in this respect Hanna was much more consistent and persistent than I – was the constant gnawing thought that we've got to do it, we've got to do everything in our power to see it through, we've got to try; that we can't go away and isolate ourselves without having really tried right up to the limit of our powers. Because if we went away and didn't try it, we'd always have to live with the awful possibility that we were isolating ourselves, bringing up our children as loners in complete isolation and alienation from the world, when with just a little greater effort we might have transformed a reality that we didn't like into a reality that our children could be at home in.

Hanna was convinced, and I agreed with her, that we could never live with ourselves in the future if we did not give this venture every ounce of our strength; that the alternative of being off and alone was so unacceptable and such a last ditch resort that unless it really was a last ditch resort, unless we really had made every effort, if we retreated at too early a stage, then we'd always have to live with the terrible doubt that we had retreated too early – that had we only made a stand, had we only really tried we could have conquered the world and made the world a place fit for our children. So through all the intense alternation, through all the intense depression, this one consideration kept us going doggedly on.

In fact, we finally made it. So the consideration was correct. But many a time it looked mighty tempting to give up this terribly difficult, seemingly hopeless struggle, and go it alone. When I look back on it, I think that the thing that gave Hanna the strength to see us through this crisis was her earlier experience with her Ph.D. thesis. Five consecutive drafts of her thesis had been rejected for five completely different, contradictory reasons by the chairman of her department, after each one of the five had been approved by her sponsor and by other professors and lecturers in the department. She went through an agonizing year where the chairman simply would not let her get a Ph.D. no matter how many revisions she made, no matter how she changed her thesis. Often she was ready to forget the whole thing. I remember how, at one particularly bleak time, a good friend told her, "You've got to do everything you can to do it – not because the Ph.D. is that important in this world, but because if you've gotten this close and you don't do everything you can to get it then you'll have to live the rest of your life with the knowledge that you gave up at the last minute when you might have done just a little more and gotten it." It just wasn't right to give up, and that conversation was a turning point that gave her the strength. It was a beautiful piece of advice given just at the right time. She made it – with agony and with tears.

And the piece of advice that she got then, and the fact that it enabled her to see the Ph.D. through to successful conclusion, I'm sure gave her the insight and the strength to keep pushing for every possible avenue of seeing through the school. And she was right. Of course we always had the backing of people in Framingham, and we always knew that we had an embryo staff, but this did not lessen the tremendous difficulties in starting the enterprise, as I am now going to relate.

Then began the great search for a campus. The main consideration at the time was financial, and there was this basic problem hanging over our heads: where were we going to get the means to launch the school financially? I don't recall the exact details of our personal finances at the time, but I recall quite clearly that we had calculated that the absolute extreme of our financial capabilities was something of the order of fifty thousand dollars, and that we were ready to commit every cent of it to this enterprise. Now for some reason that I really can't fathom at all, in all our thinking at the time – and this went right through the summer – we were not considering the availability of mortgage money, but we were thinking all the time in terms of putting up every cent of the plant purchase price in cash. That's not to say that we weren't thinking about the possibility of raising some funds in addition to what we could lay our hands on directly; but I really don't know why we never thought in terms of a mortgage.

Even later, when we were in the process of negotiating for property, it was always cash that we thought about. It was extraordinarily naive. The availability of mortgage money is an essential feature of financing. I remember at one time Fred's saying that it may be a little difficult to raise mortgage money for a school, because banks don't like to lend money to schools, they don't like to have to foreclose, and schools are so often not solvent. He worried that we might not get a mortgage loan in a time of tight money. And there were times of tight money during the year at hand in particular. But somehow the possibility of getting a mortgage just didn't figure at the time in our calculations. So we were walking around at the time with the uppermost figure of fifty thousand dollars in our heads. That was it, that was stretching it to the limit. I don't recall what relation that figure had to our particular state of finances at the time, but it sticks in my mind as being the sum that we talked about, though we hoped to do it on something less.

So what we were looking for at the time – this was in the late fall of 1966 – was something that was going to cost us no more than fifty thousand dollars. Of course, we had a double problem that we had to bear in mind, namely we had to have a place to live and a campus. It was obvious that if we were talking about fifty thousand dollars, we were not going to be able to put up any funds that would enable us to have a home and a separate campus. It's just not enough. We were hoping to find a way to separate our personal living quarters from the school, but we were also bearing in mind all along that, because of the financial realities, we would probably have to live on campus or in the school building until we were out of the red. It wasn't a prospect that we liked, but of course any prospect was better than no school at all, so it was just one of those things that we lived with.

We started our search with every assistance that we could think of. We looked at all the newspapers and all of the home advertising media. And we went to realtor after realtor. We looked at the entire greater Framingham area. We had a particular introduction to two realtors, who play an interesting role in this story. One was Eleanor Calver, who was one of the first people with whom we went to out to look at property. In fact, Hanna went out with her and immediately drove right by the Grey Nuns' property on the corner of Winch and Millwood Streets – a magnificent granite building in a story-book setting. Eleanor pointed to it and said, "I wish you could buy this, but of course it belongs to the Grey Nuns and you know the church never sells anything." Hanna was just taken by its beauty. But Eleanor was driving her to see a house owned by a developer off Singletary Lane. It was a very beautiful house, but far too expensive. I was doing most of the looking at properties. Hanna was still working at the time, but she would take days off to do some of the searching also.

The second realtor to whom we had an introduction was the realtor that had found us our home in Framingham. The agent there, Harriet Crawford, had a knack for understanding what one wanted in a house, and for showing just exactly that. We went and talked with her. It happened that one of the partners in the firm was a friend of Mal Stalker's. It was important to have introductions, because what would happen was that we would go to a real estate agent, and he would show us things in an initial flurry of interest, and then the interest would drop off. Because it was a lot of work and there wasn't that much return for it. This happened to realtor after realtor. We saw a few more than the usual number with Harriet Crawford, and then she really just didn't have anything, although she had us in mind all along, as we found out later. The person who really put her heart into it and stuck with us for a solid year, and looked high and low for us, was Eleanor Calver. She just never, never gave up. She had the particular advantage of being a long time Framingham resident, of living on Edmands Road, in the northwest corner of Framingham, which was the only large area of Framingham that wasn't yet developed, of knowing everybody up there, and of having good information as to what might or might not be available.

One of the houses we saw that looked like a possibility was in Hopkinton, and it was on five acres and had a big beautiful barn and was a big house. There was even a little cottage on the grounds. It abutted a forest in which there were miles and miles of trails. The idea was to buy the house, to have some classrooms in the main building, and fix up the barn.

Actually, I don't really know what the idea was. We went out there, and somebody pulled out of a hat the notion that it would cost about ten thousand dollars to fix up the barn to make it passable, although I have no idea where that figure came from. Much consideration was given to the place. We didn't like the location, Hanna didn't like the house at all, I wasn't crazy about it, but I thought it was all right, I could see somehow making do with it. It was way out in Hopkinton, but it was being sold for fifty thousand dollars and we could probably have gotten it for a little less, and somehow it was within our price range.

We had gone through many long weeks where we hadn't seen anything at all, and at that time we were still thinking in terms of weeks and not months, and we were getting somewhat discouraged. That house was the first house that we really had to make some hard decisions about. It was finally decided that we wouldn't make a bid because we just didn't think we ought to go all the way out to Hopkinton. That seemed awfully far. It wasn't out of range for people who lived in Framingham, but it was certainly out of range for people who lived further in. At least if you were in Framingham you had this good central location and could call on a lot of other communities for your initial population, as in fact happened. So we ruled out Hopkinton, much to Hanna's delight. But there we were with nothing.

The house that Eleanor had shown Hanna, Lane's End, the former Folsom estate, was being put up for some eighty thousand dollars. That was the figure that was being talked about for the big house and for some land around it. As soon as Hanna heard the figure and as soon as Eleanor talked to her they both knew that it was completely out of range. So they didn't talk about it any more. We went on searching and searching, until finally we were very discouraged, nothing had come of anything. As each month passed, we were getting closer and closer to our eviction date. So I thought I'd take a chance and go with Eleanor Calver to see the place again. I hadn't seen it yet. It was beautiful, just beautiful – a huge, wooden mansion, built superbly.

Mal Stalker was another person who helped look. He has a realtor's license, and being a contractor of excellent quality, he knew quality places. There are few people who know more about the Framingham area than Mal does. So he would give us a tremendous amount of advice and help. Anytime we were really zeroing in on anything he would come with us and advise us closely. At any rate Mal knew this house and he knew this area, since he was the first contractor to open up the Salem End Road area.

He thought very highly of the house. It had three big wings, it had a swimming pool, it had a huge set of out-buildings. There was a lovely cottage, there was a big coach house with an upstairs loft, and there was another garage on the other side, with an attached one-room cottage. There was lots and lots of room, lots and lots of place for facilities. There was a tennis court. There was a lovely green. There was even a little brook running down on the side. The estate had been bought by a developer who had subdivided it all into half-acre building lots. There were main subdivisions which included an aggregate of building lots. One of these aggregates had seven lots on it and the big estate house, which formerly reigned supreme over the entire area. At the time, the developer was putting up for sale the main house together with all the other lots of the subdivision to which the main house belonged. It had already been laid out and approved by the planning board as an approved subdivision, and he could have subdivided and built houses on these other lots, and just kept a bare acre around the big house. But what he was putting up for sale was a total of some seven acres. I'm sure he thought that it would be much more attractive to a buyer to have some land around such a big house. It's really very unattractive to have such a monstrous mansion, with some twenty-four rooms and three wings, on just an acre.

He was asking ninety thousand dollars for the entire subdivision. I don't know why he put it up, and in light of the future developments I don't think he knew why he put it up, but that particular time, the winter of '66-'67, was one of the tightest money periods of recent times. There was just about no possibility of getting loans, and interest rates were soaring on those loans that you could get. Of course in retrospect one can laugh, because rates were much lower than they are now. But there just wasn't money, and I think he must have been in a pinch for cash. He wanted to raise ninety thousand and raise it fast, because it certainly seemed as if he was interested in selling. There's also no doubt that he could have made more money, ultimately, by going through with the subdivision and selling the individual homes and getting any price at all on the main house. But he must have been eager for money at the time. So it was during that winter period that we came up and looked at the house.

We came up with Fred Hilton and he brought along an architect friend who had done a lot of school architecture, who looked over the building very carefully. Then we asked the building inspector and the fire chief to look over the building as well. They gave us their recommendations, which amounted to about ten thousand dollars' worth of work into the building, but this time the figure was not pulled out of a hat. This time the figure was drawn up in conjunction with Mal Stalker. The idea was that we would buy the building and the developer would do the work as part of the purchase price. This was a hard time for us, because the price was certainly well in excess of the kind of funds that we had available in any form at the time. I remember offering seventy-five or eighty and we finally agreed on a price – it must have been about eighty-five thousand dollars.

I was still thinking in terms of putting it all up in cash, and I knew we'd need some more money to start the school going, as seed money to outfit it; it was really some question as to where we'd get the money. By then our assets had increased because of some favorable turn of events in our investments, and we had been able to receive promise of a loan of some twenty thousand dollars from my father, and I think we were also planning to borrow some money from other people. Somehow, even without a mortgage – we were still talking without a mortgage – by stretching everything to its uttermost limits and really laying everything on the line twice over, we saw our way to making a concrete offer on that property.

Always in the back of our minds was the knowledge that if we had to go out and raise money to pay off debts, we were both employable. Hanna could work in industry and get a good salary, and I could go work in the academic world somewhere and get a good salary, and we'd always be able to pay off debts eventually. So that helped keep us from total despair, although we certainly didn't relish the thought of doing it that way. It was at that time that the first thoughts of a mortgage came in, and we realized that if we could raise some mortgage money then that would help. So we made the offer, and it was accepted orally, and then papers had to be drawn up.

At the time, Fred Hilton was doing most of our legal work. Fred preferred to move slowly and deliberately; he had the philosophy that if a business deal can't sustain itself over a certain waiting period, if there's a rush aspect to it, then it had better not be made. If it's a good deal it'll be a good deal a month from now for both sides, and if it won't be a good deal for both sides then, it shouldn't be done now. He's not the type to go rushing out and quickly close a deal on a momentary advantage and think that any real good will come out of that. He isn't the type temperamentally, and I don't think he believes in doing things like that philosophically.

Now there were lots of different subsidiary clauses to put into the purchase agreement when it came to actually writing it up. One had to provide that the sale would be good only if we got zoning approval – I'll go into that in a moment – and only if we got a final go ahead from the building inspector, and only subject to this improvement and that improvement and so forth. There was a considerable legal document to draw up, as well as the ordinary bill of sale and deed. All this would take time under any circumstance, but it was even more delayed than usual because of Fred's reluctance to push it, and the reluctance of the developer to consummate the sale. He knew full well that he could do better if he'd wait.

He didn't really want to sell the building, but I think he wanted the money. So he was undergoing a struggle, and unless somebody aggressively pushed him and pushed the papers under his nose he wasn't going to rush to sell; and Fred wasn't going to be pushy. So everything moved at a snail's pace, and week followed week. There were times when we didn't hear a word from anybody and I would be climbing the walls with anxiety. Sure enough, when finally the first papers began to be drawn, the developer announced that he was not going to go through with the deal.

He had not committed himself in writing, and the whole thing was off. He gave as his excuse that he was afraid of the neighbors. There had been a big furor in that area because some other contractor had wanted to put up apartment buildings. The whole neighborhood had gotten together against it and had gotten the Town Meeting to turn down a zoning proposition that would have allowed it. So the neighborhood was in a state of agitation about what was going on. He said he was afraid it would ruin the salability of his other houses to have a school in the area. We insisted that it would improve it to have a good private school in the area, but nevertheless he claimed he was very uneasy, and anyway I think that the real reason was that money had loosened very much in the interval over these months. I think he had funds, and he was no longer pressed to sell at a disadvantage to himself. Whatever the real reasons, the deal fell through, and it was now well into the spring, and things at that time looked absolutely bleak.

I would like to say a word here about the zoning question. At the time there was some question as to whether we needed some special dispensation from the Zoning Board of Appeals or from the Town Meeting to open a school in a residential area. There was some ambiguity in the by-laws. The point was really very simple. At one time the by-laws read that you could have schools, any schools, in a residential district. Then the by-laws were changed in 1963 to read that you could have public schools in a residential area. Apparently, the main reason for that change was that lots of people were starting private nurseries and kindergartens for profit on small plots of land that they had bought for private homes. They would crowd in lots of kids and it would make a terrible noise and uproar and it would bother the neighbors. So there was quite a bit of pressure to make it impossible to start that kind of an operation in a residential neighborhood. That's why the by-laws were changed.

Now whether this affected our school, which was not a profit making institution in the first place, and not just a nursery-kindergarten, wasn't clear. It did seem to Fred that we fell under the category of public schools, because there had been decisions made in higher courts throughout the Commonwealth that ordinary schools open to the public, even if they weren't non-profit, if they were bona fide operations open to the public were qualified to be called "public schools". The phrase didn't just mean tax supported schools, according to these precedent-setting decisions in the courts.

So there was a certain question involved here, and when the Town Counsel was asked his opinion, apparently he didn't want to venture an opinion. Fred was Town Moderator, so he didn't represent us in the town; but Sheridan and Randall, Bill Randall's firm, represented us in the town. They asked the Zoning Board of Appeals for an off-the-record ruling that the Zoning Board didn't have jurisdiction in this at all, that we don't even have to come to them since we obviously fall under the exemption. But the Board wouldn't do that. It's not that they turned us down, but they insisted on at least hearing the arguments before ruling on whether or not they had jurisdiction. So it looked at the time as if we'd have to go to the Zoning Board of Appeals, and we couldn't really go to the Zoning Board of Appeals until we had a purchase agreement drawn up. All in all, the whole thing was very much up in the air until much later. I'll recount in due course how it came down out of the air.

Here we were, well into the spring of 1967, utterly despairing of finding a property, all the time looking and looking. One day, I went up to Mal Stalker's house to complain about my bitter lot in the world, and there was Mal Stalker's friend, Bo Swett, who was a partner in the realty firm where Harriet Crawford worked. He just happened to be sitting in the kitchen drinking coffee, and I sat down and let off steam; at which Bo said, "what a shame that you've already bought this other place for your school and for yourselves, because just the other day we got a listing that Harriet Crawford said was just the right place for you." I'm sure they had heard that we had bought the place through Mal Stalker, when it had looked like the deal had been consummated, and Mal probably had not brought them up to date that it had fallen through. I turned to him and said, "The deal just fell through. Show us this place right away."

So out we went; Hanna and I went with Harriet Crawford that very day to Sudbury and saw the house at 171 Dutton Road. There was nobody there at the time. We drove in and I decided on the spot to buy it. This was going to be our house, regardless of what the fate of the school was going to be. When I look back on it, I don't know what went through my mind. I know that by then I had become much wiser about obtaining a mortgage. At least I knew I could obtain a good mortgage on a private home. I still wasn't sure about the status of the school. This was simply the kind of home setting that I wanted. It was one of the most beautiful areas in the whole region. The house had the kind of location and isolation well off the road, surrounded by trails and extensive woods, which made the barn in Framingham look as if it was in the middle of Manhattan.

I must have had in the back of my mind the idea that this could, in a pinch, at least in the beginning serve as the location for the school. I had only heard rumors of a covenant ruling that out, and I wasn't sure that this just might not be ignored or broken. There was the feeling that if we didn't find anything else by the time we were ready to open, we at least could open here, because there were ten acres, and that was ample land. At least this offered the opportunity of getting started, and it certainly offered us an ideal location to live.

We immediately bought the house with the agreement that we'd move in in September, as we did. That took the pressure off as far as our private living quarters were concerned. At least we knew where we were going to live. It was in Sudbury, not Framingham, but it was nearby. All of our friends in Framingham would still be near us. At least now we had a base. We could now go on searching with a little more of a grace period. We didn't have to find a combined school-home property within the next couple of months.

On the other hand, realistically speaking, we still didn't have a school campus. But I guess when we finally signed the papers on the house, it at least removed some of the pressure from our decision making. As far as Michael's age was concerned, the compulsory attendance laws of the state of Massachusetts required a child to start attending school at the age of seven, so it gave us a whole extra year. The pressure on us was to have school start, as far as we personally were concerned, not in September of '67, but in September of '68. That gave us a whole extra year to find property for the school. As it turned out, we needed that year. We needed every bit of that year. It came in very handy, and finding the house in Sudbury did solve our problems exactly as we had thought it would.

All through the spring of 1967 and through the summer we looked at land. Virtually always it was with Eleanor Calver. We looked at piece after piece. The next good prospect that came along was the M______ land, which was beautiful. There were some hundred acres, twenty of which were swamp land. It had been put up for sale in toto, for about two thousand dollars an acre. Of course this was completely out of sight as far as we were concerned. It was just land, no facilities, no water, no road. We'd have to build, and it just didn't even enter our heads to be able to purchase it outright in any way; but at least there was a lead here, and there might be the possibility, through negotiation, of either getting a piece of the land, or buying the land on option, or buying the land on a deferred payment basis over a number of years in a way that would enable us to make it with the cash we had in hand. We made all sorts of combinations of offers. M______ insisted that he wasn't going to sell a part of the land under any circumstances. That too fell through most unexpectedly when we found out that he had turned around and sold ten acres to his neighbor, presumably using the leverage of our offer. I guess the twenty-odd thousand dollars he raised that way was enough to hold him over; he really didn't want to sell it, so he kept the rest and took it off the market, at least for the time being.

Thus we had disappointment after disappointment. At the same time we were working with other alternatives and other options. One of the ideas that had come into our heads at the time is worth mentioning, because it involved a classic method of solving a problem, by creating an even bigger problem and solving the bigger problem, of which the original problem is a component. In that spring of '67 we thought very seriously of the possibility of buying a large section of the northwest corner of Framingham, of financing the purchase in the usual way, and of developing the entire area according to some advanced principles of town planning. In other words, developing a whole section of Framingham on our own, with buildings and homes and shopping centers and so forth, and with a small piece reserved for the school. We would have our school site worked into it, and in fact the school site would be integrally linked into the community so that it would eventually serve as the school for that community.

We did a great deal of work on this subject. The financial side of it involved connections through W______, a large real estate investor. We made many tentative offers. We let quite a few people in on this planning. I told Fred about it; of course, he wasn't too keen on it. He was much more interested in getting a school started and thought it would divert us from the school. One would also have to go to the Town Meeting and get considerable changes in the zoning law. It would have been quite a political campaign to achieve that. We talked about it at some length with Alan White, who knew the trade of homebuilding, knew quite a bit about contracting, and was interested in this type of thing.

Through him we met R______, an architect who was a political figure in Framingham. We got maps of the area, knew all the pieces of land we'd have to buy and piece together in order to make this a reasonable purchase, and approached owner after owner. Eleanor Calver was involved in the entire thing from beginning to end. She was the only agent involved. At one time the M______ land was one piece of the entire thing. We knew that this area would sell out very quickly, because land was getting dearer by the day in the whole region between Route 495 and Route 128, especially due west of Boston where you had such magnificent arteries as the Massachusetts Turnpike and Route 9 and then other subsidiary arteries like Route 20, Route 30, Route 135 as east-west links. Several major industries have moved in along 495, and it's going to look like 128 in a very short time.

All this was quite clear to us, and what we had hoped to do by way of developing was to take over a sizable area, at least five hundred acres, and develop a modern community in it. We had certain very specific ideas about our area. For example, we wanted it to be completely safe; we were thinking of having sunken roadways that would perhaps even be completely underground, so that the whole area could be safe for pedestrians. We were thinking of saving large areas as woods and park land, and of arranging homes and apartment buildings in such a way as to preserve most of the natural beauty. We were thinking of other things: of having it as a model for the very latest potential in communications, even at a certain loss, of getting companies like Honeywell and IBM involved in building automated homes to the degree to which it might be practicable now, where you'd have a tremendous amount of individualized computer programs to help each home owner so that much of the kitchen and much of the laundry work, much of the routine shopping and so forth could be computerized.

We knew that a pilot plan of this sort would be very expensive and not quite practical, but we were hoping that if we could get the land, and the vision to do it, and the zoning, and the financial backing, that we could also get the interest of these companies in proving that they could in fact make the next leap in home management. All of these considerations were involved in our plan. We had an open mind about the details, but we knew that we wanted something that would be a real step forward in home design and community design, in the sense that it would take advantage of many of the features of the information and communications revolution.

I can't say that I've abandoned this dream, but I can't say that I have any real intentions of realizing it. We shelved it when repeated offers to landowners just brought negative replies over and over again. We just couldn't put together the land. It was shelved some time in the summer of 1967. But in a sense it's only been tabled. The idea is still alive. If anything, it gets riper with time. I think that the ability to construct such a community would go a long way towards making evident to even casual observers the kinds of incredible new opportunities for everyday living that are available now. True, it's pretty evident that all these things are available anyway, even in the ordinary home. But if you actually went to the limits of the technology in a model situation, the contrast with living a generation or two ago would be even more striking than it is now, and probably would make a lot of the things we're saying even easier to comprehend.

So it's been tabled, but should the opportunity arise to buy a large piece of land around the northwest corner of Framingham, it might be taken off the table, especially if the school is the kind of success that we expect it to be. The development of that kind of a new town would go beautifully, hand in hand, with the development of a great school, because the education and the way of life would complement each other even more smoothly than they do in the Framingham of today.

Going Public

Other things were happening in the spring and summer of 1967 that slowly prepared the ground for the school. We were drawing up our first list of contacts for the school. We were busy meeting people. Starting in February, I believe, and extending through May, I drafted the first public prospectus announcing the school. It underwent something like seven revisions, and was finally typed on an IBM Executive typewriter by Priscilla, justified on the right hand margin, photo-offset, and folded to a size that fit into a No. 2 envelope. The title of the prospectus was ***Announcing a new school in the Framingham-Sudbury Area***. The first draft and final form are both in Appendix 3. We didn't even have a name for the school. We certainly didn't have a location for it, but we went ahead and announced the school and wrote out what the principles of the school were, and gave our first public indication of what it was we were about.

That brochure appeared in the first week of June, and throughout the month of June and in the succeeding month we mailed and distributed hundreds of them. I think all told we distributed something like five hundred, and kept track of who got them. We gave them out all around so that as many people as possible could know what we were doing. That began our first formal public relations drive to make our existence known and to make our aims known in the community with the aim of getting students.

Something that has to be borne in mind, because it set the tone for our relations with the public right through to the actual opening of the school, is that what we were doing was looking for students. We were determined to provide a physical plant one way or another, we had our staff, we had our backing; the one thing that was lacking was students, and in order to get the school going we needed students. We had a new idea in education, a new kind of school, and we needed students for it.

The point is that even though there was involved in this an exposition of our educational system, our primary goal during this entire period was not to assert ourselves as an educational institution and make a place for ourselves and actually convert the educational framework of the country to our way of doing it – that was not our aim. We couldn't assert ourselves as an educational institution because we didn't have an educational institution. All we had was an idea. Our primary aim was to create an education institution, first and foremost, and what we needed for that was students.

Once we created the institution, built it, gave it vigorous foundation, and assured its success, then we would have a product, so to speak – then we would have not only an idea but a reality. With the reality as well as the idea we could then go on to make our onslaught on the whole educational system. But it was quite clear from the very beginning that, in the order of priorities, we were first of all after students. In order to find students, our program had to be known, and we had to somehow get to the parents who were interested and willing to try this kind of an educational venture. There was no way to know in advance who these parents would be, so we just had to use a broadside, shotgun approach, and we would use every technique and every contact we possibly could dredge up in order to get ourselves known.

This stance of having to solicit for students left quite an imprint on the beginning of our entire operation. It's one thing to solicit for students. It's quite another thing to have something in hand and fight to remold the entire educational framework after this pattern. It's pretty obvious that any new institution has to go through these stages – has to go through the stage of being conceived initially, the stage of getting its first adherents to make a reality, and only later to the stage of taking the idea and the reality and trying to make its imprint on the society at large.

The first brochure contained the name of other staff members. During the spring of 1967, Ina Cooper, Steve Cooper's sister, decided to join the staff. Soon after, David Chanoff joined. He had been quite skeptical of these educational ideas, but discussions and personal experiences apparently moved him towards this conception of education. The ninth staff member was Dennis Flynn. As I recall it, he had first decided to join the staff on New Year's Eve of 1966 when we were in New York at his apartment; but it was a while before this decision became actual. There were nine staff members listed in the brochure. We had not had any staff meetings before the summer of 1967, but we had several meetings individually and in small groups, and we all knew in what direction we were headed. The spring of 1967 also saw a cooling of personal relations between us and Steve, Sandy, and Ina, which was to have repercussions for the school later on. But for the time being they remained on the staff.

Already in the spring of 1967 there was a lot of social activity, and a lot of public relations, going on for the school. I gave, however, only one talk about the school – I was later to give many – and that was arranged by Alan White for the Parent Teacher Association of the Lilja Elementary School in Natick. That was my first practice run as a public speaker on behalf of the school. It was quite an evening. There was an intense, heated debate, and I presented my ideas more or less as they were outlined in my draft manuscript.

The talk was greeted with general skepticism, although some people were quite excited by it. Many of the teachers were outraged, and I got my first taste of the kind of reception I could expect from those engaged in the educational system today. Of course it was to be anticipated that people who had a stake in perpetuating the present system weren't exactly going to like to see it challenged.

I myself was very harsh, I guess. In retrospect I can say that probably as a result of not having a school, and as a result of soliciting and trying to push something and trying to get students – as a result of all these factors, and a lack of self-confidence as well, I was probably over-aggressive in this talk. It certainly was a strong experience for all of the parties concerned, and it was a good show all in all, but somewhat later Alan very gently told me that I shouldn't come on so harshly. I should be a little more mellow, and that would go a long way towards reducing the hostility that I would inevitably raise in audiences when introducing such radical ideas.

There was another group of events that occurred all through this period that are worth mentioning. I was a member of the Conference on Science, Philosophy and Religion sponsored by the Jewish Theological Seminary. My father had been a member pretty much since its founding, around 1940. In the early sixties things began to bog down with the original group, and they felt that it was time to bring in new blood, and so a new, younger generation was invited to join. I was gradually invited to several sessions and I guess as an *enfant terrible* I made a hit or something.

In 1963 Dr. Louis Finkelstein, Chancellor of the Seminary and director of the Conference, invited me to take over some administrative responsibilities in the Conference, and I pretty much agreed to do it. Just then my publishing ventures went up in smoke, and that made me so thoroughly reassess the direction of my life that I pulled out of any active role in the Conference except as a participant. I used to go on Monday nights to seminars, and I met a great many people – that was the marvelous thing about the Conference. It was probably the first serious interdisciplinary continuing seminar in the academic world in this country. It took a great deal of vision on the part of Louis Finkelstein to organize it. Aside from any other achievements that it may have had, it brought people together from widely varying fields. I certainly met a lot of people there from different academic fields, and different realms of life. These contacts were very useful to me, both for sharing ideas and also for the connections that they made in the educational and academic world.

In August 1966 there was a Conference held in Chicago on "education for character", and I was one of the participants, in fact one of the invited paper writers. By then I had completed all but Part III of my draft manuscript on education, and I completed Part III when I came back from the conference. During this conference Dr. Finkelstein approached me to discuss the possibility of my somehow being involved in setting up a college for the Jewish Theological Seminary. Of course it was very flattering, but I told him I was in retirement at the time and not intending to come out of it in order to go into the academic world. I also pointed out to him that my ideas on education were rather radical and didn't fit into the ongoing scheme of things. I think he sort of intuited that I would have different ideas, and I think that this was something that he was looking for.

I told him that I really didn't want to discuss the matter any further until I had shown him my manuscript on education, and some of the other things I had written, so that he'd get some idea of how I think on these questions, and that even though this was a very rough manuscript and something that I wasn't satisfied with, I'd let him see it so that he'd know my thinking. I really didn't expect that he'd want to discuss the matter any further once he'd seen these various writings. So in the fall, I gave him the manuscripts, and shortly thereafter he read them and communicated with me and asked me to come down and talk with him. We had several long conversations, and he expressed much interest in a school set up along the lines envisioned there, with some suitable modifications for it's being associated with the Jewish Theological Seminary.

I mention all this because it had a continuing influence on things, which I will explain even though it goes beyond the particular chronological period that I'm discussing. At the time I turned down his offers; I felt that I wasn't ready to go to New York or to leave Massachusetts. We were already talking in terms of our own school and I felt all along that it was very important to have an elementary and high school – more so even than a college.

But the importance of these events was in the tremendous encouragement it gave me to have that kind of interest from a person like Dr. Finkelstein. It's very difficult to overestimate the effect of this. He was an outsider, a man of tremendous intellectual and moral achievement, and for him to cast a sympathetic eye on this project was terribly important to me. It gave me the feeling that there must be something of value in what we were doing that would be evident to other people of vision outside. I never doubted that what we were doing was of value, but the question was whether anybody would ever see it or whether I would have the fate that Tolstoy had. One of the most incredible sentences in Tolstoy's writing on education is where he ends his essays by saying that probably his ideas won't come to fruition for another hundred years. He wrote this in the 1860's, and described very similar educational principles to the ones we were espousing; and here it was, about a hundred years later, and we were putting them into practice! I often wondered whether the kinds of things we were doing wouldn't have to wait another generation or another hundred years. There was really no way of knowing.

But these early reactions on the part of Dr. Finkelstein were certainly a tremendous shot in the arm. He asked me to direct the next Conference on education and that it be built around the ideas that had been espoused in my draft manuscript in order for people to be exposed to these ideas and in order for us to generate some feedback as to how establishment people would react to this type of approach to education. Not that I had any doubt what their reactions would be, but it seemed to be a good idea to air their views on these problems and to get their reactions to various proposed solutions. So I went ahead; but although the program somehow did reflect the kinds of questions I was asking, and was intended to provide a platform for many of the answers, it turned out that the actual planning of the Conference took a different course.

I remember making a couple of speeches at that Conference. I was struck by the incredible lack of sensitivity of many of these educators to the tremendous crisis that education was in. They were so oblivious to it. I made a rather impassioned speech likening them to a group of French royalist ministers debating some fine points while the Bastille was being burned down. It got everybody quite excited; but that was the end of it.

At a later session, when a model school similar to Sudbury Valley was being discussed, I said rather heatedly that the participants shouldn't "bother...discussing whether [they] should or shouldn't foot the bill. I mean save the trouble! Don't worry about it! Don't foot it! Don't argue about it! The school will be built whatever we talk about here. It's going to be built and it's going to succeed. Don't waste your breath discussing whether or not society should foot the bill because the point of the paper is that it will. Therefore, if you want to discuss it at all, which is, of course, the option of the discussants, discuss whether we want to be the group that registers our consensus that we *want* to foot the bill and *want* to be in on the ground floor, in which case we have the lucky chance of going down in history." Such impassioned words had little practical value, however.

During the fall of 1968 I was chairman of a Commission to Study the Organization of a College and Postgraduate School set up by the Trustees of the Jewish Theological Seminary in the spring of 1968. That Commission consisted of a number of people whom I knew. It held several discussions and produced a report that I drafted. By this time, however, it had become clear that the Seminary would not be able to take such a radical step.

In the late summer of 1967, Hanna and the children went to Israel for quite a long while, and I joined them at the end of the summer for something over two weeks after I moved all our effects on August 31 from Framingham to the new house in Sudbury. We were all to return on September 19. All of our belongings had been piled into one room in the house, so that the former owners could live there until we returned, because they were building another house and were going to move out at the last minute. The summer was sort of a quiet period. We arranged to have two important functions very soon after we came back because we knew that we couldn't afford to waste any time.

We arranged a meeting of the nine staff members on the afternoon of Sunday, September 22, and on the same evening a meeting of staff members and other interested parties, including people who were going to be visiting teachers in the school or who perhaps would contribute somehow to the building of the school, perhaps as potential parents. That was to be a general meeting at which all these people would get together, and we felt such a meeting was very important to have in September so that we could get moving. We made all the phone calls and all the invitations before leaving.

This is where we stood at the close of the summer of '67: we had a published prospectus of the school, no name, no campus, and no idea where the campus would be; we had no students signed up at all; we were not a legal entity yet; we were committed to putting the school up – the prospectus made that clear – but we were not yet legally on our way or even realistically on our way, except that we had nine staff members, three of whom had already had a serious personal difference with us. I guess you can say that we were on our way towards the realization of the idea, but that all the concrete work still had to be done. By the end of the summer of '67 we were certainly talking in a very definite way about the school, but we couldn't point to any concrete items as parts of that school.

A Campus and a Name

Immediately on our return from Israel we launched into vigorous activity on behalf of the school. We had two days to haul the furniture and our belongings out of the living room and to make enough order in the house to allow us to have some sort of functions in it on Sunday the 22nd. During that Sunday we had our first staff meeting, as arranged, and I must confess that I don't remember too much of what went on there. In fact I can't recall that any particular issues were discussed. I don't remember anything specific that was said except for an outline of what had to be done.

The meeting that evening I remember a little better. There must have been about thirty-five people there in our living room. We taped it and we still own that tape. I gave a little talk about our hope and our expectations and where we stood and where we hoped to go. The staff was there, as well as other interested people. There was a question period, and questions were asked, and discussed. There was a fairly good atmosphere in the place. I don't know that we came away with the idea that we were going to get very much assistance from the people present, but at least we were widening the group of people who knew that we intended to go ahead, and there was the usual general expression of good will and "yes, we'll pitch in and help" that accompanies that kind of thing – an initial here-we-go session. It certainly gave us the feeling, subjectively, that we were even more on our way because lots of other people now, who were in various places in the community, knew about our going ahead. We also made it clear that we were interested in speaking at different places and in making our program known so that we could get off the ground.

The period between September 22, 1967 and July 1, 1968 lay the groundwork for realization of the ideas. It was really a very short period, and into that time an enormous amount of activity was packed in many different areas. Rather than present a chronological account, I'm going to discuss certain features of the school one by one, and relate how they were tackled during that period.

The most pressing problem was that of a campus. We continued looking at every available acre of property in detail, and we were getting more and more desperate, there's no question about that. I remember looking quite seriously at a house on Winch Street, which was by any standard an undesirable location for a school, whatever its merits as a home. It was on the market for about sixty or seventy thousand; we actually offered fifty thousand for it, which was rejected and led to nowhere.

We negotiated with a person who owned a hundred acres in the same neighborhood, and we discussed with him the possibility of buying part of his land. We found out that he was intending to keep virtually all of it to develop at a later time, which of course was the sensible thing to do. We did manage to get him to offer us one lot in one place which wasn't big enough, just an acre; and then a few acres in another place, that he offered at an average of nine thousand an acre for raw land. When we went and walked it, two acres turned out to be swamp land, being a drainage area for a number of surrounding hills. The land was obviously never dry, and couldn't possibly be filled.

And so it went. We walked land all over the place, mostly concentrating in Framingham. But we looked at properties in other communities as well when we got leads to them. There was just nothing. In the fall of '67, out of sheer desperation, I went back to the developer who owned the Folsom estate off Singletary Lane. By now I realized that the thing to do was to go for a maximum mortgage, and I went back with that in mind, and offered him more money for the same property – a hundred and ten thousand, which was considerably more than the amount we had earlier agreed on. Again he agreed. Again we celebrated, and again the same story repeated itself. We got to the point where we were going to draw up papers, and he backed out a second time, and this time it was clear that it was final; no matter what pressure was put on him he paid no attention and simply rejected the deal out of hand.

Then we found out about the Grey Nuns' property. We had heard earlier, it must have been back in the late spring, that the property, their entire holding, was up for sale. That was the property Eleanor Calver had shown Hanna on their first outing, when she commented that the Catholic Church never sells anything. It developed that in fact the Church was offering for sale many of its holdings in Framingham, and that the Order of Grey Nuns was selling its entire property, which consisted of some sixty acres of land plus a beautiful main building and a few out-buildings that went with it, and a pond.

The asking price for the entire property was three hundred and twenty-five thousand dollars, which was so absolutely and completely and totally out of range of our possibilities that we just didn't give it any further thought. Now, in the fall of '67, they were eager to get rid of it, and I think that it became clear to them that while *land* might be of some interest to developers, the big house was a hindrance to selling the property, in that it was really of no commercial value, nobody would buy an estate of that sort to live in or to do anything with unless it was an institution. A developer wouldn't be interested in the house. A developer would have to view the deal in terms of the amount of land that might be developed profitably, and then would have to think of the cost of tearing down the buildings.

So the least desirable piece of their sixty acre lot was the house and the land immediately adjacent to it. I think it was in light of this very realistic assessment on their part that they finally agreed to divide off the house and land around the house and offer it for sale, and keep the rest of the land. Everything was so dreadfully complicated because they had an agent and the agent would have to talk to the sisters and the sisters would have to talk to the higher-ups in Montreal to get the final okay and the intermediates in Lowell had to give an okay – it was quite a ladder that we had to go through, ending in the Vatican. But at any rate they obtained a go-ahead to hear our offer, and when we finally had finished our negotiations we arrived at a price of eighty thousand dollars.

There was a lot of last minute shifting around, but we arrived at a price of eighty thousand dollars for the house and the barn, ten acres of land, part of the pond (to straighten out the boundaries), the mill house, rights to use the entire pond for recreational purposes, and the dam was thrown in by them as well, because it was something of a liability inasmuch as the owner was responsible for maintaining it and it seemed to need some work, which we later did, in order to strengthen it.

The sales agreement was signed in mid-November, 1968, and when it was actually signed it was a day of great, great rejoicing and celebration. I remember buying a bottle of Chateau-bottled champagne that cost thirteen dollars, and Hanna and I going over to Fred and Nancy Hilton's, and Bill Randall came over, and we drank this marvelous champagne and celebrated the end of a long and hard quest. The actual transfer of the property was to take place on March 1. We didn't want it immediately and it gave them time to get out. On March 1 we would take possession, which we thought gave us ample time to get it ready for July 1 opening.

Of course these negotiations involved all the usual preliminaries. We had all our experts look at it: the architect, and Mal Stalker, and others, who gave it as clean a bill of health as any building was ever given. It was in fantastic structural shape. The location was superb, the fire chief and the building inspector went through it and indicated the kinds of things they wanted done, which certainly seemed reasonable and well within our reach. As it turned out, there were something like twenty thousand dollars in improvements that we made in the building during the spring and summer and early fall, but this was certainly reasonable in light of the very high quality plant that we got.

The plant was just beautiful, and the campus was extraordinarily beautiful. It was far, far superior to the Folsom estate we had twice bought and twice lost. It was close to a large conservation area owned by the Sudbury Valley Trustees, and there was farm land around it, some of which was also earmarked as a conservation area. It was a beautiful, beautiful campus in every respect and has given the school an atmosphere of aesthetic beauty and of peace that was simply a godsend for us through the first year. From the day of the signing, we knew that we would have a school. Up till that day, up till the day we actually signed for the property, we were not sure that we'd have a school, in spite of our best intentions.

In the period before that, in the fall, we had come up with the name "The Sudbury Valley School". I wasn't interested in a name that would have content to it – "Free School" or any such thing – because I thought these were all easily misinterpreted; I didn't want any cute name; and I didn't want it named after people – "Abraham Lincoln School" or anything like that. The only thing that seemed to make sense was something that would associate the school with the region and would symbolize its roots in this part of the world. The only feature that I could think of as typifying this region was the Sudbury River. In fact, Baiting Brook went through our property, and Baiting Brook is a tributary of the Sudbury River, so this was to be the Sudbury Valley School serving the Sudbury River Valley. The name was very well received.

Our first printed catalog could thus have the name of the school on it, and its location. I'll come to the catalog later, but I want to point out that the signing of the papers preceded my bringing the copy to the printer by a *couple of hours*. We were able to insert into the catalog at the very last minute a picture of the building and the location of the campus. Of course that gave the catalog a reality that no vague prospectus could possibly have.

Later I'll have more to say about what we learned from our experience with this campus. But for now it suffices to say that this campus served our purposes excellently in every way. Not the least important feature was the pond, which gave us swimming throughout our first summer and ice skating during the winter, and scenic beauty in every season.

Furniture and Equipment

A second important activity had to do with outfitting the school. I'll have more to say about this when I discuss the actual operation of the school. We felt that the school had to be outfitted with certain basic "necessities" before it opened. The period between March 1 and June 30 would be available for providing whatever physical appurtenances were needed, or we thought were needed, for setting up the school. The building we got had more than twenty rooms in it, and these were all empty. There was no furniture in it whatsoever. So we had to furnish the building, and to furnish such educational materials as we thought necessary.

The way we actually went about this at the time was to sit around and think about what there ought to be in a school, what we thought the students would want, and to go ahead and get it within the financial limitations we had set for ourselves. This meant that we got things like art supplies and paint, ordered by people who had experience in that area. We bought a certain number of books for the library. (We also got books as gifts or loans.) We bought nursery equipment so that the younger children would have things to play with.

We went from used furniture store to used furniture store to furnish the building, and used as a guide a remark made by Dennis Flynn on New Year's Eve of 1966. We somehow had casually mentioned furniture that evening, I don't remember the context, and Dennis said, as if it was clear and self-understood, that we would of course furnish the school with home furnishings, that the last thing on earth we wanted to do was furnish it like a school; that we'd have chairs and tables and sofas and armchairs, and that the rooms would look familiar and comfortable and not institutional.

At the time I hadn't thought about that and wasn't sure that I agreed. I guess I still saw rooms with more school-like chairs and equipment and blackboards in them. But as the time came to furnish the school, it certainly seemed like a very practical idea and a pleasing idea aesthetically, and it didn't seem to have any obvious educational defects to it. So we went ahead and furnished the entire building with ordinary home furniture, used; we got it at bargain prices and did the whole outfitting for several hundred dollars. The only big expenditure that we made along these lines was to buy folding chairs which were to be used in the school sort of as a filler. We would be assured that we had at least one chair for everybody, and assured that the chairs we had would be easily mobile and transferable from one room to another.

It certainly is true that from the first day that the students and staff entered the school, the place did not have an institutional atmosphere. This showed itself, for example, in a peculiar way in the bathrooms. It's well known how bathrooms in school are methodically vandalized, defaced with graffiti, and simply abused in every way. Bathrooms seem to be the favorite outlet for all sorts of vicious attacks on school buildings. Our bathrooms were never abused. Nor was the rest of the building. The same goes for the chairs and tables. School desks are always carved up, but our chairs and tables weren't abused either – nor were the walls. We were sure that this had to do with the fact that all the rooms were not institutional in nature. The bathrooms looked like home bathrooms. They had a regular toilet and a sink, and one treated them the way that one treats an ordinary bathroom in a house, which may not be with the greatest of care, but certainly not with abuse. The same was true of the furniture in the house and the walls.

It was a house. It wasn't a home, but it was a house, a regular house, and one just didn't do certain things in regular houses. It's not just a question of being in an estate type house, because you can be in an estate type house, as very many private schools and colleges are all over the country, and furnish the house with institutional furniture and convert the lavatories into institutional-type toilets, usually under the urging of the health department or whatever, and what you end up getting is the outer shell of a house but the interior of an institution. It's not just the shell that counts. It's the atmosphere permeating the entire building that counts, and when you furnish it the way a house is furnished you get a different kind of behavior.

Of course I have to tie this up with the whole attitude of the school. We probably would have gotten plenty of abuse of the building if we had been an ordinary repressive school. I'm not saying that the furniture is the key, but all these things add up. I would expect the converse to be true: that even in our kind of school, if we had had the stupidity and oversight to furnish it in the way ordinary school institutions are furnished, then that would have been very much out of line with the rest of the educational and political and social atmosphere of the place, and that aspect of it would probably have been abused. In fact we have ample evidence of this from the way other mistakes we made were corrected. For example, in those areas where we provided materials that were not the result of a real need, as I'll point out later, the materials were abused.

Public Relations

Another area of hard work during this year was public relations. The main job here was to get ourselves known in the community, with the basic aim of getting a student body. We tried to talk anywhere and everywhere, to make use of every contact that we had, in order to spread the school's name, spread our program, in the hope that out of all this effort some sort of student body would come forth. It's like a doctor hanging out his shingle. He has no idea where his patients are going to come from, but he knows that if he's going to have a practice, they've got to start coming.

People would always ask, "Well, how many students do you have?" They asked that from the very first day. They asked it in September. They asked it the previous spring. And for a long time we had to say, "None". In fact we didn't get our first students in any definite sense until March. When we went into March I think we had something like a dozen students lined up, but none actually signed up. We felt all along that in order to start we had to have something like thirty or forty students. In the second year we'd expect to double that, and then we'd go on growing rapidly after that, after the school was an obvious success, and had proved itself in one way or another.

I look back on that year and think of the tremendous exposure, the tremendous number of social events, and it really amazes me. Hanna also went out to speak to groups. In the beginning we used to go together. Then the burden simply became too heavy, and I used to go myself most of the time. There were coffees at private homes. I spoke at churches. I spoke at a ministers' conference, a temple, PTA's, at the MIT learning research center. I made contacts at, and visits to, EDC in Newton. There were other places, many other places. Afternoon teas, evening coffees, groups. I would say that during that year, '67-'68, hundreds and hundreds of people heard our pitch. It was always a little different, but it was basically the pitch that this was the right kind of school for this time and this country, and the basic ideas were presented along the lines of the catalog, the booklet *About the Sudbury Valley School*, and my manuscript.

An important part of our public relations was the first catalog and the booklet. We printed five thousand copies of the catalog. They came off the press in early December of 1967, and we distributed all five thousand by the fall of 1968, in less than a year. We mailed them, we handed them out everywhere. We had reply cards in them. We must have received about three hundred reply cards, which is not a great return but is still not negligible. We also printed *About the Sudbury Valley School* (the first edition, much different than later editions) which described the philosophy and the major ideas behind the school in somewhat greater detail, and was a propaganda piece in the sense that it appealed to the supporting statements of other thinkers and other people in education to give the impression that our ideas were not just pulled out of the blue.

Mailing was a tremendous feature of our public relations. We mailed out the catalog to everybody who had received the original prospectus, and to all the contacts we could possibly make. Everybody got the catalogue. We were very, very free in mailings. We were very eager to make our program and our name known throughout the educational establishment. We mailed a copy of our catalog with a privately typed, personal letter to every single principal in every elementary, junior high, and high school and private school within a ten mile radius of Framingham, and some every beyond that; to every guidance counselor in that area; and to superintendents of schools and assistant superintendents of schools and other administrators.

Public relations also involved extensive entertaining at home. We had many parties and dinners in our home, and some of them stand out in retrospect. I recall the party we had in December celebrating the purchase of the campus, to which we invited an immense number of people and to which something close to a hundred people showed up. There was a great atmosphere. It was a typical affair of the kind that you have to keep people aware of the fact that you're there, that you're going ahead full steam, and that you're making real progress. "Here we are with a campus now." We didn't have the catalogs yet in quantity, but we had one or two copies, and they were shown around very proudly.

We also had to develop relations with the press, and with the media. We did everything we could to get known through the public media. Our good relations with people within the Framingham community enabled us to get excellent coverage in the *Framingham News*. We got a marvelous spread on the day the school was legally incorporated. We gave out various press releases, and managed to get into a lot of local papers, and also into the *Boston Globe*. We never knew how many people saw any of these particular items, but it was clear that we got contacts through every one of them. The same holds for our appearance over the radio on WBZ. Dennis Flynn represented the school on prime time on a Friday evening on WBZ, and it was obviously a program that a great many people heard and that spread the word of our school widely. We didn't have inside connections in this respect, and all we could do was keep hacking away and keep trying to get in.

Even though we didn't have a sophisticated public relations arm, and didn't spend a lot of money or a tremendous amount of effort on it, we did manage to get enough coverage to make some difference.

When I look back on it I think that had we hired a public relations man we probably could have gotten better coverage, but in light of the way things developed for the first year, I doubt very much whether that would have made much difference or even would have been to our benefit. As it turned out, we got more than enough students.

In our situation now, we're not trying to sell a product the way a progressive educator sells his product in a progressive school, by making people think that they want it. What we're trying to do now is to open people's eyes, to make them aware of what we have. That requires a completely different approach. When you feel that you are on to something that people really want and they just need to have the veil lifted from their eyes, you have a completely different stance towards them. Your stance is one of raising the curtain, of knocking down the wall, not of that wheedling, soliciting way which aims at making people *think* that you've got a product that they really want. I guess the question can be asked, "Why did we ever have to solicit? Why couldn't we have done then what we're doing now?" And I guess the answer is that before you can open somebody's eyes you've got to provide something to look at.

At the time, we had nothing to look at. The reality wasn't there. So we had to conjure up an image, and make people think that this image was something that they really wanted. As soon as you have the reality, and with it a clear conception of what you're doing, the era of solicitation is over, and the smart way of doing it is to take a quite different approach.

You can see plenty of this in the present commercial world. In the business world, there are two categories of distribution of a product. One is represented by the tremendous public relations and sales and advertising agencies. They make you think that you want a certain toothpaste or make you think that you want a certain drink; they seek to create in you the idea that you do in fact need something. The other is the situation where the person comes to the producer fully aware of his need and does everything he can to get the product out of the producer – in other words, the reverse situation. All those producers who deal with something that is clearly a real need, where people are knocking at their door – they advertise too, because advertising is the accepted thing to do. I don't think they even realize that their advertising should be different, but even so their advertising has a different flavor to it. It doesn't concentrate so much on making you think that you've got a need they're going to fulfill, as in simply stating that they do a good job of providing your need. In other words, their advertising usually acknowledges that you recognize your need, and sells their competence.

There were two other events that took place before July 1, that were important for public relations. One was on March 10 when we had an open house at the school campus, ten days after we took possession of the property. We invited people to come in and see the place. We invited just about everybody we could think of, and we announced it through a press release that was published fairly widely. Hundreds of people came to that open house, and it was a marvelous opportunity to hand out our brochures and speak with them. We rented chairs – there was no furniture in the building – and everybody was terribly impressed with the beauty of the campus and the beauty of the building. There was no food served, just an open house. At one o'clock a meeting was held in what was later to become the playroom, and it was an overflow meeting. I gave a short address stating where we were and where we were going and what progress we had made.

We had quite a remarkable turnout, including a lot of the progressive establishment; subsequently, several of these people made themselves self-styled proponents of the school and propagandists for the school. You had the feeling that they sort of adopted the school and wanted to show that they were really in on its foundation. One of the better known of these, for example, of course didn't want to give us too much credit for originality, but he would say that one of the most important features of our school was the community aspect of it, the degree to which we were open to the community and embedded in the community, and that impressed him.

There was another meeting on June 4, which included all the visiting teachers, or all the people who said they might be visiting teachers. There must have easily been a hundred people there. By then we had a lot more progress to report, and we were in fact preparing for the opening of the school in the summer. It was just sort of a morale booster. That too was a very successful event in that it raised a lot of enthusiasm for the grand opening.

Another event that I want to make special mention of occurred when we first purchased the campus. We invited all the school's neighbors for tea at our home. We spelled out our program, in order to forestall any trouble by allaying fears. As it turned out, they raised no difficulties when we first moved in and started, and that enabled us to get going without a hitch. Later a few of the neighbors regretted our presence there, and some came to feel rather bitter towards us. They had some legitimate complaints in the Fall about the behavior of some of the students, that I'm going to talk about later. But generally speaking I would say that relations with the neighbors were satisfactory.

Staff

Another important feature of the school that took shape during that year was the staff. The first nine people had originally come together of their own free will out of an interest in the school; but in addition they had all known me personally. I want to be very explicit here in saying that these people didn't come to the school, as far as I could tell, because of me personally, but nevertheless there was a personal feature in their relationship to the school, and this had an undesirable effect on the nature and composition of the staff in the beginning. It meant, for example, that when Hanna and I had personal differences with three of these nine, this had repercussions on the entire school, and this certainly wasn't my idea of how a school as an institution ought to be run.

There certainly is room in any institution for personal relationships, but it's an unhealthy situation and an unstable one when a hybrid is made out of a personal and institutional relationship. This was a weakness in the original staff, and it revealed itself in the meetings and in the way the staff functioned in the beginning. We had a meeting on December 9, 1967 that was the occasion for quite a few bitter recriminations, and it got to be terribly personal. I didn't see any benefit coming to anybody from that, and I felt at the time that our only hope, if we were to have a good staff and the kind of school that I wanted to be part of, was to break decisively through this confusion between the personal and the institutional. And whereas the composition of the staff had remained static at these nine for something like seven or eight months, I was determined to bring about some sort of change.

At that December 9 meeting a very important step was taken. One of the key figures was Fred Newman, who had written and inquired about the school when he first heard about it. I had an extensive correspondence with dozens and dozens of people about the school, and he was one of those people. As it turned out, his path crossed ours for a very short time, and the one time that was of any consequence for the school was at this December meeting. We had met him earlier, he had indicated an interest in working at the school, but he later went his own way. I invited him to the December 9 staff meeting, and he espoused the view that anybody should be free to come into the school and to do anything he wanted at the school; and, when there, to have a full share in running the school; a full vote and a full voice in the activities of the school. His was a very loose type of "in you go, out you go" view. He expressed this view several times during that meeting, and it was a great help, since what I was fighting for at that meeting was making it possible for anyone from the outside to join the staff. Opening the staff to anybody else who wanted to join.

We discussed the whole question in detail. One of the staff members present was particularly adamant against opening the staff. He wanted to ensure that the nine people present would have a monopoly on staff positions, at least throughout the opening phases of the school. He stated it in just so many words. He thought that he was on to something radical, innovative, and historic, and didn't want the credit for the success to be diluted. He wanted history forever after to know that these nine people were responsible for it. He felt that if the staff was open, all sorts of people would rush in for the credit. We actually got down to voting on the issue, and the vote was taken to open the staff. I don't remember that we set any criteria other than wanting to join the staff. I think we agreed at the time that such a person would at least have to be present at one staff meeting and then have to make up his mind that he wanted to be a member of the staff subsequent to his being there. There was some discussion about whether we wanted to apply any particular set of standards to these people or whether we wanted to leave the decision completely up to them. But the real debate was whether or not to open the staff.

As far as I was concerned, this set the stage for obtaining a healthy institutional character rather than an introverted hybrid personal/institutional style. We had taken a major step away from having a school

based on the personal, emotional, psychiatric, and psychologically prob-
ing types of experiences that so many other new schools were based on;
and it was a step towards depersonalizing the relations between people at
the school, by declaring clearly that it wasn't important whether the people on the staff were friends or weren't friends socially. What they had
to have in common was a commitment to the institution, and whether
or not they got along personally was a secondary question completely. It
was opening the staff that achieved that step in the history of the school.

I had actively sought to bring this issue to a crisis and to a decision,
however harsh the debate and vote might be. I felt throughout the development of the school the way I feel about history in general, that it's
possible at a critical period, when factors are building up to a crisis situation, for a person to actively intervene and affect the course of events and
perhaps even guide them in a certain direction, towards a certain desired
outcome. And I've tried as often as I could, when seeing the school approach what I took to be critical turns, to precipitate crises, to sharpen
the conflicts, to bring a crisis to its culmination in as radical a form as
possible and thereby also to take advantage of the critical situation and
bring the school through in a certain direction. I'm sure that others in
the school have behaved the same way. This was the first such instance of
crisis that occurred in the development of the school. It was critical, in
my opinion, that the staff not remain closed, not remain the same group.
I thought that there would be ever increasing dissension and instability
if we did remain the same nine, and that this would really endanger the
future of the school. So I thought that a crisis, a critical situation, was
coming up, and it was therefore intentional on my part to precipitate
this crisis more rapidly by bringing the question to a head at that staff
meeting and forcing some sort of a resolution.

It was a stroke of good fortune that Fred Newman came to that
particular meeting and that the message that he had for the school
happened to be so opportune for that meeting. It certainly would not
have been opportune a year later. But his appearance at that particular
meeting with that particular message was a blessing because it brought
another eloquent voice to bear in support of opening the staff, and it
made it easier for people in that context to vote for opening the staff

without making it strictly a personal question of whether to support one view or another. Fred's intrusion into the situation made it more than just a personal conflict; it became a question of issues between an open and closed staff.

The immediate consequence of the meeting and of that one basic decision was twofold; in the first place Steve and Ina Cooper left the staff, which reduced it from nine to seven immediately; and it also brought almost immediately our first new staff member under the new policy – J. As a matter of fact, in the beginning we didn't even say that a person who wanted to join the staff should come to a staff meeting. That happened somewhere later along the line. At first, we said that all he had to do was talk to some staff member, in much the same way we said we'd accept students. There was some discussion of how we were going to accept students, and we agreed at the same meeting, although it wasn't much of an issue at the time, that we'd accept students on the basis of an interview with any staff member. That actually never amounted to much of a decision, because all of the interviews took place through Hanna and me until very late in the spring. I'll come to the question of admitting students shortly.

As far as staff was concerned, in the beginning all we did was ask that the prospective staff member talk to one of the staff members. At any rate, J. heard about the school and offered his services. He called up and told us how excited he was by our catalog and our brochure, and then invited us over to his apartment. We had a long discussion there in January, and lo!, here was our first new acquisition. The fact that there was no salary didn't deter him in the least. On the contrary, he emphasized that he wasn't looking for money, that this was the greatest thing that ever happened to him, and so forth. It was clear as a result of that first two hour visit that this was a person who was unlike any of the nine of us, who was in fact unlike anybody that I have ever known in my life. He was a character of a totally different type, from a different milieu.

Whatever my personal likes or dislikes, or my personal reactions were to him, one thing was clear as regards the school and the staff, and that was that in this person we were getting someone who was as different from all the rest of us as any human being could possibly be. It was equally clear that here was a person who was going to put our open policy to the test. As Hanna's mother would have put it: We opened the staff. What did God do? He sent us J.!

Shortly thereafter we had him to our house on a Sunday afternoon. Some other staff members were there and his daughter came. It was quite an experience for the staff members who met him and his daughter (who also offered herself as a staff member but disappeared from the scene shortly thereafter). Everybody was quite shaken by the experience, that was clear. This was not the kind of person that most of us would have gone for, and certainly not the kind of person that we felt eager to add to the staff. Yet we all realized that we had just passed a policy which made it possible for this person to join.

In a sense, that was discouraging, because when you are put to the test you've *got to* come through. It's great to love freedom as long as the person you're giving freedom to is doing the exact thing you want him to do anyway. You're only put to the test when freedom involves a person behaving in ways that you didn't want, and then you've either got to stick to it or you don't. It was the same here. It's great to open the staff in order to break the stranglehold that personal relations might have on it. But as soon as you open the staff and you get someone different like J. you begin to wonder.

From that time until J. left I would privately refer to the "J. test" that would be applied to any new prospective staff member. Namely, it would be just as much of a test for new people who offered themselves to the staff as it had been to us, whether they in fact did believe in the open policy when they met J., or met each other, and still decided to stick with the open policy and to stick with the school.

The point was that if people joining the staff could get along with a J. within the framework of the staff, then they in fact knew what it meant to have an open staff policy and to have a democratic school; and if they didn't get along with a J., if they could get along only with types that they liked, but when it came to a guy like J. they just couldn't get along, then in fact their commitment to the democratic process was by no means complete. His presence meant that the school was clearly committed to living with people who were different, and not only tolerating them – that word has something about it that I don't like – but giving them a full and equal voice in the affairs of the school to the same extent that we gave it to anybody else.

So J.'s presence in that respect was a great blessing to the school. There was a J. test for all of us. For example, during the summer we passed a rule that the school could be open if two staff members were around. Really the reason we said *two* staff members was because we didn't want to say one staff member, because we didn't want the school to be open and have regular activities going on when J. was the only person around. We simply didn't. Now that was a fair, democratic way to solving it. We didn't say, "Well, we don't mind having the school open with one person but not if the guy is J."

That in effect would have been the way it would have been done in any other institution. One would have selected people one felt were responsible enough to have the school open with, and others who weren't. But we stuck to our democratic procedure and dealt evenhandedly with everybody. The result was that it was two, no matter who the two were. That meant that Daniel Greenberg couldn't open the school alone, and Dennis Flynn couldn't open the school alone, any more than J. could open the school alone. And that was the end of that.

To complete the story, although somewhat out of chronological order, I was always convinced that J. would leave the school at a fairly early time. I was also concerned that he might do something that would make it necessary for us to get rid of him. In the fall, I felt – and others did too – that his presence was leading to activities in the school that were an overt and concrete menace to the continuation of the school. Ultimately, it became necessary for us to precipitate a strong confrontation at which the staff unanimously condemned some of his actions. We weren't talking about his style or his personality but about the things he was actually doing in the school being inimical to the survival of the school, and we asked him to resign with the clear implication that if he didn't we were going to ask the Trustees to remove him.

The result was that his resignation was forthcoming that night, and he left the school. It was a Thursday night, and the next morning, Friday morning, he was gone. And he never returned again. I'm sure he would have left the school on his own, but we didn't have the time to wait it out. So just as J. was the first to test our openness, so too J. was the first to test our determination to keep ourselves alive by taking real action against people who were doing things that were destructive to the school. In a sense our ability to confront J. – after all, we had lived with him for months by then, and we had all come to realize the value of the "J. test" – our ability to recognize the danger and to take determined action in the face of danger was a very important step forward for the staff, and an important forerunner of the kind of action we were going to be called upon to take within a few weeks thereafter.

It was the first time that the staff had actually had to get together the guts to force a destructive member to leave the community, and it was not to be the last time. It was important as a precedent for the staff, and I think it was very good that the staff set this precedent with one of its own first, before it went about its business with regard to destructive students a little later.

To get back to the story of the open staff, J. joined the staff in January, and I don't think it was until March that we had the next addition. I'm not going to go through this in any detail because the details are not that important. The only point I want to make, as far as the growth of the staff through the open policy is concerned, is that there was a period from March on when a great many people started appearing from all sorts of places and offering their services as staff members, and these people came in really considerable numbers.

The one thing that all new staff members had in common was that they were not known personally to me or to Hanna or to other staff members before they came. They came to the school and to the idea of the school directly, and their involvement with the school was direct. They came out of the clear blue, motivated by an interest and commitment to the school. As a result, the staff consisted of people who were able to work together in an institutional context without having the personal side play a decisive role.

At the end of the first year, we had a staff of twelve. Of the original nine, five remained. Thus, seven of the twelve came in later, and there were many others. There were many candidates who came and went after a meeting or two. There were many who came and stayed a while, a few weeks, a few months, and then left. What we had left after a year was the result of quite a distillation process. I would say that these twelve were something under half the total number of people who were really serious candidates for the staff from the beginning on. Many tried and for one reason or another left.

The open staff policy enabled people to come in and acquaint themselves with the school and find a place in it and see whether they belonged in this institution. We never interviewed staff candidates. We never put them in a supplicatory relationship to the school, in a position of applying for a job and having themselves judged and passed on. And we never put ourselves in a patronizing attitude towards them. In that respect the staff policy was the most correct of all our policies. We certainly might have conducted staff recruitment in a more conventional way.

I guess the reason we felt that ours was the correct way to do it was that we realized that for a person to commit a year of his time full-time to the school at no salary meant a very real, no-baloney commitment to the institution. It's a different kind of a commitment than even a student is making. Because with a student and his parents – well, you never know. Parents can send a student to the school in order to get the kid off their hands or in order just to have a place where he won't get into trouble. There are all kinds of reasons. But although it certainly was possible for a staff member to come in order to get away from things, here there was the additional factor of staying power. Escape might be the motive, and I think in fact it was the motive, with several people who came in and out of the staff. I think they did use the openness of the staff in order to somehow solve personal problems, in order to find a haven or a resting place.

But it's the staying power that counts, and to stick it out day in and day out, to do the kind of responsible work that's required of a staff member every day, you just can't do it unless you are serious and committed. As a student you don't have to pick up responsibility in the school; you just don't have that as part of your everyday function in the school. As a staff member you've got to pick up responsibility in the school, you can't survive if you're not going to be responsible. You can only survive for a short length of time, but to be around any considerable length of time you've got to be able to take responsibility. That's why the open staff policy worked for the school, and provided the school with an extraordinarily strong staff. We had our lemons on the short term, but we were strong enough to survive them because of our open policy, which got us the strong people too. Had we had to select people, I don't know that we would have recognized and selected the strongest ones.

A final word on the staff during that period. We opened the school on July 1 with something like a dozen staff members. People came and went, but throughout the first year, we always had around a dozen staff members. Sometimes it may have been down to ten or eleven; it may have gone up to fourteen or fifteen. But it hovered around a dozen. It is interesting that despite the turnover, the total number stayed fairly constant.

Enrolling Students

It's terribly difficult to convey the feeling of anxiety that we had in March of 1968 when we realized that we'd been working on the school now for close to a year and a half in one way or another and that still we had essentially no students. We had our own children, and a few other children of friends and staff members scattered here and there. But when we added up the total number of possible and expected enrollees, we would keep coming up with a fairly constant number of something like twelve, and new people just weren't coming. Now when you look at the situation on March 1, and you think that we had only four months to go before we opened the school, it's quite a sobering thought.

I must confess that at the time, when we said that we'd be perfectly happy to open with thirty students, we also said secretly to ourselves, "We'll start even if we have only twenty students, because after all the important thing is to get off the ground." But even the goal of twenty students looked terribly remote on March 1. Not because we couldn't conceive of having twenty students, but because there was no movement. Those twelve had been around for something like a year. Parents just weren't coming. Inquiries were coming, the word was spreading widely, but parents weren't coming.

And then in March the tide turned, and it turned ever more amazingly through April, May and June until it became quite a flood. By the time we opened our summer session, we had some hundred and thirty students registered, and when we opened in the fall we also had about a hundred and thirty-five students registered on the first day of opening.

The actual enrollment procedure that we worked out is a good example of the way the school has always functioned, administratively, in that we preferred always to let our experience force on us the need for new procedures, instead of anticipating administrative procedures on the basis of some abstract theory, or even on the basis of other schools' experience. There are manuals for starting schools, and there are plenty of schools in operation, so that people who want to start schools of any sort can draw on plenty of experience of other people that's been recorded in detail to anticipate administrative needs and to set up a whole administrative procedure. We could have done this.

We could have expected that we'd need a procedure in one area or another, and we could have sat around and prepared things well in advance so that the machinery would be ready to go. But we preferred not to do that. We knew that this school was unlike any other school in every detail of its operation because it was unlike every other school in its philosophy and outlook. We knew that this would mean that we would have to think through everything about the school, from the simplest administrative procedure to the most complicated educational questions, in a completely new and independent way. We knew that this was going to be a staggering job that would really have no end, that we'd be constantly improving on what we were doing and that we'd constantly be finding new areas to tackle.

So, given the tremendous number of problems that we knew we would have to cope with, it just wasn't practical or sensible to try to sit down and cope with all of them in advance. Rather than do that, we adopted a policy of thinking through each new problem as it came up through either the press of events or the persistent interest of some member of the school community. That sort of staggered the problems, and made it possible for us to give each individual problem a lot of thought.

In the matter of enrolling students, the original dozen or so were simply declared enrolled. The parents said they were coming, and they were all people who apparently knew what we were doing. It's sort of interesting to look back on it, because almost all of them left the school by the fall of 1968. These first students were just sort of enrolled by agreement. We knew we'd have to do something a little more formal eventually. We had an open enrollment policy — anybody who wanted to come could come. That was clearly in line with the philosophy of the school, and we certainly didn't want to put faith in any kind of prior records, whether school records or guidance records or anything else.

Our feeling was that if the prospective student could function in the real world and wasn't clearly disturbed or handicapped – and by "clearly" I mean in a way that could be evident at first sight – then he should be able to be a student in the school and function in the school, because it was a normal thing for normal people to be capable of taking responsibility for themselves. So we had an open enrollment policy, and yet we knew that there had to be some way for the students and the parents to be sure that they really wanted to come to this school, that they weren't confusing the school with some other kind of school, only to come back and plague us with this misunderstanding later.

The point is that we had an open policy, and we knew that the responsibility for the decision to come to the school had to lie entirely with the students and the parents, but we didn't feel that the printed literature was enough to guarantee that they would exercise their responsibility in a reasonable way. Also, I guess there was a bit of a streak of paternalism left in us. We wanted *to make sure* that the parents and the students would exercise their responsibility in the proper way. So we decided that we would require every prospective student and every prospective parent to come to an interview. We wouldn't structure the interview, we wouldn't quiz them or anything like that. The interview would in fact be a chance for them to interview us, would be an opportunity for them to ask us questions and find out what we had in mind. But we felt that we had to make sure that they had this opportunity and that they took advantage of it.

It's really a very subtle question. We forced the interview on the parents, and that very act was basically incompatible with the philosophy of the school. It put the parents and the student in the position of applying to us for something and put us in a kind of judgmental and authority position relative to them on their very first contact. That was clearly the wrong way to start. I don't think we saw that at the time. I don't think we saw it for a long time, until we restructured our enrollment procedure in the winter and spring of 1969. But I hasten to add that we didn't make the interview the standard kind of interview where we'd interview the parents and student and find out whether they're the kind of people we want.

We made the interview a situation where they interviewed us to find out whether we're the kind of school they wanted. It's not that there was anything wrong with the interview once it got underway. The only thing wrong was that we forced the interview to happen. I don't know whether we could have done differently. I don't know whether we could have just said to people, "Look, if you want an interview to find out about the school you can have it, and if you don't you can enroll without it." I think that kind of an attitude would have been widely misinterpreted as discouraging an interview. At any rate once we had the interview it was in fact the parents and the student interviewing us, and then they went away and were to make their decision on enrolling.

In the beginning we made all our arrangements by phone. We set up the interview by phone, and afterwards we let the parents inform us by phone, at some later time, without specifying any deadlines, whether they wanted to enroll their children or not. So in the beginning we hardly had an idea who came. One thing that we were very strict about in setting up these interviews was that both parents had to come. And the reason for this goes back to the way the school was structured, which I haven't gone into as yet, which gave the parents a considerable voice in the operation of the school, and made it impossible for parents simply to send their kids to the school and then forget about the whole thing. We felt also that what we were doing in the school would have great repercussions in the home.

So we were quite convinced that we didn't want people coming to the school who were not at least willing to go along with the school. It didn't mean that they had to be ideologically "pure," it didn't mean that they had to subscribe to our ideas, but it meant that they had to be aware of what they were doing and willing to go ahead and do this. In this way we hoped to avoid later difficulties, of parents and of families having tremendous crises and perhaps destroying the school in anger. We felt that there would be crises in families; we couldn't avoid that, what we were doing had too many implications about the family structure just to happen casually. But I always felt that different families would go into different crises at different times, and that the families that weren't in crisis would help those that were at any given time. What we wanted to avoid, or what we tried to avoid, was lots of people going into crisis at the same time, which we knew would be very destructive to the school. So we were always quite insistent on having both parents come.

There were lots of things about these early interviews and the way we got into the interview procedure that weren't good. For example, we didn't have the school building furnished and ready for operation until well into June, so that the interviews took place at our home, and this was a terrible thing for us. It was really just ghastly, because it was bad enough that we were both involved in setting up the school, but our home life was completely disrupted for several months by this constant trek of people in and out for interviews. Since children came as well, Michael and Talya's daily lives were often a shambles because of the intrusion of children who would just steam in and upset their games and their toys. It was really a fantastic strain on the family.

Also, in line with our stance of soliciting students, of really needing students, we dropped all the normal formalities that an institution would have – it was a sign of our desperation – we didn't keep the interviews to business hours and business days at all. We allowed people to come whenever it was convenient for them, and of course usually it's convenient for them not to have to miss work and not to have to disrupt their scheduling in any way if they can disrupt yours. So there were often interviews in the evenings, and there were interviews over weekends – it was a seven-day-week affair. That never gave us a moment of peace or privacy, and it also set the wrong tone in many other ways because it put the idea into all these people that we were out to please them at any cost, in order to attain our educational aims.

They got the idea that we would be door-mats, because in fact we were doormats in this respect. It set the wrong tone in so many ways: it put us in a judgmental attitude and them in a soliciting attitude as far as the interview was concerned, and it put us in a supplicatory attitude as far as pleasing the parents and serving the parents was concerned. Which is really the standard situation in other schools. The school people are the authority and guide in the educational area, but they're the servants and the doormats as far as servicing the whims of the parents is concerned.

All these bad aspects were due to our interview structure and the way it was carried out. There was no way of avoiding having the interviews in our home. We might have avoided having them at all hours. But we were so afraid at the time that by insisting on these formalities we wouldn't make it, we just wouldn't have any students, that we didn't insist on it. As time went on, we got more and more strict about these things, there's no question about that. By the time we were into late May and early June, we definitely had the interviews down to nine-to-five, five days a week, and in June we moved a lot of the interviews over to the school. From late June on they were all at the school. So those undesirable features of the interview procedure were eventually got rid of as our desperation waned. But they left an after-effect that took the better part of a year to wear off.

They also left another after-effect that I don't see any way we could have avoided, and that was that despite all our desires to diffuse responsibility and to make this a non-hierarchical school, these interviews at our home, conducted by us, definitely created the impression that it was the Greenbergs' school. In June, July, and August the interviews were conducted by other staff members, and certainly parents who were interviewed by other staff members didn't have this feeling. But there was such a large number of people who had been handled by us on their way to the school that again it took the better part of a year to wear that impression off.

(There were other reasons for them to think it was the Greenbergs' school. Until the beginning of school, the overwhelming majority of the work that was done in setting up the school was done by the two of us. We had both given full time to this, we had abandoned all other work just for this. There were no other staff members in a position to do that. So right off the bat that meant that we were putting more into the school, there was no getting around it. The other staff members had different jobs, lived in different places, just didn't have the time and often even if they did have the time didn't have the focused commitment yet to be involved in the school even in their spare time.

During this formative period up to July 1 when we opened I would say that there were only two other staff members, Margaret Parra and Priscilla Parris, who put in a considerable amount of work that really made a big difference. Every staff member put in some work, and certainly in the month of June, especially towards the end, a lot of staff members put in quite a bit of work. In the month of June a lot of people worked on the physical plant, painted large parts of the building, helped furnish it and so forth. Close to the opening date, more and more people really made a difference. But during the earlier months we two carried the main burden. It took almost a year of actual functioning of the school for that imbalance in the work load to dissipate itself and for the responsibility for the school to be divided more evenly.)

One of the ways we solicited students was by using the summer session. We decided to open the school on July 1 rather than in September, which would have been the proper time to open for a standard school year. We wanted to have our program run through the summer in order to give parents and students a chance to try it out without making a final commitment, to help them decide whether this was what they really wanted. This way they could get to know the staff and what the program would be like, and make a decision based on some reality. This was one of the ways we were going to compensate for the lack of a real live model for the people to see in the interviews.

As it turned out an awful lot of people came to the summer session; we had about a hundred and thirty students in the summer. When we started recruiting students we allowed anybody to enroll for the summer, even people who were avowedly coming for the summer alone, because we thought it would be good for the school to have a lot of children in it, and that we'd be better off having a full school, even if this meant having a lot of students who were definitely not coming back in the fall. A little later, when the enrollment began to fill up, we changed that and decided to take for the summer only those who were really trying it out for the year. Even so, a lot of parents said they were trying it out and in fact just used the summer as a summer camp to dump their children.

In retrospect, from the point of view of testing the school for the students, I don't think the summer was a very good idea. We got about 50% return rate from the summer to the fall, out of which I'm sure at least half would have come even if there had been no summer session, and perhaps all of them would. It's true that we got several students not to come who might have started out in the fall and dropped out and might have caused us extra trouble. But on the other hand a two month test period doesn't really give much of a taste of the school.

Any test period really isn't enough if you call it a test. As we found out, even if you say to a student that you're going to give a test period of a year, it's not enough if the student is on test all year. Certainly a two month test isn't enough under any circumstances. In two months it's still very easy for parents and students to read into the program anything they want. If you add to that all of the initial perturbations that we had to work out, I don't think that from the point of view of testing out the school for the students it was a very good idea.

But in the event, having the summer session turned out to be a great blessing, actually a magnificent idea for the development of the school. Because what we did was use it as a proving ground for all the other components of the school, and in particular for the staff. The summer was the shakedown cruise for the staff, and it really enabled us to clarify a lot of our concepts as to what the role of the staff is and what a staff member should be. Not that we're not still clarifying it, but we ended the summer with a much clearer idea than we began with. A lot of people came and left in the summer, but the staff at the beginning of the fall was for the most part the same staff that we completed the year with, with only a few exceptions.

It's interesting to see how things work out differently from what you expected. The summer didn't serve its intended purpose for the student body, but if I think of what would have happened had we not had that intense clarification period for the staff, had we started out with a raw staff in the fall as well as a raw student body, I am convinced that the school would not have existed for more than two months. The whole thing would have collapsed in October or November. The ability of the school to survive the early fall rested entirely on the fact that we had a strong and united staff in the fall, and that was formed over the summer.

Another idea that we used to induce students to come to the school never got beyond the paper stage, which is all for the best. That was the idea of having an afternoon program so that students who would be going to public school could come after public school hours and participate in school activities afterwards. That was, even at the outset, a plan of desperation. That was when we were still thinking of a school with fifteen or twenty or twenty-five students in it, and hoping simply to get some companionship for them. So that we were willing to introduce something like an afternoon community-center program if only to bring some more students around and give the regulars some social life. Happily that never got off the ground. By the time people began inquiring about it we had enough registered students to make it unnecessary, and we abandoned it. But the fact that we even talked about it is just another indication of how desperate we were for a student body.

Getting back to the enrollment of students, we soon found that we were getting quite a number of requests, and it became necessary to get some kind of administrative order into this. What we did was develop an interview form, which wasn't an application for enrollment, but an application for an interview. When people called and inquired about the school we would send this out. It just had some basic listings on it – the name and age of the prospective student, the names and addresses of the parents, and a statement at the top that we had an open admissions policy and we required an interview at which both parents were to come; and that if they wanted an interview they could send this form in and then we'd call them and set one.

That gave us a little more control over the flow of the interviews. We started getting these forms in and making calls and scheduling interviews ourselves. Eventually we realized that we were just having the interviews and letting the people go home and make up their minds, and then when they did make up their minds we didn't have any procedure for handling them.

We needed an enrollment form, and we spent some time thinking about what had to go on that form. We knew we wanted open files, and we knew that we didn't want the kind of data that would be confidential and that we didn't feel had any relevance to the students' coming to our school. Which meant that we ended up with an enrollment form which had nothing but ordinary registration information: name, addresses, names of physicians in case of emergency and this sort of thing. The filling out and return of this form was considered a commitment to enroll the student.

We then started giving out these forms in the interviews and saying that if you wanted to enroll you had to send the form in and that would constitute enrollment. We also mailed them out to all those who had already been at interviews. We didn't yet have a legal contract – this enrollment form didn't constitute a legal contract. We certainly didn't require a deposit. We were still afraid that if we required some kind of a deposit we would scare people away. We didn't even set a deadline on when these forms had to be turned in. As the interviews increased in number – we must have interviewed several hundred people during the period between March and August, with a big peak coming in April, May, June and July – when it became clear that we were in real danger of filling the school to capacity and even exceeding the capacity of the school plant, we had to start putting some sort of a deadline on the return, telling people that they had to return it by a certain time.

We closed enrollment on July 17, because at that time we had over 150 enrollment forms. Of course, as it turned out quite a few of the people who had enrolled never showed up. They changed their minds at the last minute. It wasn't until the middle of the summer that we actually had a contract that was a legal contract document. On August 1 the contracts were mailed out to all the people who had sent enrollment forms, and that finally required a signature and a written commitment to the tuition. A lot of the people who had sent in enrollment forms never sent in the contracts. So we were able to allow a few more siblings or friends in after July 17, and a few people got in by being insistent. But basically from July 17 on the enrollment was closed, though we ended up starting the school with quite a bit under our capacity – about 135, whereas our capacity was closer to 170. That was because a lot of people didn't show.

It probably would have been good to have the contracts ready earlier, and in general to have the procedure a little more formal earlier, but we had to get over our feeling of desperation, and anyway each new procedure only came up at the time when it became pressing and not in advance. The need for contracts only made itself felt after we had a big enrollment and we realized that we had to regularize the way of collecting the money. We had to put it on a legal basis so that people would in fact be legally liable for the money, and we'd be legally able to collect it. We probably should have had the contracts much earlier.

But this brings up the whole subject of how the legal side of the school was taken care of. Fred Hilton served as corporation counsel for the school from the beginning, and he did most of the school's legal work. Fred was quite aware that the school was a radical departure from other schools, and that we would be doing things in a different manner, and he, like us, was not sure in advance how we had to go about these things. So for him too it was important to pace his attention to problems according to the rate at which they came up. He also realized that if we tried to anticipate everything before we'd really worked it out we'd be running into trouble and doing wasted work.

His attitude towards the legal side of the school was very much in line with the school's philosophy, but very different from the normal counsel-client relationship. Anyway, there was never a standard counsel-client relationship between Fred and the school for many reasons. Fred was a personal friend; he was doing it out of personal friendship, among other reasons. He was even involved with our personal legal dealings in the beginning before the school took over these matters. He was also President of the corporation and President of the Board of Trustees. So we never really had a hired counsel to the corporation, who could be instructed what to do and who could render independent opinions that he would not have to then defend from an executive position.

Anything Fred did as counsel he then later had to be aware of defending as President or as Trustee or as parent. All of these aspects made the counsel-client relationship very complex. Everything went along fine as long as there was no strain on the relationship, but it buckled when we hit our first really major crisis. I don't see that we could have avoided this situation. Without Fred's help and advice we probably would not have gotten off the ground, and there was no way to have Fred involved in the school and have somebody else serve as counsel. In fact he was counsel before he was anything else. So it's just one of those quirks of history that we got into that kind of a situation. Afterwards, we finally hired counsel who was not a Trustee and was not a corporation member but was entirely independent.

To get back to the original point, Fred applied our philosophy to our whole mode of operation in that he made it a policy never to suggest on his own that certain legal work had to be done. He always let me, or somebody else, discover that a legal problem existed, and present a draft of the solution, or at least worry about the solution. If we wanted to do something we had to take the responsibility for doing it. He was there as counsel in the strict sense of the term, as adviser when we sought his advice. This is quite different from the usual relationship. Later, one of our Trustees, a businessman, would often say at meetings (in response to a problem), "Well, you just tell counsel what your problem is and let him work it out." This is in fact the way most lawyers operate for corporations. Their advice is more active; they're expected to come up with drafted solutions.

Fred's attitude was that we were the ones who were supposed to come up with the solutions, we were supposed to handle our own affairs, we were supposed to come up with the proposed solutions and he was there to check them out when we came to him, and to see that they were done properly; but we had the primary responsibility for spotting the problems and for seeing them through. Which meant that — for example, since I'm talking about student contracts — we wrote out the enrollment forms, and he didn't ask to check them, or any others, unless we brought them to him. When it came to drawing up a legal contracts, I was the one who drafted it. Fred was then given it to look at, and he made some suggested changes.

Hanna did most of the interviewing. I was so busy with other tasks that I did only a few. It came to the point, in April, May, and early June, where I would only interview if we had to schedule two concurrently or if she had to be in a different place. In the beginning we did them together, when we were learning how to do them. The pressure of these interviews was tremendous on Hanna. She saw hundreds of people. I'd say she almost never spent less than hour in an interview and she often spent much more than an hour.

Almost every interview was a grueling experience. The interviews brought out the deepest aggressions and hostilities and fears and defensiveness on the parents' part towards these new concepts. Practically every interview involved basic attacks on the philosophy of the school and often on us. It was a physical and especially emotional strain to go through these interviews by the dozens and by the hundreds. It's difficult to imagine what a terrific strain it was. By early June Hanna gave under that strain; but luckily for us she lasted into June, and by then it was possible for the rest of us to take over the interviewing for her. She kept away from it for several weeks until she sort of got her bearings back, and then towards the end she took her regular turn in the interviews. But she was especially suited to doing interviews. By temperament she could maintain an equable external balance even while undergoing an internal slow burn, which is something she could do better than I could. But she paid a heavy price for it while it was going on.

There was nothing the parents hesitated to say at these interviews. Many of the interviews involved parents reviling their children to their faces. Many of the interviews were so tense that the parents spent much of the time concentrating on utterly trivial questions such as how the transportation arrangements would be made, or would there be food or not or something like that, just to avoid talking about the educational issues. It is an important thing to point out that we made it clear at the interviews – this was our policy always – that once we got the people to the interview, once we got their interest, we certainly didn't have a soliciting stance toward them in any overt way. We did not try to convince them that this was the school for them. On the contrary it was always our policy, certainly mine and Hanna's, and certainly that of most of the other interviewers in June and July (although there may have been some exceptions) – it was certainly our policy to discourage people from coming to the school.

We would point out all the difficulties involved, all the ways in which the school was different from other schools, all the strains that were going to appear, all the unaccustomed outcomes that parents should expect. Our policy was to discourage them, unless it was really what they wanted, unless they really wanted this kind of freedom. Because we did know, we were certainly always aware, that if we got people there on false pretences, if we got people there who really didn't want to be there, we were going to be in for a lot of trouble, because as soon as they woke up and found out what it really is they were going to be very unhappy and seek to destroy it. As it turned out, that came precious close to happening anyway. But at least we always knew that our hands were clean in this respect. We did not engage in any active solicitation or any deceit whatsoever that would avoid the basic issues in enrolling the students. We were clear in saying that this was a very different school, and that you should not come unless you really wanted it. And there was a large drop-off rate from the interviews. Dozens and dozens of people came for the interviews and did not return. They were discouraged. So I would say that at least in that respect the interviews were in line with our way of viewing a healthy enrollment procedure.

Early Finances

The finances of the school during this initial period of 1967-69 can be taken care of rather briefly. We knew that we'd need seed money to get the school off the ground, and, as I've pointed out, we expected to put up that seed money personally. It was always our idea that the school would run on tuition. We didn't expect to require any kind of contributions or any kind of outside help. The only thing that we needed was seed money to start with, for a down payment on the campus and then to fix up the campus and to equip it for starting. As soon as the school started we expected to be able to cover its operations through tuition income. We also realized it would take some time for the tuition income to build up to a level sufficient to cover staff salaries, because the school population would take time to build up. That's why we said from the very outset that there would be no staff salaries at all during the first year. So that in effect the staff would be providing additional seed money for the school, in the form of their salary for the first year.

No other school that I know of has started off with this kind of an initial subsidy on the part of the staff. It amounted to an effective subsidy of over a hundred thousand dollars for the first year. This made the founding of the school possible. As for the cash seed money, it required $24,000 in down payment on the $80,000 property, and it required something like another $16,000 in seed money to cover the initial repairs and modifications that were required to make the school conform to standards, the initial outfitting and furnishing and public relations and catalogs, and so forth. This meant a total of something over forty thousand dollars in cash that we put up personally.

The way that was arranged was that we wrote a one year note for the entire sum. The idea was that during the first year of operation we would work out a regular method of repayment. Fred looked out for our personal interests in a very careful way. I was at the time still naive, and ready to bank on a lot of good will. I was ready to forego formal repayment procedures, and I was ready to see the money returned over fifteen or twenty years. Hanna was much wiser. She insisted on a more regularized procedure, and Fred supported her wholeheartedly, much to our benefit, and made sure that we would not commit ourselves beyond one year, so that we would have a chance to see how things were going at the end of the first year. That certainly was a great protection as things turned out. It made a tremendous difference.

The bank mortgage constituted a long term loan which subsidized the school at the outset to the tune of $56,000. That was not an easy mortgage to get. As I've already mentioned, banks were not eager to lend money to schools; we tried at several banks and all of them turned us down. The winter of 1968-69 was also a tight money period. Not as tight as the year before, but also relatively tight. Interest rates were rising. To give some idea, that was a time when ordinary interest rates for good home mortgages were in the vicinity of 6-1/2%. When I had gotten my home mortgage six months earlier the rate was 5-3/4%. So we're talking about a ¾ point rise in the mortgage rate in half a year. Of course we've become used to that kind of rise since then.

What happened was that thanks to the community sponsorship of our school, and thanks to Bill Randall's involvement with the school, we were able to obtain a mortgage from the Framingham Trust Co. for $56,000 at 7%. This was a high interest rate, although not above the rate that would be normally given to high risks. But since we couldn't get a mortgage from any other bank, we gladly paid 7%. It was a great thing that the mortgage came through, and one of the key breaks that we got in the formation of the school.

The tuition rate was set at $700 for full time students and prorated for part time students. We allowed all sorts of part time attendance. Again, that was another way of getting students to come. We allowed attendance at the nursery school level for two days a week, two mornings a week, three days, three mornings, part time in every conceivable way, so that we'd match the flexibility allowed in other nursery schools. We hoped that would induce parents to send their children when they were still very young, and get them used to this kind of an educational system at a very early age. Now a tuition rate of $700 was clearly not going to do anything as far as the finances of the school went in the first year. We expected that 30 students paying $700 would just about cover the out of pocket cash expenses the very first year.

The way we set the tuition was by reference to public schools' expenditure per pupil. During the year 1967-68, which was the year just before our opening, the average public school expenditure per pupil was around $700 in the reasonably better systems. That wasn't the top per pupil expenditure and it wasn't exactly the average; it was a bit above average but still close enough to be considered a reasonable average. It certainly was far below the tuition of any private school in the entire area. The idea was that if we could make this kind of school work financially a lot of people would take a second look, because certainly the first thing that anybody looks at with a new school program – anybody on a school committee or any administrator, and even teachers – the first thing they look at is what it costs.

We were determined from the outset to make it competitive with the public school system, and we were convinced that the finances would work out, including staff salaries, when the school became big, because we were sure that we would operate more efficiently than any public school system in every respect.

We were sure that we'd have fewer expenses on educational materials because we would just be filling needs and we wouldn't be buying the tremendous excess of equipment that the regular public schools buy in the course of forcing all the kids to do what they don't want to do, and equipping them to do it. I already had some experience of the tremendous savings that can be achieved, when I had established a free laboratory in Barnard and saw how each student could do far better experiments at far less total cost because we didn't have to duplicate everything needlessly. So we were sure that our curriculum costs would drop. We were also sure that our expenses on the physical plant would not be excessive, because we didn't think we had to worry about grandiose buildings – more about that later. We were sure also that our pupil-teacher ratio would be more favorable than the public schools'. In the public schools they run about twenty or twenty-five students per teacher, and here we felt that when we were running at full steam – well, we just had no idea, we certainly were sure that we wouldn't need more than one teacher per twenty or twenty-five students, and the economics of that works out to good salaries. But we anticipated that our ratio as the school grows would go up and up and up, to 30, 40, maybe even 50 to 1. We really had no idea.

It remains to be seen what it's going to be. We also knew that we were going to save tremendously on administrative expenses. In fact we were going to just wipe away the administrative overhead at one sweep. We weren't going to be burdened with any kind of administrative structure because the staff was going to share all the administrative tasks as equitably as possible, split it up among itself and not have that expense to burden the school with. So on all these counts we were convinced that we were going to have a much more efficient operation, and that we had no reason to think that our per pupil expenditure would exceed that of the public schools.

When I come to the financial considerations that led to the raising of tuition for the second year, I'll have more to say about that again. But our principle didn't change at all. If anything, the economic realities of the first year bore out all these feelings and convinced us that, provided we got a school that is large, we would in fact operate far more efficiently, and with better salary scales and better equipment all around, than any public school system. Even the idea of apprenticeship in our school goes a long way towards providing the very best equipment possible, because as soon as a student is ready to specialize in any area and to learn the techniques of any area in depth, he goes out into the real world in an apprenticeship program and uses the very latest equipment that's in actual use. So you don't get this guaranteed obsolescence and fakery that exists in every single school situation, even through the college and university level, where students are trained on "student" equipment that is already many years behind the times, because by the time the school equipment manufacturers get it it has already gone through its regular course of obsolescence in industry. And then to make things worse, the equipment is specially designed for students, so that it's not the real thing anyway. It's a minor miracle that anybody ever gets out of a student laboratory or a student situation into the real world, because anyway they have to be retrained from scratch. I remember this vividly because I had gone through all the laboratory courses in physics, and yet when I was playing with the idea of becoming an experimental physicist I had absolutely no training worth a dime that I could call on.

The Structure of the School

I want to discuss in some detail the administrative, organizational and legal structure of the school that was put together during those months. In the first place there was the question of incorporating the school as a non-profit educational institution, according to the laws of the state of Massachusetts. We had to do a great deal of thinking about the kind of legal structure that we wanted and the kind of by-laws that we wanted to operate under. There were some features of the school that required special consideration before the legal structure could be worked out.

We knew that we wanted the internal governance of the school to be carried out by the School Meeting, and all the other affairs of the school, the general policy and the external affairs and the contractual affairs and so forth, to be governed by the general corporation, which would include the parents – because we felt it was right to include the family – and which would also include members of the public and the staff. We were sure that all these people had to have a voice.

We didn't want a staff cooperative – that didn't seem any more correct to us than having a school run by a headmaster. We didn't want a parent cooperative – that didn't seem right either because that left out people who were daily involved in the school, such as the staff. And we didn't want just a public board of Trustees. We wanted all these various sectors involved in the school. But there were a number of thorny points. For example, an ordinary corporate structure, which is incorporated under the laws of the Commonwealth of Massachusetts, has certain requirements. You have to have a President, you have to have a Treasurer, you have to have a Secretary, and you have to have a Board of Trustees. It seemed that in order for this to be a legal corporation these various offices and structures had to have certain powers that were rather considerable. And that seemed to run counter to our wishes to avoid a hierarchical power structure in the school.

This required a lot of thought. Normally a President is the chief executive officer of a corporation and has a lot of decision making power. The Board of Trustees usually has the full power of running the corporation. This is true of ordinary corporations and is certainly true of charitable institutions. There is usually a general membership, and if the general membership does anything significant that usually consists of electing Trustees, although many Boards of Trustees are self-perpetuating. The general membership may have some other token powers, but by and large the Trustees run the place in all policy making aspects, and the executive officers carry out the decisions and have a wide latitude of decision making power. This did not reflect the kind of school we wanted. We did not want to have any specific individual distinguished by decision making powers that made any difference. We wanted the internal governance spread among the entire community of students and staff, and the external governance spread among the parents, the staff, the Trustees, and public members. The way we saw it, the Trustees would be elected by the membership at large, and we wanted the Trustees to be like the executive officers; we wanted them to be responsible for carrying out the policy decisions, while we did not want the executive officers to have important powers at all.

There were additional requirements dictated by our conception of the democratic structure of the school. We knew that we wanted a Board of Trustees that was up for re-election every year, so that you couldn't get any entrenched group. We wanted a staff without tenure. We didn't want the concept of tenure, we wanted people who were there on their own merits, and who were good enough to get jobs elsewhere if they had to.

It wasn't clear at the outset that we could do everything we wanted to in a corporate structure. We had a rather long meeting, at which several staff members were present, late in September of 1967. Bill Randall was there too, and of course Fred. We discussed at some length just how democratic we wanted to be. There was some feeling at the time for having all the students have a voice in the corporation. The principle was the usual democratic one that those affected by decisions should have a hand in making them. So we wondered whether the overall decision making structure shouldn't also include the students as well as the staff, parents, Trustees, and others because the students were involved in all the consequences of the decisions.

Fred and Bill doubted that you could make minors corporation members in Massachusetts. So the question then became one of looking for some other structure that would give minors the equal voice we wanted. I remember Bill Randall's shock that we would even consider giving four year olds any kind of voice in decisions – it was a shock that was to remain with him and with many other people throughout their association with the school. It would come back and express itself when the School Meeting made decisions about the internal affairs of the school. Then the question would always be, "How can you let four year olds vote?" The only way to get around this as far as the legal structure of the school was concerned seemed to be to depart from the corporate structure and to try to set up some form of a trust. So we also explored ways of setting up a trust, the point being that a trust is like a partnership agreement between the people concerned. If you're drawing up a trust agreement you can really draw up any sort of agreement you want – you can even allow minors a voice. We followed that line of thought for a while, and Fred drafted some possible outlines of trust agreements.

There were several considerations against setting up a trust form. One was a financial one. Drawing up a trust agreement would involve a tremendous amount of legal work. Then there was a much more important objection. In a trust, because it's an agreement, every detail of the agreement has to be spelled out. You can't rely, as you do in the corporate structure, on the body of corporate law that covers all corporations and sort of takes care of a lot of specifics that you don't have to spell out every time. In a trust there is no such thing, because every agreement is different. You've got to spell out every single little detail and facet of the organizations functioning. What this means is that your trust by-laws have to be practically a book and that they're constantly subject to revision and updating. Every time you want to make a little change you've got to go through a tremendous rigmarole.

Now if we were going to hope to be a model for a mass school system in this country, it hardly made sense to start out by organizing ourselves in such a complex fashion that a person had to master a whole book of by-laws in order to figure out what we were doing. Imagine if a school administrator came up and said, "I like the way your place is running. Could you get me a set of your by-laws so that I could set up one?" and you handed him a book 200 pages thick with every step spelled out in detail. It would be a legal monstrosity, and it would certainly put a damper on the ability of our ideas to diffuse in a mass way.

A corporation is a corporation. That already has been diffused for us. The corporate structure is something that is already understood throughout the country. So from the point of view of being a model for a mass educational system, you would be far better off being able somehow to adapt to the existing corporate structure and having a set of by-laws that are reasonably comprehensible, rather than go into the trust form. That was a big consideration.

We finally decided on a corporate structure, and we realized after further study that we were able to include most of our democratic principles in an ordinary corporate structure, because we didn't have to give the executive officers the kind of power we didn't want to give them, and we didn't have to give the Trustees the kind of power we didn't want to give them.

As a result, we produced our first set of by-laws (Appendix 4). There were two things in this first set of by-laws that were serious departures from either what we originally had in mind or what later turned out to be what we wanted. I'll touch on these briefly. The first was that, because of our hesitancy to mention minors at all in the by-laws, we left the School Meeting out completely. The School Meeting was described in all the literature and all the discussions that went on. But nowhere in the by-laws were the powers and duties of the School Meeting spelled out because we didn't feel that binding decision making powers for minors could be included in the corporate by-laws.

The second point had to do with the staff. The one part of the school that has always been hardest to focus on sharply is the staff. What exactly is it doing here, what are its responsibilities, what powers does it have? Even the simple concept that the staff was responsible for the day-to-day maintenance of the school took months to elaborate, and that very phraseology only came out towards the end of the summer, and entered our literature and our by-laws after we'd gotten under way. The staff did not have the responsibility for overall policy (that is for the Assembly), it didn't have contractual responsibility (that is for the Trustees), it didn't have responsibility for the internal governance of the school (that's for the School Meeting) – the staff had a very peculiar responsibility as the agents of the corporation responsible for the day-to-day maintenance of the school.

Furthermore it didn't have any disciplinary powers, being unique among all staffs at all schools that I've ever heard of in that it didn't have any power to back up its responsibility. It had to work through other organs. It had to try to affect internal discipline through the School Meeting, and any enforcement power that couldn't be exercised through the School Meeting had to be exercised through the Trustees.

If the staff made certain decisions that neither the School Meeting nor the Trustees nor the Assembly would back up, then you had a real problem on your hands, because then the staff either had to modify the decision or had to be fired. Because the staff in this structure was given no authority of its own. That's a very difficult concept to understand. I would say that this was very hard for many of the first group of Trustees and parents to figure out because they often expected the staff to take things into their own hands the way a normal staff would. I mean, what are you hired for? What are you a staff for, if not to do a, b, c, and d? It was very hard for people to get to the idea that the staff's role in our school was different from what it is in other schools, had a different character.

That was hard for us to formulate. The question of how the staff got chosen and hired and fired was terribly hard to formulate. In the early prospectus and in the early thinking on the staff I felt that the staff ought to be self-perpetuating, that the staff ought to select new staff. But that really didn't last long. Part of the revolution that opened the staff also made us less protective all around. We decided to open ourselves to additions and we also decided to open ourselves to criticism. We always felt we shouldn't have tenure, now the question was, who was it that we were serving?

The feeling at the time we drafted our first by-laws was that the staff was after all responsible for the running of the school and hence should be accountable to the full membership of the corporation. So the hiring was put into the hands of the Assembly. The firing, on the other hand, was not put into the hands of the Assembly, but into the hands of the Trustees. I didn't have any strong feelings about this one way or another.

Fred had very strong feelings about it, and I think rightly, because he felt that firing was going to be an extraordinarily unusual situation, especially since we don't have tenure and can simply drop a person at the end of his term. Firing would usually be for very unsavory reasons, and it wasn't the kind of thing that you wanted to air before the membership at large, because it was no good for the school to have these things aired in public and it was also extraordinarily damaging for the person involved. Fred's idea was that if the Trustees couldn't be trusted to have extraordinary restraint and discretion in this matter, then what could they be trusted to do? This was something that ought to be the domain of the Trustees. They could handle it quietly and yet with dignity and with care. I think he was right at the time.

This caused quite a ripple in the spring of 1968. Sandy raised tremendous objections to it, and several other staff members expressed serious doubts about it because they felt that the Trustees were sort of a sword hanging over them and that if they didn't behave they'd be fired right away. It took a great deal of argument to convince them that they had to trust the Trustees, and also that they had to let the thing work for a while and see what happens. Eventually that issue just sort of faded into the background and the experience of time showed that it was a good decision.

Another aspect which wasn't dealt with in the first set of by-laws had to do with getting rid of students. We had no stipulation about letting students come in or getting students to leave. I guess the assumption was that this didn't have to be put in the by-laws since the school would run like any other school — that the staff would somehow find a way to enroll students and select them and if need be would get rid of them. But there was no specific provision in the by-laws, and as we came to know the by-laws better and to understand them it was clear that a staff that had no disciplinary power whatsoever was not going to be the group that would be empowered to throw students out of the school. That was perfectly ridiculous. If they didn't have the power even to discipline in minor instances, you certainly weren't going to give the staff the power to throw a student out if they didn't like him.

We were sort of in limbo there. There was no provision in the by-laws for throwing out students who were obviously destructive. On the other hand it was clear, once you thought of the problem, that the Trustees had to do that for the same reason that the Trustees were the ones who were going to throw out staff if there was staff to be thrown out. The analogy with staff clearly applied. But on the other hand you could argue that just precisely because the Trustees' power to fire the staff was spelled out in the by-laws, while their power to throw out students was not spelled out in the by-laws, that they didn't have that power. That's a standard legal argument and it could have been presented.

In fact, the only place where you could argue that the Trustees were given the power to dismiss students was in the provision that they had power to run the general affairs of the corporation in a beneficial way. You could say that in times of crises when a student did something terrible it would be part of the general powers of managing the business of the corporation that the Trustees could throw him out. That was in fact the power under which the Trustees finally did act when they had to expel a student, but it was very much to everybody's disadvantage that this wasn't spelled out, and it cost great delays and doubts in the Trustees' actually assuming this power. This error of omission was to play havoc with us later when we had our first great crisis with students.

The papers of incorporation were drawn up and signed at the organizational meeting of the corporation held February 19, 1968 at our home. That was a great occasion. It was covered by the *Framingham*

News. We had champagne for everybody. There was a brief organizational meeting according to the law, at which officers were elected: Fred Hilton was elected President; the Trustees were elected; Alan White was elected Secretary; and Dennis Flynn was elected Treasurer. There were a total of twelve original incorporators. That included the seven incorporators that were required by law for the purpose of incorporating a non-profit corporation, and all the Trustees; there were eleven original Trustees, and Dennis Flynn, as an officer, was also one of the original incorporators. That was the total membership of the corporation in our organizational meeting.

We had our first corporate business meeting on May 6, and one thing is worth recounting here. We had a provision in the by-laws that a quorum for an Assembly meeting is ten. Of course, that is a small quorum, and was set so that we could always carry out our business; for the very first business meeting, however, when we had only twelve incorporators, to have a quorum of ten meant that just about everybody had to show up. It was quite a business on May 6 to get everybody to show up at least long enough to elect other members of the corporation, namely staff and public members, and bring up the total number so that we wouldn't be strangled for a quorum ever again.

There wasn't any official staff in the school until the Assembly could hire them on May 6. The reason for that was that you had to have your papers approved. They had to be drawn up and sent to the Secretary of State for his approval. That took some time. You couldn't actually transact any business until the papers were approved and the charter was issued, and we had our first annual Spring meeting as provided in the by-laws on May 6 at which we transacted our first business. I'm going to come to that shortly.

I want to point out two other aspects of the school's organization that were written into the by-laws and were not part of the legal structure of the school, but yet were very much part of the printed literature and part of its way of operation. They had to do with the relation of the school to the community. We had a school that was completely open to visitors. Anybody could come in. It was our aim to be part of the community, not to close off our doors in any defensive stance, not to regulate the visitors, not to register them, not to make them feel unwelcome in any way, but to open our doors wide to anybody who wanted to come in, to make them feel welcome on the premises. The only limits to this openness had to do with expense. A person couldn't come in and use our facilities in a way that would cost us money without covering that expense; but that was a provision which we never really had to worry about.

This openness to visitors was something that a lot of people questioned on many grounds. Most new schools discourage visitors. Our feeling was always that if the school was really as much in contact with the real world as we claimed it was, openness would in no way disrupt it. There was no reason to fear adult intrusion; adults didn't have any particular authority in the school, and there was no reason to think that they'd disrupt. They had to be civil, and the visitors had to obey the same rules and regulations that everybody else in the school had to obey, but to the extent that they did there was really no reason to think that they would disrupt anything because the atmosphere of the school was one of openness to the world, and therefore completely compatible with an open visiting policy. It turned out that we were ultimately disappointed in our expectations, especially because of continuing hostility from visitors. But for a long time we maintained our complete openness.

The other part of the structure that wasn't spelled out in the by-laws, was an important feature and was, I would say, a colossal failure – I think our one and only really colossal failure – namely, the visiting teacher program. This had to do with some early mistakes that we made about the role of the teacher in the school. Although we were always clear that learning would take place in the school only at the initiative and request of the students, we did feel that the interests of students would be so varied and cover such a wide spectrum that it would be important to have available a wide spectrum of teachers either on the premises, or regularly visiting the premises, or associated with the school, so that we could satisfy any request.

Where we went wrong was in our understanding of the nature of learning that is self-motivated. I think we underestimated the amount of progress that a student can make on his own if he's really bent on learning a subject. We were a little overanxious. We were a little too eager to have somebody there at the first sign of interest, not to let the interest die because it had encountered some obstacle, however small. It's sort of like Fred's principle that if a business deal is good it'll stay good. I don't think that we realized that if an interest is real it'll be pursued, and that there will be repeated attempts made to overcome obstacles — that this is part of reassuring yourself that your interest is real. It's really part of establishing a real interest — seeing it through and fighting it out. We were just a little overanxious to have someone ready and waiting just as soon as the student expresses his first interest in a subject.

So we had all these visiting teachers lined up. That naturally led to going just a little further, to making sure that everybody knows that you've got these people available — you announce them, you make their presence known, you give their names, you give their fields, you express in writing and orally their availability and willingness to teach, and that they'll be there these particular days each week, and you even go a little further, saying, "I'm ready to give a course in this or that to anybody who's interested at a certain time." It's all sort of a continuum: as soon as you're over-eager to jump at the first sign of curiosity that a student shows, you can very easily lapse into making this over-eagerness obvious and sort of making it clear that you hope the students will show an interest in your direction. And that's just a short step away from the good old progressive idea that you've got these wonderful things to offer, you're hoping they'll take it, and the idea that they'd please you an awful lot if they did take it.

Now I think all these things iron out in the wash, and in fact in our school they did iron out in the wash when it became clear, for example, that even if students did please a teacher by taking his course, no material rewards came out of it, he didn't get an A, and he didn't get a pat on the back, and he didn't get a good report card or anything like that. The effect of it was really transient and the students dropped out if they really weren't interested. And they dropped out like flies, so that most of these overanxiously constituted courses were failures. Soon we didn't do that any more. We learned very quickly that this was an unstable way of doing things and an incorrect way. But there were certainly dangers in the beginning that our overanxiousness would give us some of the aspects of a progressive school, which had offerings that it wanted the students to take advantage of.

I think that the staff in the school erred in this far less than the visiting teachers. But the fact that we went a little overboard and made sure that we had a good list of visiting teachers, made sure that everybody knew that we had a tremendous range of activities, led to somewhat of an overanxious atmosphere to please and to service and perhaps to encourage learning, if you will, that shouldn't have been present at the outset. I don't think that we ever crossed the really sharp dividing line between our kind of school and a progressive school. We never introduced all those institutional rewards and punishments that would back up a progressive attitude. But the visiting teachers certainly lent some color of progressivism to the school, though it rapidly faded out, as it became clear that the only way anybody was going to learn was if he really wanted to learn.

The students quickly realized that it didn't pay to satisfy people by learning things that they didn't want to learn, and the visiting teachers rapidly found out that there was no future in it for them if they came and hawked their wares, that nobody was going to give it support, that nobody was going to pat them on the back. If they came to the school it was because they wanted to come. In that sense too the program turned out to be a tremendous flop, because the visiting teachers almost never showed up. The number that ever showed up even once was probably about 50% of those who said they'd come, and the number that made any kind of a contribution could be numbered on one hand.

There were a few visiting teachers who came all summer fairly regularly, but only two came on a regular basis during the school year. Aside from that, the program just fizzled out. I don't think it had any catastrophic effect on the school, but as a conception it was all wrong because it stressed a type of overanxiousness that shouldn't have been in the school. As soon as that was realized by all parties concerned, by the visiting teachers, by the students, by the staff, by everybody, the program sort of faded away.

If, in the real world, you want to learn something, the guy doesn't come to you except under extraordinary circumstances. By and large you go to the person and learn on site. You don't expect anything else. That's the way to extend the range of offerings. To make the range of offerings in the school as wide as the real world, which is what we said we were going to do all along, means to make the whole real world easily accessible to people in the school. It doesn't mean that you artificially try to transplant into the school images of the real world, which is the way schools usually do it, unsuccessfully. It didn't take long to sort that out, but there was a short term perturbation which certainly added to our problems of getting ourselves straightened out when we first started functioning.

I have yet to recount how the original Board of Trustees was composed during the fall and winter of 1967 and early 1968. The first group of Trustees was, in addition to Hanna and me, essentially the neighbors who had given their support from the outset. Fred Hilton of course was deeply involved from the beginning. I asked Lorna Johnson to be a Trustee, and I remember having a conversation of several hours with her. She had become a member of the Framingham School Committee and felt that she would be interested in somehow being involved in an educational experiment. She certainly didn't subscribe to our theories, but she joined out of an interest in the experiment. She often used language analogous to the language she used as a medical researcher: that here was an experiment she was interested in, and that she was willing to help supervise in a professional capacity as a Trustee.

Harvey Ammerman joined, and then Bill Randall. The other early Trustee was Alan White. That gave us a total of seven. Those seven would have been the original incorporators, except that it was not a good idea to have husband and wife as original incorporators. In fact, generally it isn't a good idea to have a husband and wife on a Board of Trustees. It was only because of our extraordinary financial stake that we both were on the Board of Trustees to begin with, to protect our financial risk to the extent possible.

During January and February 1968 we added four more Trustees in time for our organization meeting on February 19. These were Gene

Wilson, who was at the time in the Harvard School of Education and was in the process of forming his own company. Gene was President of the Framingham Choral Society, and he was also the organist and choral director of the Unitarian-Universalist Church in Framingham. We met Gene through Stanley Kass, another Trustee, whom we met in turn through Alan White. Stan was a project director with Raytheon. He joined not out of identification with the philosophy of the school but out of an interest in seeing a different kind of a system tested out. Wally Rubin became a Trustee, and eventually an officer. Wally was a stockbroker; we had met him through his wife. Joan Rubin and Myrna Aronson were sisters who were very much involved in the League of Women Voters and who were among the recipients of the first prospectus, along with a personal letter. The responded, and they came and talked with us and became very interested in the school. Joan at the time was thinking of somehow being involved with the school on a part time basis. She was teaching art part time. The fourth Trustee added at that time was Marx Wartofsky, Chairman of the Philosophy Department at Boston University, whom I had met through some friends shortly after we moved to Framingham. I had many long discussions with him about the philosophy of science.

During the first year, several Trustees resigned. Stanley Kass was the first to resign, in November of 1968 at the height of the crisis that I'll be describing later. Fred Hilton was next, then Marx, Lorna, and Harvey. Five out of the original eleven resigned, and then Bill did not return after serving out his year term. So by the end of the first year we had lost six of the original eleven Trustees, which is very much in line with the general 50% attrition rate that we experienced all along. I'll come back to that later. I don't really know the significance of that attrition rate, except that it appeared in place after place in the initial phases of the school. These positions were almost all filled as they became vacant.

I should say a word about the public members who were elected to the Assembly as people from the community at large who had expressed some interest in the school. One of the public members was Edna Frank, who was also on the Framingham School Committee and was known for her interest in educational innovation. Mal Stalker was a public member. He was of invaluable help throughout all the phases of remodeling the campus, and he was the main contractor for all of our work. He supervised all the physical transformation that the place underwent with tremendous care. He really made every effort to do things for us well, and as efficiently as possible.

Charles Gaines, minister of the First Parish Unitarian-Universalist Church became a public member. There were other public members in addition to these. Several were elected in the September '68 corporation meeting, which takes me a little ahead of myself; they had been candidates for the staff but had changed their minds, and they wanted to continue some official association with the school.

Another public member, elected at the May '68 meeting, was Nancy Hilton, who was going to become a member of the corporation as a parent but who was so helpful in so many ways that we felt that we wanted to make her a public member immediately in order to involve her right away in the functioning of the corporation. By one of those twists of history, she became the last member of the Hilton family to remain formally associated with the school. Fred resigned as Trustee and President, Timmy withdrew as a student, but Nancy remained through May '69 as a public member of the corporation.

We called on some of the public members who had shown real interest in the school to replace some of the Trustees who resigned. That's how Charles Gaines became a Trustee after Stanley Kass resigned. Joel Gordon, a parent, was elected to cover the vacancy caused by Fred Hilton's resignation. He was the only parent who was heard by the Trustees during the critical upheaval of the school in the fall, as the representative of the parents who were satisfied with the way the school was running. After Marx resigned, Sheldon Penman was elected a Trustee. Sheldon was a long time personal friend, going back to 1956. We had been students together in the graduate department of physics and we never lost contact. He had been Hanna's boss at MIT. When the news broke that the school was in a lot of trouble, Sheldon immediately called and offered every assistance he could. He was our "academician" in place of Marx. The other two vacancies occurred in the late winter and early spring, and we didn't feel a need to fill them in until the May '69 meeting. These were filled at the May meeting, along with the vacancy created by the termination of Bill Randall's term, by electing Edna Frank; Barbara Chase, a parent of three students in the school, who was eager to participate in school activities; and Dennis Flynn, who under the new by-laws had to become a Trustee as Treasurer.

It's sort of interesting how the composition of the Trustees changed over the first year. It started out with our neighbors as the nucleus. That gave us an absolutely essential starting point. But many of the early people were not really identified with the philosophy of the school or ready to go on the line for the philosophy if it was under attack. These were replaced by people who had some involvement in the school as parents or as interested members of the public, who were sympathetic towards what the school was doing, and could identify themselves with the school in crisis.

Myriad Details

Another thing that had to be done before school started was to obtain all the legal permits necessary for operation. We had to get an occupancy permit from the building inspector, which gave us the right to use our building as a school in Framingham. That meant that we had to submit ourselves to inspections on the part of the inspector and fire chief. We certainly cooperated in every way because we were determined to be well within the bounds of the law. As radical as our program was in education, we certainly didn't want to shirk our duties as law abiding citizens. We wanted to fulfill, and we wanted to be known as fulfilling, all of the laws and ordinances of the land because we wanted to make it clear that our philosophical conceptions of education were entirely consistent with a system of laws that is set up in a democratic society. We were always clearly set on the path of being a law abiding organization; and the authorities with whom we worked recognized this. We always cooperated with them to the utmost, and they recognized this and cooperated with us in return. For example we installed a beautiful fire detection system in the school, which the fire inspector and the insurance underwriter said was one of the finest systems they had ever seen. It had ample detection heads and in no way tried to cut corners. This was typical of everything that we did.

We had an initial inspection in early spring, and we had a final inspection just before we opened the school; and we got our occupancy permit with no difficulty whatsoever. The underwriters approved our fire system. We put in an extra fire escape over and above what we had to do. We did expensive work on the dam over and above what we were required to do, even though the damn was structurally still quite sound. And so it went.

We also had to obtain the approval of the Framingham School Committee to operate as a school. To that end I had an interview with the superintendent of schools, discussed the school's program in detail, and sent him all the information about us. The superintendent of schools recommended it after clarifying that we certainly intended to comply with the attendance laws, that we were open at least 180 days a year and the proper number of hours a day for the students who fell under that law, and also after he was assured that we had available instructional capabilities equivalent to those of Framingham's high schools. He recommended approval of the school and the School Committee unanimously voted it.

As for the question of zoning, which had seemed as if it might be a problem, when the question finally came up it just evaporated. The building inspector apparently saw that we were in fact engaged in a bona fide operation and understood that the law entitled us to open a school in that area. He issued a permit without any difficulty. So in the end we didn't have to go the Zoning Board of Appeals route. We were issued the permit in a perfectly straightforward fashion.

We also took pains to hire a certified lifeguard for the summer, who was not a member of the staff. In fact he's the only person who was at the school in any kind of a teaching capacity who got paid regularly for his services during that first year. He got paid the regular rate paid lifeguards during the summer of 1968, and that gave us the full protection we felt we needed on the waterfront. The pond was a beautiful swimming area, and I think without the swimming we would just have never made it through the summer. We also had to arrange many other things, such as insurance. We had the benefit and the assistance of a good insurance company and were covered comprehensively in every way.

For the first summer we committed ourselves to organizing transportation for a fee. That took a great deal of organizational work, far out of proportion to what it was worth. Several staff members, with the idea that they might get some income out of it, drove students along pickup routes to and from school. It turned out to be a major miscalculation, and it just didn't work out. It wasn't possible to collect fees that would make any money for the staff members, and the complaints about the way it was done and the way it was organized were unbearable. At the end of the summer we swore off ever again having anything to do with transportation for the students.

There were a lot of details which had to be taken care of during that period. The library had to be organized. We went down to the Bureau of Library Extension of the Commonwealth of Massachusetts Board of Education and made contact with them and registered with them. We got the right to use the facilities of the Framingham public library, and bit by bit we set up ties with the various institutions that we would be called upon to cooperate with during the year.

I say all this simply to point out that at every turn there was something else to be taken care of, and all of these details were taken care of cleanly and thoroughly and professionally. There were no loose ends left, to the extent that we could locate them, because we were determined that the school would run as a completely professional and polished institution. Even such a thing as picking stationary for the school involved many phone calls until we found somebody who bid most reasonably on it, and involved going down and ordering it and picking it up. Everything was taken care of in detail, so that the school was prepared to open on July 1. We had as clear an idea as we could have been expected to have of what it was we were going to do: there was a staff present and ready to go, and a student body, all our papers were in order, there was a Board of Trustees, and so forth, and by the time July 1 came around we were ready for the test of reality.

On May 6 we had our first corporation business meeting (after the organizational meeting of February 19), and at that meeting we approved an annual budget for the next year which we knew would hold us through the summer and would require revision in September. There wasn't much debate at that meeting. Things were sort of laid out and cut and dried. But in holding the meeting we had taken our first step towards a town meeting form of government, even though there were no parent corporation members there and there wouldn't be until the December meeting.

With this I've reached the end of the preparatory period '67-'68, and I've come to July 1, 1968, which was the day on which the school opened its doors for operation. On the day that it opened the staff was raw. The corporation was raw. Everything was raw. We weren't experienced in any way, and the only thing we had going for us was our idea of how we wanted to shape American education. If we hadn't had that idea there would have been no school. It was the idea that kept the school going and welded all these raw elements into the final form of an experienced and functioning institution.

The Staff Comes of Age

In discussing the school's first year of operation from July 1, 1968 through the end of June 1969, it is not my intention to give a daily log of events but instead, in the same way that I've been proceeding till now, to discuss certain problems and topics that came up during that year, and follow them through the year. The first subject that I want to discuss is the one that was the major concern of the school during the summer: defining the responsibility of the staff, what the staff was in the school, what it meant to be a staff member, and what the staff's role was in this institution. As I have already said, when we started out on July 1, we knew that we were there but we didn't exactly know what we had to do. I guess you could say that we had the feeling that whatever had to be done, we would see to it that it was done, but that we really didn't work out the implications of that stance. But it certainly didn't take long before we had an opportunity to face the problem of the nature of the staff, because within the very first two weeks of the school's operation the entire matter came to a head and a crisis.

As might have been anticipated, the basic problem with the staff was defining the meaning of the word responsibility. Everybody understood that the staff was to be responsible for keeping the school going, and everyone also understood – in theory at least – that the idea was to diffuse this responsibility throughout the entire staff. That is to say, the idea was to have neither power nor authority nor responsibility concentrated in any one member of the staff or in any small clique of the staff. The difficulty came in translating this idea of diffusion of responsibility into a behavior pattern on the part of staff members that would in fact be identifiable as the concretization of the idea.

One of the important things we learned in this initial period was how to avoid a common misconception about diffusion of responsibility in a democratic society. The democratic ethos calls for equality of opportunity for everybody in a society. Nowhere does the democratic ethos imply that people are equally endowed either hereditarily or in any other way. The important point is that everybody has an equal shot at anything available in the society, and the important thing is to make this equality of opportunity real. On the other hand no one can say who will take up any particular pursuit, and no one dictates how the equally available opportunity will in fact be grasped by the various individuals in a society. In particular, nowhere does the democratic ethos specify – indeed, in no way is it compatible with – the equal allotment of available resources or available opportunities or anything else available in society. Equal allotment is as repugnant as unequal allotment. In fact equal allotment is just the other side of the coin of unequal allotment. They're both imposed by external authority, they're both a regimented form of allotment of resources; and it would come as no surprise, for example, that dictatorial governments introduce social reforms that move towards equal allotment of resources. Equal allotment is just as arbitrary as unequal allotment. What is not arbitrary is equal *opportunity*, which then makes it a matter of individual choice and individual responsibility to determine just how any one person is going to take advantage of the opportunity. A person has a right to take advantage or not take advantage. Just as, for example, a person has a right to show up at town meeting or not to show up at town meeting, or, in the school, to come to the School Meeting or not to come to the School Meeting.

As long as you are guaranteed an equal opportunity, you have no complaint later if you don't take advantage of it. It then becomes a matter of individual choice to exercise whatever degree of opportunity you wish to. The same holds for the concept of responsibility in the school. Certain things have to be done to keep the school going on a day to day basis. (The very words "maintain the school on a day to day basis" came to be used to describe the staff's work as a result of these clarifications during the first few weeks of the summer session.) These things constitute the collective responsibility of the staff. They have to be discharged by the staff if the staff is to fulfill its overall responsibility to keep the school going; if this total amount of work is not discharged by the staff, the school will not function and a new staff will have to be found.

The idea of the diffusion of responsibility among the staff says the following: there is not a priori unequal or equal subdivision of this responsibility among the staff members. No one has a monopoly over the responsibility, no group has a monopoly over it, nor is it a matter of any one person or even of the group *in toto* assigning the responsibility in any given way. Rather, the responsibility is there for every individual staff member to grab hold of, to the extent that he wishes and can. A responsible staff member is a person who will take as much of the responsibility available to the staff as it is equitable for him to take. That's of course a very difficult concept. It means that he won't grab more than his share and it means that he won't be a slacker and allow everybody else to pull his weight for him. Of course, the word "equitable" in this context is very difficult to pin down because it has to do not only with the total amount of work available but with the individual interests and capabilities of the various staff members, and this is something that has to be worked out between each individual staff member and himself primarily. Of course, to the extent that he's an agent of the school, that part of the school community that's responsible for hiring staff members has a right to judge at some point whether or not any individual staff member has in fact taken a fair portion of responsibility on his own, and to either continue the staff member in the employ of the school or to let him go on the basis of this evaluation.

All this was extraordinarily difficult to get clear, because we are embedded in a society in which there's still a tremendously strong tendency to arbitrarily assign and regiment and subdivide responsibility through some authority, either equally or unequally. In our society the idea that first comes to mind when one talks about diffusion of responsibility is that somebody's going to carve up the pie. To say that in fact nobody's going to do any carving, either equally or unequally, but that each member is going to have to do his own carving for himself and is really going to have to seize responsibility on his own, on the basis of his own evaluation of his capabilities and of the needs of the school and of what is appropriate and right – this is a terribly difficult thing to get across. I guess one can say in retrospect that we were very fortunate to make such rapid headway with the idea and to get so far so rapidly.

A prime example, because it's so simple, was the question of cleaning up the school. This came up over and over again. A lot of outsiders thought we were terribly preoccupied with cleaning, but in fact this was just the most obvious and simple example of what I'm talking about. Many of the staff initially thought that the overall cleaning of the school should be subdivided among the staff members much the way this is done in other groups, and then each person would do his allotted task. What happened was that this system showed itself immediately to be completely ineffective and completely out of line with what the school stood for. A subdivision was made. First of all, it was arbitrary and therefore had no relation to the interests and capabilities of the various staff members. Secondly, each staff member wasn't called upon to take really responsible action. Instead, he was called upon to act automatically by simply fulfilling an assigned task.

The result was quite predictable: staff members who were behaving responsibly and who would have been capable of arriving at their own conception of how much cleanup they ought to do were doing their part of the cleaning well, and responsibly, and those who were not responsible weren't doing their allotted part well. The former ended up doing the cleanup of the others as well, because they felt a responsibility for keeping the school clean. This was discussed several times at several staff meetings. At first it was so difficult to understand how else it could be done – so difficult to imagine saying, "Look, you don't have to subdivide the cleaning of the school. You don't do it that way, by assigning it to various people. The school has to be cleaned and everybody knows it, and people should look at the school and say, 'I'm going to see what has to be done and I'm going to do it.' If they see something that has to be done they simply go ahead, and if they're responsible people they do it. They won't pass a piece of paper lying on the ground and say, 'Well, I don't have outdoor pickup today, the other fellow will pick it up.' And they don't walk into a room in which something has just spilled and say,

'Well, I'm not assigned this room today, the guy who's assigned it will clean it up.' They simply do what has to be done."

Now, it's terribly difficult to make this transition from a regimented society to a responsible society. We're used to the regimented society, to having everything laid out in a linear fashion, and we're used to thinking that that's the way things get done because in a highly efficient technology that's in fact the way things get done. But in responsible behavior, initiated in a democratic society on the basis of individual initiative, you're not dealing with a linear situation. Even in cleaning. The linear element is the one that keeps the school clean according to some defined set of standards, and that's a very small element. That can be taken care of very easily. The non-linear element is much greater – in other words the element that provides a school that is aesthetically clean, that is aesthetically presentable – this already is not a linear concept. This is a matter of judgment, and this is a matter where each staff member really is called upon to exercise good judgment in his own way. People had to get used to the idea that the aesthetic character of the school, as regards cleanliness, came about as a result of each staff member's aesthetic conception of cleanliness, provided that each staff member is in fact trying to form such a conception in his own individual way.

The first objection that comes to mind is that something won't be done if it's not assigned. What's missed is the idea that by assigning you're not only preventing the assumption of responsibility, but you're also not taking any steps in the direction of developing the aesthetic aspect of the school.

We simply hammered away at this over and over again. In the beginning we did make assignments. We erred in that direction; we realized the error; we cancelled the assignments; people went ahead and did what they could; and gradually members began to develop a sense of responsible judgment as to what's appropriate and what isn't. It was really quite an experience to see this transformation take place over the summer. In the beginning of the summer it was terrible. Towards the middle of the summer a small number of staff members actually carried most of the work of the school. Then, towards the end of the summer, each staff member who remained really began to grapple with the problem and to find his own way, his own niche in contributing to the maintenance of the school. For example, by the end of the summer what you had was a completely spontaneous cleanup. You might have days in which more people would clean than on other days, but the point was that people would carve out tasks for themselves.

I remember the feeling of amazement that went through a lot of the members of the staff towards the end of the summer and the beginning of the fall to see that the school really was pleasantly clean. It wasn't a question of meeting minimal standards in a linear way. There was a character of presentability that went together with no graffiti and no vandalism of the school and so forth. The school was clean, and yet I would say that it wasn't compulsively clean – it wasn't kept shiny and polished and people weren't run after and told not to touch the walls and not to touch the chairs. It was well used; the school got normal use. But it was kept up in a reasonable and conscientious way by all the staff members. And there was a feeling of amazement that everybody on the staff had found his way towards this, and the place was actually kept clean without any need for making assignments of any sort whatever.

The same thing applied in every other realm of responsibility. There was clerical work to do. There was admissions work to process. There was a tremendous correspondence with other schools and organizations to worry about. There was a correspondence with people who inquired about the school, with people who were just plain interested in being in touch with the school, and with people who applied for jobs. There was routine correspondence that had to do with the financial aspects of the school. There was taking care of the physical upkeep of the school, keeping in touch with the plumber and the person who had to mow the lawn and do the snow removal and so forth. There was balancing the checkbooks and keeping the accounts. There were loads of areas of responsibility, and these were not parceled out, but slowly, very slowly, one after another of the staff members carved themselves out areas for which they wanted to take responsibility.

As this happened, the original concentration of responsibility diffused, not because people were forced to take on work, but because people took it over on their own; they were doing it as a matter of judgment, and they were capable of exercising judgment in the areas that they took over. In this way we got a real diffusion of responsibility, because when a person did take over an area he was in fact acting responsibly for that area, and not passing the buck to you because you had assigned it to him.

I would say that one of the greatest successes of the first year was the development of a staff in which all of the areas of maintaining the school were diffused among the various staff members. We had a staff in which the running of the school was rather fairly divided by the free, individual choice of various staff members to take over responsibilities for certain areas. This was very much in line with our open staff policy, where we in effect said: "We don't know whether you belong in the school or not, and we're not here to judge whether you belong in the school or not. Come. Look at the school. Look at what its needs are. Study your own capacity and see what you can do in the school, see if there's a place for you in the school, see whether there's something you want to do in the school, whether there's an area in which you can exercise responsible judgment and contribute to maintaining the school. If there is, then you belong in the school, and if there isn't then you yourself know that you don't."

This method of staff recruitment immediately eliminated everybody who's looking for an assignment, everybody who's looking for somebody to tell him what to do. In the beginning, we had a staff who came without a clear conception of what they were going to do in the school or in fact even what it meant to be responsible in the school. Once we worked this idea out, new people didn't come unless they had already found for themselves a niche in the school where they could make a responsible contribution to the maintenance of the school.

Another problem hit the staff during the first few weeks of operation of the school, and kept rocking it throughout the summer: the problem of confusing personal relationships with institutional relationships; looking for personal friendship and affection to be part of the school, part of its institutional character. This had to do with the whole question of interpersonal relations among staff members and between staff members and students, and the question of what a proper form of interpersonal relation is in an institution such as ours. This was related to the problem of responsibility, because what we had in a number of our early staff members was an inability to be responsible, which meant also an inability to define one's own character, to form an integrated concept of one's place in the school or in the world, a difficulty in formulating one's own individual makings. I think this is very closely related to a need for personal friendships as a means of shoring up the individual concerned, a means of filling the vacuum created by his lack of self-esteem and lack of well defined character. What such an individual is looking for, to fill this vacuum in himself, is other people's intimate intrusion upon himself, other people's getting into him and becoming part of him.

I think that this dependency on interpersonal relations, this insistence on other people showing intimacy, was a crutch, a substitute for not being able to stand on one's own two feet. Such people sought a hybridization of the institution, a mixture of the personal and the institutional; they looked for affection and guidance and love in the interpersonal relations of the people in the institution.

It's not that I think that a person who has a well defined concept of himself is incapable of close personal relations. Quite the contrary, I think such a person is capable of real, deep, intimate affection and personal relations with others – but a kind of relation which is deep and lasting and yet not cloying or possessive, not dependent, not one that is needed by the person in order to keep him going but one which is freely given and freely accepted by the person, and is a relationship of equality and mutuality between the people concerned. That, I think, is possible only with people who have well formed concepts of themselves. So I'm not saying that whole people are incapable of interpersonal relations. That's not the point at all. But they don't hungrily seek them out at every turn as a substitute for their own undeveloped personality, and they don't insist that every institution of which they're a part provide this for them.

In an institution based on the democratic ethos, responsible people will form personal relations with other members of that institution on the same basis that they form it with any other member of society. But irresponsible people, people not capable of taking responsibility, will need supportive relationships in a democratic institution more than in any setting, because the democratic institution calls on them to exercise responsibility, demands it of them, and they're always conscious of their inability to do this; and they're therefore more than ever in need of a dependent relationship on other people to support them because they've got to have that as an escape from responsibility. To the extent that the institution will cater to this need, it will make even more difficult and more impossible the exercise of responsibility on the part of these people.

All this can be seen in other contexts. One of the classic ways repressive and regimented institutions keep themselves going is by providing a dependent relationship for the people involved in the institution, by creating paternalistic relationships or cloyingly dependent interpersonal relationships among the members of the groups in order to perpetuate their need for dependency, and in order to push off any tendency towards individual responsible behavior.

This confusion of personal and institutional relations was a very serious matter in the school in the beginning, and wore, as one might expect, a very personal aspect. Those staff members who felt that the appropriate personal relationships, whatever they were to be, were missing in the school, naturally turned on the remaining members of the school community with severe personal attacks, accusing them of lacking the desirable personal characteristics they were seeking. So we had accusations that some of us were lacking in love, lacking in the ability to relate to people, and so forth. After we survived that onslaught we had the first departure of a number of staff members. Two staff members (one of them an "acting" staff member, not yet formally hired) resigned at that time, and it signaled the first rift in the school. To be sure, the school continued to function, but the effect of that rift continued to be felt through November. For, while perhaps the most extreme exponents of these views left, others remained with similar less sharply focused feelings that a certain type of interpersonal relationship was lacking in the school. These feelings hovered as a lingering disease in the school, until those who felt this way either left the school or changed.

The ways in which this milder continuing confusion kept gnawing at the school were varied. For example, from time to time certain staff members would want to bring in people who had some experience with T groups or various other kinds of encounter groups or interpersonal relation centers. Usually they would want to bring such people into the school in order to improve the atmosphere of interpersonal relations in the school; or they themselves wanted to introduce some of these methods or techniques into the school for the same reason. This met with a great deal of resistance from people who weren't looking for this kind of thing in the school, until eventually this whole theme died away.

Another point that I want to discuss is the way the staff solved the problem of salaries. It became quite clear that the school was not going to have enough students in the second year to provide anywhere near enough income for the staff unless either the staff was radically cut or the tuition was raised or possibly both things happened together. By any "normal" standards of student/staff ratio the school was terrifically over-staffed, and by any ordinary accounting the tuition was terrifically low. So it became clear to us, from December on, that something was going to have to give if we were in fact going to have a second year of operation of the school.

We realized that one thing that couldn't give was the tuition, at least not enough to make a difference. The tuition could rise, but in order for it to rise enough to provide staff with a reasonable income it would have to go near $2000. We were quite sure that we couldn't do this on any grounds. It was the worst thing to do. It would deviate from our whole conception of the school as we wanted it. So the answer did not lie in that direction. Of course it would be nice if we would grow and add a tremendous number of students, but the reality for the second year didn't seem to lie in that direction.

And then there was the possibility of cutting down the staff radically – e.g., in half. That possibility was not desirable from anybody's point of view, because almost all of us wanted to return, and we all expected the school to succeed in future years, and we all knew that the greatest asset that we had in the school was the strong staff that we had. We knew that if the school was to have any future it depended largely on the staff. We would be jeopardizing the future of the school to solve the short term problem by cutting the staff radically. This was the argument that swayed the Trustees later, after we had reached our own conclusions on the subject. It was also clear that for the school to be able to grow we had to have available a large staff. This meant that we had to sustain a certain imbalance, as far as the financial capabilities of the school were concerned, through the next year.

So the question then became how to get through the second year. There were extremely strong feelings on the part of the staff, completely consistent with the philosophy of the school, that again highlighted the difference between our school and progressive schools: no one on the staff felt he was doing the school a favor by working for no salary the first year. In fact it was quite the reverse. It was more the psychology of the dollar-a-year man in government. Our working at no salary was the ultimate expression of our individual dignity, and the way in which we expressed most clearly our desire to work at the school – the fact that we were working at the school because we really wanted to be there. This desire transcended every other consideration. The members of the staff always felt that it was a tremendous privilege to be staff members at the school. Far from doing the school a favor by being here, we were being accorded the cosmic privilege of being involved in the birth and develop-ment of a great institution.

We never deviated from this feeling. Yet, as a staff that went through one year without pay, we were getting hungry. So we faced the problem of raising some cash to cover our needs. The one thing that we knew we didn't want to do was work for small salaries, for two or three or four thousand dollars, or whatever the school could afford; we weren't going to "do the school a favor" and work at that salary so the school could make it. In other words, we didn't want to fall into this pattern of being "good hearted" teachers who were willing to work for a pittance of a salary for the good of the school. We also weren't going to do the parents a favor and say, "We know how hard it is for you to put up the money, and we're going to give you a break."

What we were doing at the school we were doing first and foremost for ourselves, and secondly for the good of the institution to keep the institution going, and we didn't want to transform our commitment to the institution into a favor towards the parents to spare them the pain of higher tuition rates. That was a very tricky thing, because that meant that we just couldn't accept progressive-school salaries. Yet we didn't want to accept no cash at all. We wanted to get whatever cash we could from the school, but we didn't want that to be our salary. That seemed to be a very difficult box to get out of.

We tried all sorts of approaches, some of which were proposed in various memos drafted in the Spring, that can be found in Appendix 5. In the end many factors contributed to an ingenious solution, that gave us the dignity of the relationship that we wanted and yet made available to us whatever cash the school could in fact afford.

The components that went into the solution were varied. Some of them were suggested by the solution that we found for repaying the seed money debt that the school owed Hanna and me. (I'll discuss that when I discuss finances.) The key idea was that a certain percentage of the income would go to staff salaries; it turned out to be 75% of the total income. That figure was rather interestingly arrived at, because it's generally known that salaries of teachers and administrative staff and personnel in public school systems come to anywhere from 80% to 85% of the total budget, and sometimes even higher.

We were so sure of being able to operate more efficiently than the public schools that we were perfectly ready to accept 75% as the percentage of the total income that should be allotted to staff salaries. That established a basic institutional commitment to the staff. The staff in turn exempted from this commitment the first $40,000 of income, the minimum needed for effective functioning of the school through the year. The second commitment of the school was to an excellent wage scale, with a minimum salary of $10,000 and a maximum of $25,000. One of the factors that went into our deciding on a $10,000 minimum was Jan McDaniel's eloquent description, which he presented not only to the staff but also to the parents at a parent-staff meeting, of how in the public school system $10,000 was the figure at which a teacher had really "arrived". Since our whole conception of staff was that nobody on our staff would be there if he didn't really belong, everybody on our staff had "arrived". The $25,000 figure for our top salary was sort of pulled out of a hat, though it corresponded roughly to the top salary for administrative positions in public schools.

So we had an excellent salary scale which was compatible with the best of schools and yet not out of line with salaries being paid in public schools. What we then said was that since the school had committed itself to this excellent salary scale and committed itself to putting aside regularly a fixed percentage of all the income to pay these good salaries, we in turn would be ready to accept in actual cash disbursement in any given year whatever funds were available in the salary kitty that constituted 75% of the income (after the first $40,000).

To the extent that the money available in the salary fund didn't pay off the school's obligation to us in salaries, the school would owe it to us in future years and would pay it out from the salary fund of future years should that salary fund develop a surplus over the requirement of the given year involved. We were confident that the success of the school would mean such efficient operation that excesses would develop in the salary fund and would make possible the school's honoring its obligations to pay off these arrears. As one of the Trustees put it, this was sort of a pension plan for the staff, and indeed it was. This solution meant that we could sign for salaries with dignity, and it enabled us to take whatever funds were available, whether $2,000 or $4,000, without being "$2,000 teachers" or "$4,000 teachers" doing a favor to the school.

The salary plan was the result of many long, hard meetings during which these ideas were worked out. This brings to mind the kinds of staff meetings that were held all through the year. During the first week of school, in July, we had a staff meeting every day at the end of the day to evaluate the day, so that we could keep on our toes. Then we had a meeting once a week, at night. We used to go home after a long day of work, have a quick dinner, and then have a long night meeting. Often these meetings went deep into the night. We were notorious for our late night meetings. The meeting in the summer at which two staff members resigned must have gone to all hours of the morning. It happened over and over again, whenever we had a serious issue to discuss; and this continued into the fall.

Somewhere along the line we changed our meeting times to the afternoon. There were still several occasions on which our meetings went right through the night; in fact, one started in the afternoon and went right through till four in the morning. Later, we had our meetings Wednesday afternoons, and then finally Monday afternoons. Eventually, we were able to settle most of the outstanding issues during weekly meetings that lasted two or three hours usually. But there were still times when we'd reconvene or have special meetings and go deep into the night when we had a particularly thorny problem.

We always made it a staff policy to confront our problems and work at their solution without consideration for the time element, if we had to. The staff never hesitated to do this. A lot of times outsiders charged that we were crazy to meet so long, or that I drove the staff and kept them late at meetings, but I certainly always felt that it was a general desire on the part of the staff to solve problems when they came up even if it meant long, late meetings.

One other aspect of the staff that I want to discuss involved a change in the by-laws. I'll talk about by-laws revision later, but I do want to mention this particular change now. I mentioned how difficult it was for us to determine how the staff would be hired and fired, how originally we had thought that the staff would be self-perpetuating and then we figured that the Assembly was the right group to hire the staff. We were scared off from that by the Fall crisis that I'm going to talk about very shortly, when among other things it became clear that the parents were not the group most directly affected by the staff, and that the parents weren't the people who bore the direct consequences of the choice of staff. They bore the consequences inasmuch as their children were affected, but the parents could select one kind of staff or another kind of staff and then go home.

The staff did not interact with the parents on a daily basis. It was the day-to-day school community that was most affected by the nature and constitution of the staff. Once we realized this, we realized that the right group to make the basic decision on who should and who shouldn't be a staff member was the group affected by that choice, namely the members of the School Meeting. It was this group that was able to evaluate the function of the staff, and the degree to which a staff member had in fact assumed responsibility, and it was this group that had to take the consequences of the decision; if they decided well they would have a good school, and if they didn't decide well then they would be the ones to suffer most.

So the School Meeting was given the first crack at deciding, by vote, who should be on the staff, and those people who were elected would be the pool from which the staff was hired. Nobody the School Meeting rejected could possibly be hired as a regular staff member of the school. These elections had to be held at least once a year, because there was no tenure, and only those elected by the School Meeting would be eligible to be hired as staff.

The second step in this procedure was that the Trustees would hire from this pool; and that was in line with the Trustees being the fiscally responsible agents of the school who made the final decision as to how many actual salaries for the various staff members. We achieved a delicate separation of powers: the School Meeting was given the authority to determine who would be eligible for the staff, but was not given authority in the fiscal area of negotiating contracts and deciding on the number of staff because they weren't responsible for the consequences of that decision; and the Trustees were given the responsibility for making the fiscal decision because they were responsible for that, but they could only choose from people that the School Meeting had elected.

This new method of choosing staff was adopted during the course of the first year, and the necessary changes in the by-laws were made; and the staff for the second year of operation of the school was selected in this way. Two different elections were held to determine the pool of candidates for the staff during the first year of operation of the school. Fourteen people were put up as candidates, and out of these fourteen, twelve were elected candidates for the staff. People were exercising judgment, splitting their ballots, and thinking about the various candidates.

Then this pool of twelve was presented to the Trustees, and there was considerable discussion among the Trustees as to how many of these it would be fiscally responsible to hire under the new salary funding plan that the staff had recommended, and that the corporation and Trustees accepted. There was some division among the Trustees, some feeling that it would not be responsible to run up a high salary arrears debt for the school, and that the staff should be cut radically. But the overwhelming majority of the Trustees went along with the original idea that had motivated the staff to seek the solution of the problem in the first place, namely that the staff was the school's greatest asset, and that we should do everything we could to keep this staff with an eye towards the growth of the school during the second and subsequent years.

That concludes my discussion of the various aspects of the staff and its development during the first year of operation of the school. The summer was the key factor. It was during the summer that the main outlines of the staff's function and the nature of the staff's responsibility were drawn, and those members of the staff who came through the summer came through with quite a well-formed idea of what it was they were called on to do in the school, what kind of a school they wanted to have, and what it meant to be individually responsible for one's deeds. This rather well-formed idea was crucial to the staff in dealing with events at the school.

Trouble with the Students

When we started the school on July 1, we had an enrollment of about 130 students, and many of these – as it turned out, the majority – were students who were there just for the summer. It's hard to describe the atmosphere of the summer, except to say that it wasn't the real thing as far as the school was concerned, and certainly not as far as the students were concerned. To begin with, summer is traditionally a time off from school, so that there really was no pressure on anybody's part to do anything academically constructive. It was like the atmosphere of a summer day camp. In fact a lot of the parents kept calling it a summer day camp, and that of course expressed their attitude towards the place as well as their kids' attitude. So the fact that we didn't force anybody to do anything could be taken in stride by everyone.

The school was, for most people, just a very free and liberal summer day camp, and even the other aspects – for example, the School Meeting – well, they were "all right"; people got the idea that this was a summer camp at which the kids and the counselors together made the rules. To be sure, there aren't many summer camps that do that but somehow this isn't quite the same as doing it for real, when it counts, the year around. This pronounced difference between the summer and the regular school year, which I think was very unfortunate, could be felt in the attitudes of many of the students who did return in the fall.

Many students who came back in the fall were filled with doubts as to whether the kind of thing that was going on in the summer was really going to continue, or whether now it would be, "Let's get down to business and study." I'm sure a lot of the students felt that for the summer they had been "allowed" a lot more freedom than they'd be "allowed" during the year, as if there was somebody around allowing these freedoms and parceling them out.

Nevertheless, on the positive side, because of this summer camp atmosphere, because there wasn't pressure on us, we had a chance to work out a lot of the routines of the school, and, as I've already pointed out, we had a chance to get our conception of staff clear and to form a unified staff.

In general, aggressive or destructive attitudes don't vent themselves with much fury in a summer camp. There's plenty of rowdyism and vandalism and so forth, but somehow the object of hate isn't all that focused. So while we had an awful lot of irresponsible behavior – in fact, I'd say that irresponsible behavior was characteristic of the student body during the summer – it had sort of a "light" quality of irresponsibility. A lot of littering, a lot of things left undone that should have been done, but still, everybody wanted to have a good time and there wasn't anybody who really wanted to poison the place.

By the same token a lot of students who were more seriously irresponsible, or who harbored more serious resentments, didn't show up in the summer. They signed up for the fall. They didn't want any institutional structure during the summer. It was enough for them to come around in the fall. I remember Hanna saying that it was an ominous sign that a lot of these students didn't come for the summer; that if they were really interested in the school and what the school stood for they would have come in July; that they should hardly have been able to wait for school to open, and they should have got going right away, to put things into shape right away. She felt something ominous about people who signed up in the spring but preferred to wait for the fall to start because they *really* wanted to be free in the summer. It said a lot about how they pictured the school, and what kind of an idea they had of the place.

When the fall came we had quite a different student body. First of all, about half were new students. And an awfully high percentage of those were teenagers, high school age kids. Both in the summer and in the fall, indeed throughout the year, we had a full spectrum of ages, but it was a little weak on the high school ages in the summer and rather heavy on the high school age kids in the early fall, while it sort of evened out a little during the year.

We felt the different atmosphere in the school instantly, on the very first day of the fall – a definitely different, more sinister atmosphere. It was felt by all of the staff to whom I talked about it. We had a large group of people who were wild looking, who behaved wildly, who played loud rock and roll music all over the place – and the more disturbing the better – who carried on in an unbridled way. A lot of them walked around with hostility clearly showing on their faces; they were unfriendly, especially to adults. The only word I can think of is "sinister" – there was a sinister atmosphere about the school, and many of the students who had been there throughout the summer, who had really been looking forward to the opening of the school in the fall, were struck by this too – were thunderstruck by it would be the more correct way to say it – and very depressed at the prospects. One students who had been there in the summer visited us at home together with his parents, and they were very worried. This was about two weeks after school began. They couldn't really put their finger on it, but they felt the presence of a very undesirable element. And in fact there was an undesirable element. But at the time, I pointed out that we'd have to give it time and see how things developed. We had to have some patience, we couldn't take action immediately after a couple of weeks. I imagine what they wanted was somehow to remove these students, somehow to get rid of them.

What had happened here was actually very simple. In retrospect, I think the issues were much simpler than the more complex ones that have since faced the school. There was a group of students who had decided not to act responsibly in the school, for whatever personal reasons; they had decided that this was a school like any other school, and that they were going to act in this school like they would act in other schools. They wanted us to be like other teachers, they wanted us to take responsibility out of their hands, they wanted to be pushed around, they wanted to hate us in return. They wanted to resent us; they never gave up, they never wavered in their resentment of the staff.

I used to think that if we just held our ground, they would see eventually, after several weeks, that we were not going to impose ourselves on them and that they had no choice but to take responsibility in their own hands and be responsible for their own behavior. But no amount of time helped. They had made a decision not to act responsibly, and they were determined to force us into being like the staff in other schools. They hoped either to goad us into being repressive (and then they could expose the fraud of the school, which would be a good way to vent their anger), or they probably hoped and preferred to finally drive us into being a progressive school, into being sweet to them, being "good" to them, guiding them, taking an interest in them and having a concern for them, babying them, so that they could still hate us and still resent us and still not act responsibly, but at least their existence wouldn't be painful all day. They could have their hatred and still not suffer too much as a result.

They manifested their decision not to act responsibly through many, many modes of behavior. In the first place, they were completely contemptuous of the internal government of the school by the School Meeting. They flouted whatever rules and regulations were made, and they mocked the ability of the School Meeting to enforce its regulations. In the second place, they advocated all sorts of phony classroom experiences that could take their minds off of themselves and take their minds off of what they really wanted to do. They agitated for us to give courses, to provide instruction, to entertain them. And to the extent that they couldn't get us to do it, they tried to organize it among themselves. They were really determined to keep up a program of entertainment.

Also, they filled the school with hostility, as far as adults were concerned and as far as many other students were concerned – for example, some of the summer students and some of the new fall students who were in fact interested in what the school stood for, and who were consistently bombarded with contempt and hostility. Also, they insisted on imposing their image on the entire school. They would congregate in the most obvious places, out in the front, in the main lobby, so that anybody who came would immediately see them and take them for the school. In addition, they were particularly ornery in their behavior towards little children. They would find it amusing to lead little kids into trouble. There was an unending atmosphere of immature irresponsibility and hostility about the place due to this rather large contingent of students virtually all of whom were of high school age.

One could understand the sociology and psychology of it, but such understanding could provide no solution to the complete incompatibility between them and the school. There are, to be sure, ways of forcing a person to become responsible. For example, one can just take him and dump him in the middle of the woods in Alaska and leave him there. That does wonders, as a lot of people have discovered who have taken juvenile delinquents or others who have exhibited difficult behavior and placed them off in their own Boy's Towns or own colonies, and really made them provide for themselves. That does wonders. But of course we weren't the ones to impose this kind of regime, because we weren't crusading to make people responsible, we were expecting responsible behavior in the school.

With a number of these students a particular manifestation of their inability to care for themselves was that they were hooked on drugs of various kinds, some of them on pretty serious stuff, others on the so-called lighter stuff like marijuana. Some of them were pretty regular and heavy drug users, something which I must say we were at the time rather naive about. It took us some time to discover that there was a lot of this going on and that many of them were regularly bringing drugs onto the campus. Now if there was one thing we were sure about it's that we weren't going to have illegal activities on campus. We were always careful to act within the law and we respected the law. We wanted the law respected on the campus, and we were of one mind on the subject. So that as soon as we became aware of what was going on, we knew it was going to lead us into some sort of confrontation with at least some of these kids.

I must say that the whole thing had a kind of a nightmarish quality about it. Those first few weeks of the fall term were very painful to me, and they got more so as time went by. I'm sure part of it was due to the fact that Hanna and I had been working under great pressure for a long time without letup, and we certainly were aware of the need for rest and to get away from things. We had planned to rest in the intersession between summer and fall sessions, but an accident in the family forced cancellation of those plans, and in fact increased the pressure and tension that we were undergoing personally. So I'm sure part of this nightmarish quality of my recollection has to do with my own state of nerves at the time.

But I remember being very conscious of hating to come to the school and of being very sad at a situation where finally we had the realization of our dreams in concrete terms, and I didn't even want to go there. Hanna felt the same way. It was just too hellish. It's interesting that one of the complaints that these students leveled against us later was that we filled the school with hatred and hostility. Of course, they were leveling it at us because we wouldn't accept them as they were, and so they felt rejected and objects of hatred. But as far as I was concerned, it was they who permeated the place with an atmosphere of viciousness.

The degree to which these students were destructive to the school as far as the public was concerned was almost unbelievable. Several of them would go riding around in the neighborhood in convertibles or with arms and legs hanging out of open car windows – all during the school day. Or they would thumb their way through town in sizeable groups during school hours and make themselves very conspicuous. They simply flaunted the freedom of the school in ways calculated to irritate the townspeople.

Hanna and I decided to take a vacation, come what may, so that we could really clear our minds, rest our nerves, and try to get a perspective on things. We went to the Caribbean, which always relaxed us even a short exposure. We set our departure for October 7.

During the week before, it became clear to everyone that the school was going to have to take action against drug use and drug traffic. At the time, I was chairman of the School Meeting, which I'll discuss later in greater detail. I remember calling a Special School Meeting on the Friday before we left – we left on a Sunday – for the purpose of discussing what we would do about the drug issue; and making it very explicit that one of the things that the staff was responsible for was maintaining the legal operation of the school. We were determined to see through this responsibility and make sure that there would be no illegal activities on the campus.

I asked for, and got, a resolution that there would be no illegal activities on the campus, and I also asked for consideration of a resolution that drug users could be punished in some appropriate fashion. The School Meeting did not finish discussing the latter resolution, and there was some other business left over to a Monday meeting. At any rate, Hanna and I went away for ten days and the drug issue resolved itself during those ten days. I say "resolved itself" because the essential points of the issue were clarified as far as the school was concerned during those ten days.

I don't know the details. I've heard many of them, and other people who were present at the school during those ten days will have to speak for themselves. But there was a clear determination on the part of the school not to tolerate drugs on campus. This involved a decision on the part of the Trustees, it involved a decision on the part of the staff, and on the part of the School Meeting. As far as I can see, there was never an issue of principle here. What was at issue was the way the school would enforce its rules again the presence and use of drugs on the campus, as well as other rules. It is easy to see that to the extent that you have members of the student body who are determined not to obey School Meeting resolutions or cooperate in enforcing them, to that extent you're going to have a problem on your hands with drugs and with everything else – and indeed it was with everything else.

On the Monday before we left, something occurred that really broke my heart, since it was to me a sign of great trouble for the school. Medical supplies were being stolen right out of the medical cabinet in the nurse's room, which was of course not locked. We knew that some little kids were involved, and we also knew that some teenagers were involved; one teenager had taken tremendous quantities of adhesive tape and wrapped it around her leg for some reason or another. We discussed this at length at the School Meeting – it was a desultory discussion, but nevertheless it went on for a while, and nobody had a solution. The only motion that was offered and finally passed was that the medical supplies should be locked up. There was a lot of talk about how only little kids were to blame, but we all knew that this wasn't true. This was the first and only lock that was ever voted in the school; and the vote was later rescinded. But the idea that we were going to have to start locking things up in the school was so contrary to the kind of atmosphere of respect for the law that we were bent on having in the school that it was to me a clear sign that something was very, very wrong.

We came back on Thursday evening, October 17, and we returned to school the next morning, Friday, October 18. I was struck by the worsening of the general atmosphere in the school. If anything the atmosphere was darker, the hostilities were deeper, and there was a general feeling of despair everywhere: in the hostile students, because they weren't getting what they wanted out of the school, and in all the rest of the students and in most of the staff, because the school just wasn't what they had thought it would be.

I remember coming back with my mind cleared, with my strength restored, and with a very firm conviction that if matters had not radically improved by the time I returned I would press hard to take decisive action and remove from the school the students who were bent on behaving irresponsibly. We simply could not survive the presence of this group. We had no way of changing them. We would either knuckle under and become the kind of school they wanted us to be, or we were going to survive, which meant either removing them or perhaps precipitating a change in some of them.

I was completely determined to precipitate a severe crisis in the school, especially after everything I saw that Friday. It was just a question of deciding how to move, but we had to do something very soon. On Sunday I went to Fred's house and had a conversation with him in his living room. We talked for about an hour and a half. He was, among other things, very complimentary about the staff's behavior during our absence. It was then that I confronted him with my feeling that we had to do something radical in order for the school to survive. We discussed how we could expel students, what the grounds would be, and what the procedure would have to be. I told him that I felt that we had the authority to do it and he seemed to agree. He introduced me to the concept of "bad att." – "bad attitude," which he said was used widely by private schools as a reason to expel students. I came away from that meeting with the distinct feeling that we would be able to remove these students whom we felt we had to remove by having the Trustees expel them.

As I recall it, the chronology of events was then the following: on the basis of this conversation with Fred, which I interpreted in the way I've just said, I called a special staff meeting on Monday evening, October 21 – this was one of those meetings that lasted into the early hours of the morning – to discuss which students we felt would have to be expelled. We reviewed the list of students over and over and over again, and came up with a list to bring to Fred and the Board of Trustees for discussion and action. I don't recall the exact number on that list but it is my recollection that it was somewhere around 26.

With this in hand we went to sleep Monday night (Tuesday morning). The school operated as usual on Tuesday and I called Fred Tuesday evening with the intention of discussing how we could convene a special Trustees meeting as soon as possible, in order to discuss the list and see what we'd be able to do. To my surprise, he told me that he had thought the matter over, and decided that the Trustees should not expel anybody – that he didn't want to carry through this kind of an operation. The conversation was relatively brief and threw me for a loop. I had no idea what he expected us to do in order to survive. I knew he was aware of the problem. He had been aware of it almost before anybody else. In effect he was now handing it over to the staff. That was essentially the last conversation I had with him about the school.

The Crisis

From that point on matters came quickly to a head. We had a staff meeting on Wednesday which again lasted into the early hours of the morning. I announced Fred's decision, and we all felt that we couldn't survive as a school the way we were going, that the one apparently straightforward avenue of egress had been closed. We went over and over all kinds of alternatives of how we could keep the school going, because as far as we could see the school's fate was sealed. It was this feeling on the part of the staff that the school was definitely, unquestionably doomed to failure, unless we were able to change its course, that led us to throw everything we had into our final desperate gamble.

We knew we were going for broke, we knew that there was no return, we knew that we'd have to do something radical and stake everything on its success. The reason we were ready to take this kind of a risk was because we were all convinced that otherwise there was no hope of succeeding with the school. For my part, it is worth stressing that I had the advantage of thinking these things through during a peaceful vacation away from the school, and that I don't feel that this decision was in any way induced by tension or exhaustion or tiredness or giving up on alternatives.

During the course of that Wednesday night meeting, we realized that the only authority left in the school that we could hope would support us was the School Meeting. There was just a possibility that we, together with enough of the students who did want the kind of a school that we thought we were creating and that they thought they were getting – there was just a possibility that these two groups together could attain a majority at the School Meeting and could put the School Meeting on record as wanting the removal of certain students.

We felt that if we could get School Meeting support, we could go the Trustees and say, "It's not just the staff that wants this, but the School Meeting as well. You've got to take action." We realized that even with this the Trustees might not act, but there were no other paths that any of us could see that had even a remote chance of succeeding. So we turned to the internal governing organ of the school as our last hope. And it was right that we should turn to them.

In fact, had things been constituted differently, we would have taken this problem up with them in the first place. Had the original by-laws been framed differently, this kind of a problem would have been discussed naturally in the School Meeting right away, and the School Meeting's recommendation would have received serious attention from the Trustees. But the role of the School Meeting was not then that clear, as far as such a drastic action was concerned; and the role of the staff was still unclear. Perhaps we should have gone to the School Meeting right away anyway.

The reason I first turned to the Trustees (through Fred) was because I knew that many of the Trustees still wanted the school to operate in as traditional a manner of authority as they could get it to operate, despite the democratic principles that underlay it. The general mood of the Trustees was definitely to encourage us to try first to work in a "quiet" way, to work through the staff, to work through the Trustees, perhaps through the parents concerned, and not to invoke the kind of democratic procedures that one might want to invoke in this kind of a school.

I yielded to this mood because I thought I had no reasonable alternative but to yield. In the end, as one might have predicted at the beginning, yielding did no good whatsoever. The crisis that came was just as strong; we had to have recourse to democratic principles in the end; and we lost the people who were not committed to these principles anyway despite our effort to keep them. So in retrospect we might have been better off had we gone to the School Meeting right away.

At any rate, the decision was made Wednesday night to go to the School Meeting on Thursday, to lay the problem before it, to make it clear that the staff was not going to continue working at the school under existing circumstances – that the problem of students seeking to destroy the school, as we put it, was one which had to be solved by the School Meeting if the staff was going to remain. And we were quite aware of the fact that if the staff left, the school was bound to close.

We were really laying it on the line; we weren't kidding. We were saying in effect that we had an idea of the kind of a school we had hoped to set up, that we had placed this idea before the public, that there were in the school many people who subscribed to this idea and who wanted it, and that we were ready to continue working towards the realization of this idea with the group of people who wanted its realization, but that we would not work in a different kind of school. If this meant closing the school, still it was no concern of ours to keep it open as a different school than what we had intended to set up.

There's an incredible twist to this whole story. There wouldn't have been a crisis had Fred gone ahead and expelled the "bad atts" via the Trustees. There would have been an uproar, but there would have been no crisis. The students would have been expelled in due course, the Trustees would have taken the action, there would have been no legal challenge to this perfectly legal act, and the school would have gone on functioning.

But if this had happened, the solution to the school's problem would have come about by resorting to methods that were out of line with the basic principles on which the school was set up! The real reason there was a crisis was because in the last analysis, when we were pressed to the wall, when we had a clear choice of compromising the foundations on which the school was set up — and it was something we were urged to do over and over again [all we had to do was give a few courses, be a little nicer to the students, guide them a little, and "everybody" would have been satisfied] — if we had compromised, we wouldn't have had this problem.

It was just because we stuck to the principles on which the school was based when the chips were down, and appealed directly to the democratic position of the School Meeting — that's why there was a crisis. That's what really precipitated the crisis, because we laid the basic issues right on the table, where there was no avoiding them and there was no hiding behind procedures which might somehow resemble procedures in other ordinary schools.

We announced our position on Thursday morning to a shocked Special session of the School Meeting. People certainly were expecting something to happen, because rumors had been rocking the school for several days that some action was going to be taken against some students. We announced a special School Meeting, for the purpose of discussing the "closing of the school," in particular to discuss the problem that was destroying the school and threatening to close it. The meeting was started by reading the resolution of the staff, and immediately plunged into discussion of how the School Meeting was going to cope with the problem of having in our midst students intent on destroying the school.

The School Meeting started at about 11:00, because of the two hour notice period required for special sessions. Our first session ran for two hours, and we ran through Thursday and through Friday in consecutive two hour sessions, with one hour breaks in between. The first session was taken up with how we were going to cope with the problem, and the only solution that anybody had to present was that the destructive students had to be recommended for expulsion from the school. Nobody had any other idea of how to deal with the problem.

It was decided to go through the list of the entire student body, to discuss each person in turn, and to determine by vote who were the students that the majority of the School Meeting felt were being destructive and should be recommended for expulsion from the school. During that first session there was a major speech made by Dennis which presented his ideas about the types of destructive activities that were going on in the school. He listed forty-two students by name whom he thought to be destructive to the school and wished to see out.

This speech gained a certain notoriety among the students and the parents. It's interesting how contradictorily they viewed it – on the one hand, as a sign of personal viciousness on his part towards the students, and on the other hand, at the same time, they viewed him as speaking for the entire staff and as presenting the staff's list. It was actually quite clear to everybody at the meeting that this list was not presented by the staff and that Dennis was speaking for himself.

The roof fell in on Thursday because these students ran to the phone and called their parents, which was to be expected from their overall behavior pattern of dependency. As quickly as possible, they brought down the wrath of their parents on this entire procedure. That night was absolutely hellish. Parents started coming in late in the afternoon, and from 5:00 p.m. until after midnight a stream of parents showed up at the school to register their disapproval in vitriolic terms. This continued all through Friday. There were attempts made by parents who descended on the school Friday morning to stop these meetings from continuing on Friday, but the School Meeting voted to continue the meetings. A parent protest meeting was subsequently held on Saturday night, October 26.

The point that I'd like to make here is that throughout this uproar, right through to the end of Friday's meetings, the actual School Meetings were conducted with tremendous dignity and care by the student body and the staff. The students were extraordinarily cool in the School Meeting, and presented their cases and voted methodically. It was quite clear that the one thing in this entire picture that disturbed the parents more than anything else was that we were in fact giving the students a serious share in deciding the fate of the school as a whole. That was the rub. I'll have occasion to deal with some other aspects of this major crisis when I discuss the parents, but the key issue was student responsibility and the students' role in governing the school.

When the stakes were down, when it was clear to all that we meant it when we said that students were to be given an equal voice with the staff in determining the internal governance of the school and that they could say things that really were going to make a difference, then the roof fell in. Because, as we were told over and over again by the dissident parents, the staff were the ones who were really supposed to guide the destiny of the school. Again and again we were asked, "How do you expect young children, young adolescents to make decisions like this? How can children be allowed to talk about one another and to judge one another?"

Of course, the parents of those who were not behaving responsibly were by and large the most vociferous in this – it was like a self-fulfilling prophecy. It was their continuing lack of confidence in their own children's ability to act responsibly that created a pattern of irresponsible behavior in their own children.

The Saturday night protest meeting had every aspect of a lynch mob to it. I'm sure somebody with literary talent is going to write the history of this, and will describe the atmosphere there much better than I can. The meeting was organized by certain dissident parents, and the staff was invited to it as an afterthought. Later the staff was bitterly reproved for not having had the school building prepared for the meeting and not behaving as hosts on an evening, the purpose of which was to rake the staff over the coals.

The atmosphere was so charged and so ugly that it was virtually impossible for members of the staff to speak at this meeting. I took the floor several times and was interrupted each time, and finally I said that further interruptions would lead to my leaving for good; further interruptions were forthcoming, and I left.

The staff walked out, quite spontaneously, with me. We considered that to be our resignation from the school. We considered that the overwhelming majority of parents disapproved of the kind of serious democratic structure that we intended to present to the school; and that under the circumstances we had no choice but to leave. We could not continue. We had staked all, but this was the end, because in fact we were not going to be backed up. We might even be backed up by a majority of the School Meeting, but we were not going to be backed up by a majority of the people who would soon constitute the bulk of the corporate membership of the school, namely the parents. Even though they weren't corporate members yet, nevertheless they were the people who made the school and it was their decision to bring or take away their children.

The meeting continued after we left, discussing among other things the idea of trying to staff the school with other people. (Eventually several dissidents and their own staff formed their own kind of a school.) At the time, we considered ourselves to have resigned. We spent an all-night "wake" at Dennis' house. It was a moment of deep personal tragedy for all of us because the product of all our commitment had apparently gone down the drain.

An urgent Trustees' meeting was called the next day, and the Trustees then learned that we really meant that we had resigned. It was quite a charade there for a while, because some Trustees at first took this as a kind of a bluff on our part, and even had some light-hearted comments about it until they found out that we really meant it. They couldn't believe that we would abandon something that we'd spent so much time putting together. It was only after they really did believe it that they buckled down to the job of either seeing to it that the school continued to function in the way that it had originally been intended, or abandoning it themselves as well. They had to face the question of whether they wanted the school to close or not.

It's one of the ironies of fate that a majority of the Trustees eventually ended up by thinking that the school ought to close, and the school probably would have closed had they made up their minds all at once. But they didn't reach this conclusion all at once, and there were always enough Trustees interested in keeping the school going to keep a majority voting in favor of action that would keep it open. And the school survived.

There was more to it. At the moment of crisis, the interests of staff and Trustees were curiously different. The staff of course wanted the school open, but only if the basic principles underlying it were not compromised; otherwise, their very commitment to these principles led them to prefer no school at all to a compromised school. The Trustees – or at least the majority of the original Trustees – in principle wanted the school closed, if it was to be the kind of school they now finally understood us to have had in mind; but they preferred at all costs to see it remain open in practice, and to find some way of keeping it open, in order to avoid the onus of having been the sponsors and supervisors of an institution that failed before it had hardly begun.

Thus, it was uncommitted Trustees who in the last analysis kept the school open, whereas the committed staff had been prepared to have it close. An interesting twist. The result of this situation could have been foreseen: the Trustees in fact succeeded in keeping the school open, by yielding all points of principle to the staff. The result was that the staff could now work in the kind of school they had always envisioned, while several Trustees, recoiling from the kind of school they now perceived this to be, resigned. Which all goes to show, if it needed showing, that it is not solely through the efforts of the committed parties that institutions survive their greatest trials.

At the Trustees' meeting on Sunday, the "ex-staff" was present. The immediate problem was getting the school to open the next day and then determine the immediate future of the school. The main outcome of that meeting was that the ex-staff was prevailed upon to open the school on Monday, in order to announce that the school would be closed for the rest of the week; and the Trustees committed themselves to come up with some sort of solution within a week or two (this was never really clear) so that the school could continue functioning.

Monday, as can be imagined, was a day of incredible gloom around the school. From the staff's point of view, it was the end. From the students' point of view, it was a matter of deep shock. I'm sure that the students who were destined to leave knew very well that whatever happened, they weren't going to return. As for the other students, who had hoped to have the kind of a school we hoped to have, they must have felt very much like we did, that everything now was in the balance and that the likelihood of a successful outcome was very slim.

The newspapers had got hold of all this, and gave us terrible publicity. We got repeated coverage, which consisted only in very small part of press releases that Fred prepared on behalf of the school. Most of the coverage came from the dissident parents and from the more irresponsible of the students, and of course put the school in a terrible light. There were severe personal recriminations involved; many of us received letters during that period that contain a level of personal hatred that's almost unimaginable, in addition to incredible personal attacks made face to face during meetings and conferences. One would expect, by the nature of the problem, that there would be a large emotional personal outburst involved in it, but it was very hard to take while we were going through it. Seen in perspective, the charged emotion was to be expected and was not the central issue involved.

The basic question was, were the Trustees going to get rid of these students one way or another or were they not? The meetings of the Trustees during that week went on night after night until one and two a.m., and for several weeks to come there were meetings on Sundays, nights, and weekends until a final outcome was reached. This lasted till the end of November. There was something like a month during which Trustees' meetings were held at all hours and at all times. The movement was slow but inexorable.

The first break occurred when Bill Randall saw clearly that this staff was simply not going to return to the school with the disruptive students still there. While others argued the pros and cons of whether we had an obligation to keep these students, and whether it was right on our part to expel them, Bill saw that the staff was not going to return as long as these students were present; and he wanted the school to continue in operation. He hoped eventually to reach a generally satisfactory solution, if he could just get the school going again. He was the one who proposed the solution that was finally adopted, namely to suspend those students that we felt had to be removed; and he asked the staff to review the question and bring in immediately a new list. The staff met and went over the matter again, and came up with a list that finally numbered twenty-nine. So the Trustees suspended twenty-nine students by letter, hand-delivered on Friday of that week, the suspension to continue pending a conference and further negotiation.

This enabled the school to re-open on the following Monday, without these 29 students, and without some others who sympathized with them. The attendance varied between the high sixties and high eighties for a couple of weeks while the issue was in doubt. But the very first day school reopened, the atmosphere was felt to be different by everybody. It was a new school. The pall of hatred and hostility that hung over it had disappeared. There was a tremendous agony of tension, the issue was still in doubt, but the pall of hatred and the deathly grip of irresponsibility and dependency had gone.

We just knew we were on the right path, and I say this even though there were terrible things still going on. Many of the students who came were still often destructive, and were close friends and sympathizers of those we had suspended; but we had hopes for these students. Many of the dissident parents came in and out – we had the strength of our conviction to keep that school open to visitors throughout this period. We never closed it to visitors, even though we certainly would have had every justification to close it to outsiders for a couple of weeks and lick our wounds. As a result, we had people coming in and out of the school all the time, some of whom were just plain busy-bodies and others were dissident parents who were going through our files, trying to get together information that they could use to fight us. Yet we kept the school open, and we kept the files open, and we stood by our basic principles; that was the whole point. We laid our principles on the line and we stuck to them through thick and thin. That's why we succeeded.

The situation as far as the suspended students were concerned was that they were given the opportunity to set up conferences with groups of Trustees. There was a terrific amount of maneuvering. There were threats of legal suits, there was all kinds of concerted activity. The dissident parents were not members of the corporation yet, but they hoped somehow to take over the corporation, to use the democratic aspects of the school's organization to take over the school. Under the by-laws, they wouldn't become corporation members until December 1, and the Fall meeting was scheduled for December 9, which was quite a way off. In the meantime, they were not members of the corporation and couldn't take any direct action. The delay saved us.

It's interesting, if a little out of context, to go back and recall how the three months delay in corporation membership came in. In my naiveté, I was perfectly ready to have parents have the vote immediately, as soon as they enrolled their children. Both Hanna and Fred felt that there should be some kind of a residency period until they got to know the school. I think Fred preferred a year, and finally we compromised and made it three months. There's absolutely no question that as far as the survival of the school was concerned, that three months period went a long way toward saving us: I don't say it alone saved us, and I'm not really sure that had we had a political confrontation in the Assembly in November we wouldn't have won. Nevertheless, that three months cushion made it a sure bet.

The suspended students at first didn't even try to arrange conferences because they hoped for some other kind of settlement. It was clear that Bill and some others hoped that through these conferences the following scenario would take place: the students would come back a bit contrite and say, "We'd like to come back to the school and we'll behave ourselves. We'd just like the staff to yield a little and be more supportive." We would then say, "You've been naughty and misbehaved. Now you're going to behave, and in return, we're going to hold your hands and guide you." After this, they'd all end up coming back. Certainly this was the expectation of several of the Trustees. However, it was not our intention ever to see them back. Nor did we think they'd come back – we knew better than that – certainly not as long as we were the staff and gave the school its tone. Also, we were not about to change our educational approach. It was, again, our persistence in sticking to our principles, and the support we got during this period from many of the Trustees, that kept us going in our intended direction.

It was obvious that the dissident parents were trying to drag out the entire process until the December 9th meeting, and that they were just trying to buy time. Some of these parents were even enrolling their children in other schools. It's absolutely remarkable. The children were enrolled in other schools and attended other schools, but in the mean time they were kept formally enrolled in The Sudbury Valley School for the sole purpose of giving the parents the vote in order to take over the school and recast it. They were clearly hoping to buy time towards this aim. But buying time works in many different ways, and one by one people who saw that they weren't being allowed to return to the school and that no progress was being made in their direction started withdrawing. We had several early withdrawals.

Every now and then we encountered a parent who understood that what we were doing was being done honestly. One of the most moving experiences we had was when one parent, who was himself a college administrator and a man of great integrity, came to our home, at the very beginning of the crisis, and said, "I know my daughter has been doing everything she could to destroy the school. I've heard her on the phone with her friends plotting the most bizarre escapades to degrade the school. I know this is the case. I just want you to give me any more information you can so that I can see whether it might be possible to help her in some way." This was an honesty which wasn't matched by any other parent, although we did have a few parents who came in and were fair enough to say, "Look, we have no prejudgment on the question. What is it that is going on?" and then heard us out. But the overwhelming number of parents were blindly angry, doubtless because the whole atmosphere in their home, the whole way they raised their children, created the very dependency and irresponsibility that they were now trying to shield and excuse.

Eventually it became clear that we'd have to take some action against the indefinite procrastination. The Trustees kept meeting, and one of the key breaks came when there was pressure, especially on Bill's part, to take some action *vis-à-vis* some of the suspended students who had already completed their conferences. Bill was hoping that some of them would be returned to the school; that if there was an indication that one or two were being acted upon and returned, the parents would see that we were trying to bring about a compromise settlement. We of course didn't want this, and since the Trustees had said that the parents could come to a second and final interview, it was difficult to take final action before the second interview was over.

There was a fateful Trustees' meeting on November 12 when it was decided to announce publicly that a couple of students had been reinstated and that the talks were continuing. In exchange for this, I pressed hard for a concurrent announcement about the staff. I said, "The whole school is being undermined because these people are waiting for staff to be fired by the Trustees," and I kept pressing this point over and over again! The Trustees either had to support the staff or not.

I pressed for an announcement that the Trustees were not going to fire any staff members now. This finally carried by a majority vote. It was at that meeting that Fred Hilton resigned, and that Marx Wartofsky handed in his letter of resignation (although he stayed on officially for several more meetings). That was certainly a fateful meeting on the way towards resolution of this whole situation. We operated for a while without a President, until Alan White was elected. Later, the Trustees finally

announced a deadline beyond which there would be no more conferences, and then all final decisions would be made.

We came in night after night for the conferences. At each one there
would be two or three Trustees, usually three: I, as a staff representa-
tive/Trustee, and other supposedly "unattached" Trustees. We would
talk to the parents and the students in these long, vituperative, agonizing interviews, which I am not able to look back on without a feeling of
horror. Actually, the conferences had one good effect, of showing at least
some of the Trustees at first hand the kind of wild behavior that we had
been talking about. We had often pressed to give the Trustees specific
instances of destructive behavior. But this is so difficult to catalog, especially in a school like ours, where you don't have people watching over
students. You know that everything in the demeanor and carriage and
behavior of a student is meant to destroy the democratic functioning of
the school, and yet if you are called upon to actually enumerate specific
acts it's almost impossible to do.

The interviews finally came to an end. The Trustees finally had to
expel a couple of students — actually, they weren't expelled. The Trustees
decided they would terminate their enrollment, but they were allowed
to withdraw and get their money back. There was also the whole question of a refund of money. The Trustees felt, and I went along with this
100%, that we should refund all the money to these people. This was
a concession that I was ready to make. It was like saying, "Well, we
may also have been partly responsible for this trouble because we may
have contributed to your misunderstanding of the nature of the school,
and that's why things didn't work out." Actually, I don't think that we
were liable for misleading the parents, and I don't think we were legally
obligated in any way to give back the money to anybody. But I'm glad
we did.

The next and final step in ridding the school of this component was
that the Trustees sent a report to all the parents saying that the interviews had been completed and that most of the suspended students had
withdrawn; and we then offered a full refund to anyone else who chose
to withdraw up to Wednesday, November 26 (the Wednesday before
Thanksgiving), no matter what the reason for withdrawal. We did this

because we recognized that a lot of people had second thoughts about the school, and that it wasn't exactly what they had thought it would be; and we were now offering them an opportunity to clean the slate.

It's really amazing how this refund offer pushed people over the brink. A lot of people would have kept their kids in the school just because they had made a certain investment and they weren't ready to lose the investment. But the minute we offered them a few hundred dollars back they took their children out of the school. They would have been ready to keep their children in a school that was, in their eyes, no good, simply for the sake of a couple of hundred dollars. It's really staggering.

Of all the suspended students, a handful returned, those who we really felt deserved another chance, who had really recanted, and some of whom had made very moving pleas. Of those who were suspended and returned, maybe half a dozen students in all, only two remained regular students in good standing till the end of the year, and signed up to return the next year. I'm glad for the sake of those two that we allowed the others back, that we didn't simply cut them off. But I would say that it is a remarkable verification of our diagnosis of the problem, that even among those who were seared by a suspension, and who came back after that searing experience, all but two couldn't make it through the year.

A large number of students and parents took advantage of the refund offer. Charles Gaines said repeatedly that this offer made it possible for us to retrench back to the group that was really with the school, and he was absolutely correct. We were left with something like sixty-five or seventy students. We were left with about half of our original student body, but the group that we were left with was by and large the group that wanted to be in the school.

Settling Down

From December until the end of the first school year, another handful of students dropped out – something like another half dozen or so at the end of January and a few more during the Spring. For various reasons. But that was just a scattering. The overwhelming majority of students remained. And though the atmosphere in the school had improved immediately on November 4, the atmosphere changed radically from December on, when the population had stabilized and there was no more anxiety about whether the school would continue or not, and when the final constitution of the student body became clear. You could really feel it.

It was in December that the school year really began. The summer wasn't really representative of the school, and the early fall wasn't. It was really from December on that the school began to function. Later, when I talk about the development of the School Meeting, we'll see that a real turn took place in the School Meeting as well – that it became a serious legislative and judicial body from December on.

The final turn of events came after December 9 when the Fall meeting of the Assembly was held. There was still lingering worry on the part of some people that dissident parents might show up, even though they were no longer registered in the school, or that something would happen. Actually the December 9 meeting was no problem whatsoever. On the contrary, if anything it was clear that the school intended to survive; and from then on anxiety about the fate of the school diminished.

That means that even though the school completed its first year on June 30, 1969, it had in fact been in existence only half a year, after a birth that had involved tremendous trauma. In general one thinks of the first year of a school as a collection of good experiences, with a lot of enthusiasm and all the pluses that go with a first year. We had the pluses, we had the "pioneering spirit" and all that, but we had a first year that was only about six and a half months long (less four weeks of vacation), and preceded by a series of unsettling and unnerving traumas.

The student body remained at a level of about sixty-five throughout the first year. Many of these were part-time students under age 6. There were something like 50 to 55 full-time students. A lot of the students in the school, even of those who remained, were sent on a one year trial basis; that is, their parents said, "We'll let you go for a year and see how things work out." Most of the students re-registered for the second year, plus several new students. The total number of full-time students registered for the second year at the end of the first year was 56.

It was decided in March that the school would open a second year only if there were a minimum of forty paying students signed up. A deadline of April 1 was set for re-enrollment, and we waited to see whether we'd have the minimum number we needed. This was a purely financial question of covering the bills. So you see that there was an unsettled atmosphere over the school and over its future as far as the students were concerned right through the winter and early spring.

Really it was only after April, when it was clear that the school was definitely going to open for a second year, that the students could know that they were involved in something that was going to go on. And by the time they were sure that they were involved in an experiment that was successful enough to continue, the year was about to end. There was no summer session in 1969. All things considered, the first year can be viewed as a succession of traumas and anxieties and interruptions and vacations. It's amazing that anything positive got done. It's almost a miracle that the student body held together at all, much more so that it held together resolutely and went from strength to strength as far as the growth of inner discipline and responsibility was concerned.

It's worth recounting at this point the development of our student admission procedure. As I've already related, we had an essentially open admissions policy right from the beginning, but we required an interview. In the aftermath of the November crisis, as one might expect, we came to doubt a lot of our procedures, especially our admissions procedure. The fact that several Trustees kept hammering away at the staff that it was our fault that all this was happening, that it was our admissions procedure that had let all the destructive students in – and that's why we'd have to keep them – the fact that the Trustees didn't accept the validity of the idea of self-selection in admissions didn't make life any easier for us.

We gave a lot of thought to the question of whether perhaps we might have instituted a better system. For example, one of the students who was suspended and finally withdrew had a police record and was on parole, and we hadn't even known that. We began to think that if we had had a decent admission procedure that really looked into people's backgrounds, we wouldn't have gotten a parolee. So we got to thinking that maybe we had to tighten up our procedure, maybe we had to find ways to distinguish between the kind of students who are going to make it in the school and those who aren't.

That sounds logical until you really look beneath the surface, and then the whole thing comes apart at the seams. Because the first thing you realize is that the main reason these students didn't make it was because they decided not to make it. They decided not to behave responsibly, for whatever reason – psychological, social, you name it. If they had decided to make it – as they could have, and as others did – then they would have made it. We had a number of students who had worse records than some of those who left, and who made it beautifully. One of the students who did best during the year was an absolutely hopeless case from every point of view, as far as his background was concerned.

It's a matter of internal decision; you can make it if you decide to make it. We came to realize that what we were talking about was a person *deciding* to be a responsible human being, and that's a decision any person can make. A parole board has no idea which of the people it puts on parole are going to behave responsibly or not. There's a 70% return rate, they still can't tell you which 7 out of 10 are going to be back and which 3 are going to make it. They just don't know, and there's no procedure for weeding people out that is good enough for you to stake a person's life on it. You might even have some studies that say, "Well, those who were breast fed as babies are going to make it better than others," or something. But you're not going to have such a high degree of correlation that you're ready to stake a person's future on it and say, "This guy's got these and those characteristics, he won't make it and therefore I'm going to keep him in jail now." You just can't do that. And by the same token you can't say to any prospective enrollee, "Based on your record I know you're not ever going to behave responsibly. You just can't be in the school." A human being is always capable of making a decision to behave responsibly.

Once we realized this we realized that there was no way at all for us to do better than we had done in predicting the behavior of students in advance. Nevertheless, we eliminated the one inconsistency of the old admissions policy, namely the compulsory interview. We eliminated any aspect of patronization or supplication or any of the unhealthy relationships between parent, school, and prospective student that we had before in the interview situation. Now we've gone right down the line in saying that the parents and students have to make up their own minds and have to find their own way of making up their minds. In addition, we came to expect a more successful admissions record because we now had a school in which there was a tradition of responsible behavior, in which there was something to see.

Of course, one can still see what one wants to see in any institution, I guess, but it's a lot harder once the model is there. People can still visit the school and read the literature and get a misconception of what the school is about, but it's not as easy to go wrong. And then we added to the admissions procedure an enrollment fee, and an advance on the tuition, and a contract saying the signee will abide by the by-laws – we added a good legal contract and a businesslike approach, and all these little changes reminded a prospective student that every aspect of his decision had to be made carefully, that nothing was going to be done sloppily in an "I'll do you a favor, you do me a favor" atmosphere. The whole approach became more self consistent, so that the admissions policy became completely integrated into the school, from a practical and philosophical point of view.

I want to say one more thing about the student body during the first year, about numbers. I pointed out that we had originally hoped that we'd start with something like 30 students. Then the terrific influx came, a lot of it due to a misconception of what the school was about, to a desire for a progressive school in an area where there was no particularly well-known progressive school available. Thus, we were flooded with students relative to our initial expectations. This caused an interesting destabilization in our growth projections. We had expected something like 30 or 40 students the first year, at the most; somewhere about double that the second year, and then some major subsequent growth.

The sudden influx of some 130 students the first year meant that, for reasons we couldn't fathom, we had reached a size not dreamed of reaching before the third year. That threw all our planning off, because the way we saw it at the time, the next step after having 150 students was an immense number – 500, 1000, 10,000 – because once we got into large numbers we expected a snowball effect. When it started to happen the very first year, it was as if we had to telescope our whole projection and time scale. So there was a lot of talk during the summer, especially in Trustees' meetings, about how we had to start worrying and planning for a new campus and new buildings in order to accommodate the hundreds of new students that we now expected to come the second year.

That bit of fancy came back to plague us later. We still get ribbed quite a bit – I do especially – about how I expected 700 students the second year. In the event, we shrank back to a number that much more represented the realities of a first year in this kind of a school, namely somewhere around 60 full-time students. Even that was a little high. And we went into a second year with 56, which grew to the 70's.

The dynamics of the growth pattern are the following: At the very beginning, you expect to pick up, randomly, the few people who somehow are tuned in more or less to the kind of thing you want to do; and you can expect that in a population pool of around a million people there are going to be of the order of magnitude of individuals or tens of people who will be fairly close to each other on any view. I mean, if you pick some crazy far-out religious view, you'll probably find 10 or 20 or 30 people in the Boston area who share it; and this is true of anything else. So you expect to pick out a few such people in any population. The only problem is to get to be known well enough so that the initial few will know you're there. Then you enter a proving period, of unknown length. You expect to pickup a few more units as you get better known, but the real growth occurs only after the basic proving period. It takes time simply to get started, and then you've got to start producing a working model that people can see and react to, and that's got to be studied and talked about. Slowly people start spreading the word that it's there, until finally its influence on local thought snowballs. Finally, when a lot of people start to send their kids, you can expect the experts and the public opinion leaders to study the working model and to say good things about it.

Concerning the number of students, I want to mention that right after the November crisis I received a telephone call from the President of the Summerhill Society in New York. He said that he had heard terrible things about the school, he'd gotten awful letters from several people, and he called me to find out what was going on. I told him some of the background of the crisis. Then he said, "How many students do you have left now?" I said, "About 65." And he said, "My goodness, I thought you were talking about a school that had a total of 20 people in the first place and had split into ten and ten. But 130 to begin with! Why, even now, after the split, you've got more students than virtually any other alternative school in the country." I thought that was an interesting observation, because it threw things into perspective. Regardless of how we compared to other alternative schools, we had one thing in common with them, and that was that we were considered quite different from ordinary schools. His comment shed light on the dynamics of population growth for such schools all over the country.

There is one other point that I want to discuss: the development of a post-high school. It was always clear to us that it made no sense as far as the school was concerned to segregate ages. It made no sense to stop at eighteen. The whole idea of elementary school, high school, college really had no relation to what we were after. So it was just a question of time until we would open the school to people of all ages, so that it could be a place of learning for all members of the community. Towards the end of the first year we began taking steps to extend the school to students of all ages. Appendix 8 is the first draft proposed along these lines, presented by me to the Trustees in June 1969. Action on this matter was taken during the school's second year.

The Parents and the School

I've mentioned why we gave an important role to parents in the school. It turned out that there was no parent involvement in the school at all in the summer. Come the fall, the parents' presence was felt a little more, by and large in a fairly standard way; namely, there was a tension between the parents and the school which was similar to the tension that exists in all other schools, and this was in line with the expectation that a lot of parents had that the school would be really like any other school. So during the early weeks of the school we had this feeling that there was a school and a staff on the one hand and there were parents on the other hand and there was going to be a lot of argument and hassling back and forth – the way you always have in PTA's or community-staff groups.

This of course was not the kind of thing we had in mind when we set up the school. We were interested in parent involvement in the school, and we meant *involvement,* we didn't mean this kind of sparring from the outside with an "inside" authority structure. So in the area of parent-school relations we had the same lack of consistency with the school's principles that we had with certain students; and it was often the parents of these same students who created the problem.

What stands out in my memory was the parent-staff meeting held in early October. We felt that it would be a good idea to promote parent involvement in the school by having regular parent-staff meetings which would be open to the students as well. In other words, sort of a regular open house for corporation members, parents, students, and maybe other interested parties, once a month – the first Wednesday of each month – at which the various issues that were confronting the school would be discussed openly; and these meetings could also serve as occasions for socializing.

The first meeting was in the beginning of October, and featured an address by Dennis on boredom. This was a subject we had discussed at a staff meeting, and we thought it would be a good idea to bring it up because some of the students were complaining about being bored because we weren't entertaining them. We had made the point that boredom was an essential phase for these students to go through because they had to reach the point where they were not being entertained anymore, where they were getting bored, and then realize that they would have to provide their own inner drive to get along. Dennis' talk, which included many provocative things, was not received well by the parents. It was clear from the initial reaction that we were dealing with a tremendously hostile group; that October meeting was a real harbinger of things to come. It was the direct precursor of the October 26 protest meeting.

Interestingly enough, the hostility centered around a central point of the school, the point of giving the students the right to choose what they want to do with themselves, how they want to spend their time, and what they want to learn. The parents were just outraged that we weren't providing more guidance, and more instruction; that we were really letting the students be on their own. We were given the same old arguments about how do you expect children to learn and this and that and the next thing. In fact one parent got up and talked about how there had been psychological studies made which showed that humans placed in an environment in which there was no sensory stimulus present suffered psychological disorders. Well, you can imagine the height of absurdity, regardless of the merits of our approach, in talking about a student in The Sudbury Valley School as an analog of a human being placed in an environment without sensory stimuli! The absurdity of that analogy is so great that you could see how these parents were straining to negate the basic premises of the school. To these parents not entertaining a student, not guiding him, was the direct equivalent of putting him in an environment of sensory deprivation.

After that hostile confrontation it was clear to us that an awful lot of parents weren't with the school. We hoped that time would change them. But things developed as they did, and the second confrontation on October 26 followed the first one, on an equally fundamental issue.

The next situation where we were together with the parents was at the December 9 corporation meeting. That was the corporation meeting at which the parents were voting members. We had had our first organizational meeting in February. Then came the May 6 meeting, which was the first real business meeting, at which we elected staff and passed budgets – those were the first staff elections by the Assembly. Then we had a September special meeting, right after the summer, which refined the budget for the year, and also added some staff. The fourth corporation meeting was held on December 9, and this was the first meeting of the kind that we'd originally projected, where parents had a large say. It took place after the main brunt of the great crisis was over.

By now we were left with mostly parents who were sticking with the school. There were to be sure some parents who were not satisfied, but who were nevertheless sticking with the school, and a few voices were raised in protest; but the general atmosphere pervading the December 9 meeting was one of extreme caution. Everybody was so aware that the school had just survived a threat to its existence and had barely made it through, that nobody really wanted to rock the boat. Nobody wanted to raise any issues that might split that meeting and lead to the demise of the school. So the atmosphere was one of great caution. Even the remaining dissident parents muted their voices. I guess they figured that there was time to make their opinions felt, and that the business at hand was to see to it that the school continue. There were two parts to the meeting. The first part was the business meeting, and then there was an informal discussion.

Appendix 6 contains two reports made at the business meeting. A few questions were raised in the informal discussion about our program but there was really not much action. Everybody heaved a sigh of relief at the end of the evening that we had made it through the first meeting and that we were on our way to some form of parent-school cooperation and involvement rather than antagonism. Some parents had expressed a will to help and to participate, and we hoped something would come out of that.

Alan White chaired this meeting, as our new President. He made a very moving opening statement that compared the school to the colonial pioneers, the first small band of settlers at Plymouth, who came through the first winter with their numbers cut in half, but who survived to leave their imprint on the entire future of the great American continent. That was certainly very encouraging to hear at that moment.

The actual degree of parent involvement in the school increased from December very, very slowly. Some of the more actively dissident parents simply left but others, even among the dissidents, slowly came to identify themselves with the school in one way or another. I don't want to exaggerate, but I do think that we felt a slow but steady growth of identification of the parents with the school, over the six months following the December meeting.

We had an informal meeting in January, and one in February, at which we discussed the financial situation of the school and the admissions question. We had several open meetings to discuss admissions policies, meetings at which some parents showed up. In March there was a fifth corporation meeting, a special meeting called to amend the by-laws and to pass certain financial arrangements – the salaries and the debt repayment (I'll come to that when I discuss the by-laws and finances) – and each of these meetings showed a greater degree of parent participation and involvement. The questions asked were much more serious, and grappled with the issues.

The corporation meeting in March didn't have a cautious atmosphere. There were only one or two parents who voiced any kind of serious dissent and there was some sharp debate, but it was a different kind of atmosphere. There wasn't the walking-on-eggs business. It felt more and more as if people were gaining confidence that the school would survive.

Then we had our regular corporation meeting in May. This was the meeting at which officers were elected for the second year; it certainly conveyed a feeling of looking towards the future. We elected a Board of Trustees and officers for the next year, voted on a budget – everything looked forward to next year. We knew we were going to have a next year, and the parents felt that this was something they could count on.

Then in June we had a big dinner party, preceded by cocktails, to which everybody brought a dish; this was an opportunity for parents and staff to socialize and meet each other. All these meetings were open to students as well, and we had a fairly good student attendance throughout, which indicated a student interest and involvement, and a willingness on the part of parents to let the students participate along with them, which of course is part of the idea of the school.

There's really nothing very dramatic about any of this, it's just that it takes a long time for the parents to get to know their own minds, their own attitudes towards the school, for them to get to understand the school, for them to get to know each other, to have confidence in each other and in the school. I feel that we gradually got a greater sense of identification of the parents with the school. It was a very slow process. It doesn't happen quickly because, as many of the parents said to us, you've got to reexamine your whole life, and you've got to reexamine your attitude towards your children. Since the parents are not at school everyday, they can postpone this kind of reexamination.

I do want to mention in this connection one of the most outstand-ing experiences of the first year, during the special corporation meeting of March 6, where amended by-laws were passed. The significance of this meeting was that for the first time the corporation at large, includ-ing the parents, had a chance to reexamine and study the principles of the school, and the way these principles were put into practice in the by-laws. The original by-laws had been handed to the parents; they were drawn up and prepared before there were any parents in the school. Even if parents said, "We subscribe to the by-laws; we've read them and we understand them," nevertheless they were handed these by-laws, and they had not had any hand in forming them.

When the amended by-laws were presented for discussion and voted on paragraph by paragraph, the parents now had the opportunity to look them over carefully and to express their opinions on these by-laws by voting. The issues were thought about and debated at this March meet-ing, the parents voting paragraph by paragraph to affirm the by-laws of this school, to affirm a school whose structure was clearly laid out along the lines of responsibility, freedom, and the democratic ethos. This was a moving experience, because it was like the rebirth of the school in many ways. It was like a mass reaffirmation of faith. That meeting gave me more confidence than any other single parents meeting or corporation meeting, because I felt that from that day on we had a group of people who had knowingly affirmed their support of this kind of a school, and that even though some of them may later leave, what we had here was a real institutional reaffirmation of principle.

I guess what I'm saying here complements what I said before when I discussed the student body and the crisis: the first year consisted not only in the birth of the school but in its being put to the test several times. Not merely surviving several times, but being reborn in a strengthened form several times during the year. And these successive rebirths – after the crisis, after the December 9th meeting, after the March meeting, after we knew that there was going to be another year, after the May 9th meeting – these successive rebirths and reaffirmations were tremendously important factors in strengthening the school and in assuring its future.

New By-Laws

The development of new by-laws for the school was a very important phase in the school's refinement of its concept. The old set of by-
laws somehow did not set out in a clear enough manner the principles of
organization of the school. It's not that they weren't there, but there was
something about the presentation that veiled what we were doing just a
bit. For example, there were clauses saying that the Assembly can set up
such committees as it sees fit to carry out its work, and that the Trustees can set up such committees as they wanted to carry out their work.
Both of these provisions look innocent enough. Actually they reflected
the idea that the way the school would really run, when it got down to
the nitty gritty of how the ideas were really going to be concretized, was
through some sort of a committee structure.

The idea was that it's very nice to have these big town-meeting-type
groups, but the real work, the real decision-making would be done in
small groups that would hold the really effective power in the school.
What I'm saying is more a matter of tone than of specific stipulation. It
was perfectly possible to have a democratically run school under these
by-laws. In fact there's no question that such a school was encouraged
and set forth. But provisions of this sort were put in purposely to provide
the potential for a somewhat more traditional and autocratic structure
under the umbrella of a democratic one.

Another example was the complete absence of any mention of the
School Meeting. Again, it's true that this was done largely because the
School Meeting contained minors and in general the by-laws didn't refer
to structures that contained minors. Still, the absence of any mention
of the School Meeting was another symptom of a tone that just slightly
revealed some reservations. I don't think that it was a question of betray-

ing principles. I want to be quite explicit on that. But it was a question of not having enough confidence in them, of setting them forth a bit ambiguously with some protection in case they don't work. It was a matter of lack of self-confidence and lack of confidence in the ideas, that they could form the basis of a viable organization.

One has to be a little careful about faulting the original by-laws too heavily because one has to remember that these reflected no experience with the school, and they also had to be drawn up at a time, back in the winter of '67, when many of the ideas of the school had not really been worked out. When there were many areas of the school that we had clear in overall outline perhaps, but not really in detail. Obviously the most flagrant example of this was our conception of how the staff ought to be hired, which went through repeated refinements. Another example was the lack of clarity in the role of the Trustees. I remember that Fred used to say at the early meetings of the Board of Trustees, "I can't figure out what the Trustees are for." And he had drafted the by-laws! It took a long time for the function of the Trustees and for their place in the organization to be worked out. In short, the original set of by-laws were written without the benefit of understanding through experience. And when you're setting up a completely new institution under a completely new legal structure you've got to be prepared to have several areas that you're not really clear about when you start out.

Initially, the impulse towards reworking the by-laws came not from any feeling that we had to do the whole thing over but from a realization that certain paragraphs were inadequate and should be cleaned up. Actually the first spur towards revising the by-laws was the student crisis. And the need to be explicit on the question of expulsion. In addition, we wanted to clean up some minor inconsistencies in the wording and to look a little more carefully into some of the provisions that had been shown to be weak during the crisis.

For example, we had to revise our residency requirements, or at least we had to look a little more closely at them, because we certainly didn't want to get into the situation that was threatened (although it never actually came about) that people would enroll their children and then pull them out, or the students would be absent for a long time or would be suspended indefinitely, and yet the parents would still have a full participatory vote in determining the fate of the corporation. This was absentee landlordism and absentee voting at its worst. Things like that obviously had to be cleaned up. As we started turning our attention to them we suddenly realized that if we were going to have a meeting of the Assembly that would pass amendments, this was an opportunity to go through the by-laws carefully and do over the entire set.

What we got was new by-laws in which the School Meeting is described in a forthright manner, the student body is discussed clearly, as is the staff, and the fact that we have open files, and so forth. There was no provision for a committee structure to govern the school. The new set of by-laws was clear affirmation of our principles in practice. I repeat, I don't think they could have been written earlier, not only because of the personalities involved, but because they required an understanding in detail of how the school operates. But I do think that once we got into the first year and got to understand things better, it was important that we do it.

We didn't anticipate that after the new by-laws would be presented to the Assembly, the discussion and voting would represent a review of the entire school and a reaffirmation of the Assembly's faith in the school. That was an added benefit that we got from rewriting all the by-laws instead of just amending a sentence or two. Had we realized that in advance, we probably would have set out purposely to rewrite every paragraph, if only to change a comma here and there, in order to be sure to attain that very important reaffirmation.

The School Meeting

I've talked about the School Meeting in several connections, and now I'd like to discuss some aspects of the development of the School Meeting as an important and strong organ of the school. The first School Meeting was held at the end of the first week of school in July. Ever since then the School Meeting has been a continuing legislative and judiciary arm of the school. The School Meeting started by simply being called by the staff. I, in my role as chairman of the staff, took the chair at the first meeting, although there was no reason for me to do that. I opened by saying a few words on what the School Meeting was: that it was the internal governing body of the school, and that it would operate according to Robert's Rules of Order, which I must confess I had a very sketchy knowledge of. (But I knew they existed, and I knew this was a set of parliamentary rules that was widely used; and I felt that we had to operate in a formally clear manner in order to be an effective governing body of the school. We had to have structure.) And that's the way the School Meeting got launched. We never really voted on operating according to Robert's Rules, but that procedure gained general acceptance and became a tradition of the School Meeting.

There was never really any discussion of what the School Meeting was. I remember some people complaining – I have difficulty evaluating whether these complaints should have been taken seriously or not – about how arbitrary the start of the School Meeting was, how the advice of the students was not, and should have been, taken into account even in setting up the first stages of the School Meeting. I didn't feel that. I felt that we knew what the organization was to be and that the idea was to get it started; there were all the mechanisms that one needs within the organization to change what one didn't like, which in the event was what happened.

During the summer the School Meeting began to function in its anticipated role, and yet as I've pointed out the whole atmosphere of unreality in the summer kept things from being as serious and as effective as they might have been had it been the fall. The School Meeting did pass regulations but it really never got down to the matter of examining the school and the areas that needed regulation. It sort of relied on the good will of most people and on the good feeling of the summer, and also to a certain extent on the tradition from other institutions that in a pinch the staff was going to see things through. It certainly developed no effective means of enforcing its resolutions. There was virtually no enforcement all summer, and whatever enforcement there was in the school was very casual all around. Obviously the only reason the school survived was because enforcement wasn't that necessary.

The debates varied widely in quality. There were some that were very good, that reflected a lot of thought about what was going on. And there were many that were light-headed, and gave the feeling of people "playing government," of a student-government type of thing where you debated and raised points of order for fun rather than with any serious consequences in mind. I would not say by any stretch of the imagination that the School Meeting during the summer was frivolous. But it lacked that element of sobriety and seriousness that the entire summer lacked.

There were some important achievements of the summer that are worth mention. For example, attention was rightly given to selecting a chairman of the School Meeting, and a procedure was set up for electing the chairman and limiting his term – an example of how the School Meeting remedied the arbitrariness of my picking up the gavel and assuming the chairmanship. That was a very important step because that was the first time that the School Meeting took on itself in a serious manner the consideration of establishing democratic procedures within itself.

There were also several discussions of how one could enforce rules, and there was the introduction of the first attempt to make the School Meeting an effective enforcer of its own rules by introducing a "gripe session," by making the second item on the agenda a gripe session, during which people brought up their complaints and alleged instances of infractions of the rules for action by the School Meeting. There was an element in this gripe session of letting off steam, and of hoping that things would be settled through some of the discussion. But on the other hand there were also at least the rudiments of an enforcement system.

Another achievement of the School Meeting during the summer was that it established itself as a continuing body that operated according to serious rules; this was a long hard struggle that took long into the fall to settle firmly. There was a sizable contingent of students, which became larger in the fall, who looked for encounter-group-type meetings, who looked for emotional sessions where one vented one's feelings, one spoke freely, where there weren't regulations and rules governing procedure, where you had cross conversation and you reached agreements by consensus rather than by formal decisions and votes. By now it should be clear that we had a group that was interested in this kind of thing, because it was completely in line with their emotional needs and with their general fear of responsibility and the kind of independence and sober self-evaluation that responsible behavior entails. They wanted always to create situations in which there would be a kind of emotional undercurrent, an emotional shoring-up of each other's weaknesses.

So another important achievement of the summer was our success in withstanding that tendency. As a result, we were able to establish by the end of the summer that the School Meeting operated within a well defined structure. It was terribly important for us to have well defined rules. It was part of the style of the School Meeting. We were doing serious work, and we understood that rules of procedure are developed in order to enable serious institutional work to take place without the intrusion of personal relations and personal difficulties that would create the hybrid interference between personal and institutional relations that we were trying so hard to avoid. We understood that this was the function of rules, and that's why we wanted rules. Of course, we weren't wedded to Robert's Rules. We made many departures that we found more effective for our own needs. But we understood the use and the function of rules in an institutional setting, and that was a very important feature of the school.

I would say that at the end of the summer we had an embryo School Meeting, though there still wasn't that solidity of tradition that would assure the School Meeting's continuing vigor. Through the early fall the quality of the meetings definitely degenerated, because the presence of a rather large group of students who were in fact undermining the very principles that the school stood for was a tremendous damper on any kind of effective School Meeting, just as it was a damper on the functioning of the school in every other area.

The first real step towards giving the School Meeting a serious role in governing the school was the series of meetings that I've already discussed, where the staff threw the question of the survival of the school into the School Meeting's lap. That was a rather sudden and traumatic growing up, and it was reflected in a rather sudden change in the degree of concentration and involvement and understanding of the School Meeting and its role that was exhibited on the part of all students, including even the very students who were the object of our considerations.

The level of debate that the School Meeting saw during those sessions discussing expulsion was much higher than that of earlier meetings. I think everybody realized that finally the School Meeting was being called upon to play a role that was crucial to the survival of the school. I guess we needed a traumatic awakening to make this clear. In fact, the School Meeting had been critical to the survival of the school from the very first day, and had this been realized, had people taken it as seriously all along as they learned to take it through the traumatic events in October, then October never would have happened. But at any rate it did happen, and that was sort of an instantaneous maturation of the School Meeting. Everybody realized this: when the parents attacked what was going on, they attacked the School Meeting, as I've already pointed out, and most of the Trustees too felt that to give the School Meeting the scope that we were giving it wasn't proper. The Trustees even passed a resolution that forbade the School Meeting to discuss indefinite suspension or expulsion – even to discuss them! – and directed that every problem requiring radical treatment was to be referred directly to the Trustees without this kind of discussion.

That was the only time in the history of the school that the powers of the School Meeting were curtailed in an arbitrary fashion by anybody. Of course there was no real way that the Trustees could enforce this rule. They didn't even realize, much to my amazement, that the rule itself had within it the seeds of its own negation, because discussing whether a student should be referred to the Trustees or not was in fact the equivalent of discussing expulsion. But at the time there really wasn't much point in arguing about whether the Trustees' resolution was legal or proper or not, because the Trustees had the power to make it stick; because during this period the Trustees in fact had to arrogate certain powers in running the school, in order to keep the school going.

Now the very fact that the Trustees passed this kind of a resolution indicates what a change the role of the School Meeting underwent at that time; for the Trustees acknowledged through this resolution that the School Meeting was in fact the critical organ of internal self-government and that all *other* aspects of internal self-government were legitimate concerns of the School Meeting and were recognized as such by the Trustees – in a negative way to be sure. So in a sense the Trustees' assault on the authority of the School Meeting was a recognition of its importance.

When the school started functioning again after the four day closing, and without the suspended contingent of students, it was clear that we were embarked on a new phase of the School Meeting. From November through January, the School Meeting proceeded to examine very seriously what its function was going to be and to set up a series of procedures and organs for dealing with the effective running of the school.

This was the period when we thought through the judicial system of the school. It was quite clear that we were going to need some effective way of enforcing School Meeting regulations and, in general, of providing for law and order in the school. I remember discussing in early November the idea of having an investigative group, of having some regular organ of the school discuss and investigate alleged violations and suggest remedies. This was a very unformed idea at the time. I suggested that we have something modeled on a grand jury, without even knowing what a grand jury really is. That was the occasion for a good deal of controversy as well as progress. Shortly thereafter Dennis came up with a proposal for establishing a grand jury in the school, and this ultimately led to the establishment of a Committee on School Affairs.

The words "grand jury" were ultimately dropped for many reasons: Many of us felt that we didn't want a body that brings indictments, but merely investigations. We wanted indictments to be done in a different way. Also the very words "grand jury" suggested in many other people's minds an inquisitorial organ, which is an interesting reflection of the state of law in the country at large; because whereas the grand jury probably should suggest a group of people dedicated to unearthing evidence of probable malfeasance and then turning this over to a complete investigation by trial, people's attitude towards law has become so clouded that vigorous enforcement of law has became associated in people's minds with inquisitorial techniques. Many of the Trustees and parents felt very strongly about not having something like a grand jury in the school. That the words were just too "harsh".

A lot of people in the school, and I was one of them, felt that it would be unwise to insist on a grand jury. First of all, if it offended so many people this wasn't the time to stand on form. Also, there was an overtone of criminal proceedings in grand juries, and we wanted an organ that would deal with all types of infractions and wouldn't imply that it was dealing with criminals. We also wanted an organ that could arbitrate, which a grand jury can't.

I felt that the main problem was investigative: we had no means of getting an idea of a given incident, and what we really needed was an organ which would take testimony and try to reconstruct the incident well enough so that an account of it could be presented to the School Meeting, and then the School Meeting could decide where it would go from there. At any rate, in an open letter to members of the School Meeting, which can be found in Appendix 7, I presented my views on the legal system, and these were debated along with the views of others until we finally came up with a legal system that started functioning in January and reached a state of highly efficient operation by the end of the first year. It took that long.

It took many months of the Committee on School Affairs to work out its method of procedure, for the School Meeting to work out a good trial procedure, and so forth. But in fact the important steps came during those months of December and January.

At the same time, the School Meeting started turning its attention to the kinds of regulations needed to make the school the kind of place we wanted. A new series of resolutions was passed that had a different tone about them as regards the seriousness with which they were taken. So I would say that a critical period in the maturing of the School Meeting was during the aftermath of the traumatic growing up of the October 24 and 25 meetings.

Subsequent to that there was a new chairman in the spring, and throughout the spring the School Meeting proved itself over and over again to be a sophisticated and mature organ of the school. You could see it in many ways: the procedures were refined, a good School Meeting law book was prepared, a case book was prepared, which gave the traditions and trials and history of all the rules and regulations so that people could study them and develop a serious legal tradition in the school. Many good rules and regulations were passed. In particular, rules governing the legislative process were passed, so that we had a procedure of first readings and second readings for all rules and amendments; this gave a whole new dimension of consideration to rules and regulations that we couldn't have when motions were simply presented on the floor and voted on immediately.

I would say that throughout the spring the School Meeting operated in the way that it had been envisioned. Towards the end of the spring it had a legal status endowed through the by-laws as the master of the school's internal affairs. By the end of the first year, then, the School Meeting was firmly established as a continuing executive, legislative, and judiciary body. This I think is perhaps one of the greatest achievements of the first year of the school, one of the things that really establishes the school as coming through on its promise to be a truly democratic institution.

The School and the Community

The public relations situation during the first year is an interesting story in its own right. I've already pointed out that the first phase of our public relations, which occupied us up to the opening of the school and a bit beyond, was directed towards getting the school known broadly throughout the community, with the primary aim of soliciting students and obtaining the personnel with whom to start the school. Once that goal was achieved, it was important to realize that that phase had to be abandoned as quickly as possible, because a stance of solicitation is basically not in line with the idea of the school. It's a necessary evil with our present communications network in this country, in order to get the school started, but it's not the kind of thing that we wanted to keep going.

Once we had a school, the next important task was to make it a going concern. This meant that the second phase was one of turning inward, of concentrating our efforts on understanding the school and determining what it was to be. And that meant that during most of the first year of operation, our efforts were concentrated inward. This was reflected in an almost complete lack of extroversion. We weren't looking for platforms, we weren't looking for publicity, we didn't hand out press releases, we didn't seek forums in which to speak, we didn't write articles, we didn't look for people to write articles about us. In fact, we discouraged this kind of thing; when people inquired as to whether we might be interested in speaking or being publicized we would generally discourage them.

As a result, during the first year we had very little by way of publicity, except for the notorious sort in October and November because of the crisis. That was splashed all over the papers and even on television and radio through the dissidents. Actually if anybody read those articles carefully and thought about what was said in them, they turned out to be not so bad for us, because the kind of people who read these articles and who as a result of them kept away from the school were by and large the kind of people who wouldn't want to be in the school – namely, people who were similar in their outlook to the dissidents. Whereas a different type of person could read those articles and say to himself, "Well, this is really a school bent on maintaining a respect for certain values."

To be sure, I'm not exactly recommending the kind of publicity we got during the crisis as a means for developing good public relations, but I don't think that it did us all that much real harm. The one major piece of positive publicity we got came quite by accident: a fifteen minute television show in color on CBS-TV in metropolitan Boston at prime time – Saturday night at 6:30. This was a show for which the TV crew came out to the school and filmed on location. We had quite a discussion in the School Meeting as to whether we wanted it. Most people weren't too eager for it, but we figured that we really had nothing to hide. As it turned out, the show was done in a very balanced way. It was a good piece of publicity for us, and the people who were involved were actually quite favorably impressed with the school.

During the year, we had a tremendous number of visitors. They came in and out, but we didn't cater to them, we didn't hold seminars, we didn't have organized programs in the school, or anything of this sort. I think that this was completely proper. We needed the time and the energy to turn inward and I don't think it would have done us any good to simultaneously turn outward during this phase, because so many of the fine details of what we were doing, so many aspects of our style were still in the formative stage.

As the year came to a close we became ready to enter the third phase, of going out into the world from a position of strength. We had an institution, it had character, much of its style had been worked out, and it had the strength and resilience and wholeness that enabled it to become a factor in affecting the course of education in the country. I want to make it clear that when I say the school had a wholeness, I mean a cultural coherence. It's not that we were static. On the contrary, if anything typified the school it was an accelerated rate of growth. New ideas were more frequent in coming. We broke new ground in all sorts of directions. So it's not the wholeness of staticity that I'm talking about. It's a wholeness of style. It's a cultural matrix for the school which gave the institution an overall style and an overall stability as an institution. What differentiates a relatively stable institution from one that falls apart rapidly is that the stable one is capable of responding to change within the overall matrix of its style. And that's what we had.

The school was now ready to go out and affect the course of events in this country. To make our philosophy known, make what we stand for known, to find every way to make sure that we're not going to be overlooked, and that nobody is going to be able to dismiss us by turning the other way. That's the only way that we're going to be able to play a role in this country. And that was the whole point of setting up the school. There is no point in asking us, "Well, what do you care about playing a role in this country? Why not just go on and carry on your own little school?"

The whole point of creating this school in the middle of Framingham, in the middle of the country, open to the community, embedded in the community, was to be part of the current overall American reality, and in turn to affect that reality and to push it into the alternative that we're proposing. Had we wanted to be isolated, had we wanted to "do our thing" off in a corner, then we would have gone way off somewhere, away from things, in a different location. But we didn't. And the school will either exist for a long time or not, depending on whether or not the character of the overall society is compatible with the style of the school. What we're going to try to do is see to it that the character of the overall society *is* compatible with the school. If it turns out that the society will turn in a different direction, then the school will not be able to coexist within that society for any length of time; it will take on the aspect more and more of an isolated island, and we'll eventually have to remove ourselves bodily or build some kind of isolation from the rest of the community – both of which would change us in a fundamental way. So it's very much part of the design of the school to have to get into the battle, to affect the course of history and be affected by it. There's no chance of escaping this in the conception of the school.

In line with this we wrote and sent out a new catalog describing the school. Our original literature had a tone to it that was without any doubt soliciting on the one hand and incomplete on the other. We all knew this, and we all said that we were aware that our first catalog had been a first draft of a catalog about the school. As we got to understand the school, we were able to write something different. The new catalog had the style of the school embedded in it to a far larger extent.

The Physical Plant

We got a great deal of insight into good campus design accidentally. We went out and looked for a place and found our campus, and it happened to be an old, distinguished estate. We might have ended up with a plot of ground on which we had to build; or we might have ended up with any number of other things. I don't know what we would have thought then, but probably we would have been thinking along pretty standard lines had we designed a campus from scratch. We would have tried to decide what kind of design would best suit the needs of the school as we envisioned these needs in advance, and we doubtless would have come up with an art center, and information center, and this and that. It's called campus planning. But as it turned out, none of this came to be, because we had a ready-made building. And we found out something from our experience with this building that, not surprisingly, reflects much of the very early centers of learning in medieval and early modern Europe.

We found out that there was something extraordinarily suitable about an estate-size building, a building planned and built as a large estate, as a design for a school. Let's put it this way. You can start by pointing to some of the features of a planned campus, in the standard sense of the term, that really are inappropriate to the kind of school we're talking about. The main feature is that it's planned in a linear fashion: there's a planned use for each building, there's a restricted degree of flexibility. You build a laboratory and that's what it is. You build a library and that's what it's designed to be. There's a tremendous degree of linearity to the use of the buildings, which reflects the linearity of the institutions they serve and is very much out of character with our school. There isn't the kind of flexibility, the kind of give, that could respond to change and fluctuation in needs of various student bodies. You program what can be done at other schools so tightly that you lay the groundwork for channeling a student's possibilities for activity.

The second thing wrong with these buildings is that they're like jails, they're cold, they're mass produced, everything about them smacks of the regimented linearity of the industrial age. Long corridors, big rooms with lots of chairs lined up in them, toilets with urinals lined up next to each other, cafeterias where everybody eats at the same place at a given time, and so forth. They have a character that's very compatible with modern society. When you look at modern architecture the thing that's striking about it is the basic similarity between structures; and that's to be expected because they all share the linearity, the aspiration to linearity and the aspiration to regimentation, that modern society has. So whether you're looking at a place of entertainment, a shopping center, a prison, a school, a college, a factory – whatever you happen to be looking at, you get the same kind of structure that has become almost synonymous with the word "institutional." And that's really what's wrong with modern campuses.

Another thing that is also not in character with our school is very small intimate buildings like homes. There are a lot of educational reformers who talk about small family-type units. This is a tremendous fad in education. They talk about the "family" group and the "family" room – we used to call it "home room," now it's the "family grouping." Or they talk about reorganizing schools into small units – tens and twenties – with a teacher who has a sort of parental role. For our school, this can be ruled out on the grounds that I've already discussed, because it hybridizes the personal and the institutional relations of people in a way that we're not interested in.

The thing about large estate type structures is that they avoid linearity on the one hand and the small homey family intimacy on the other hand. What's a big estate? You've got all sorts of rooms, and you've got a lot of them, so you're never in danger of falling into the trap of thinking you're a family. There are rooms of all different sizes. They're comfortable, they're thought of more in terms of human comfort than regimenting the activities of their occupants. You get design in an estate that looks to the comfort of the inhabitant, looks to a wide variety of multipurpose rooms; so you have much more flexibility, hardly any linearity at all, and a sense of ease and comfort. This is enhanced as I've already pointed out, in furnishing the place with comfortable home-type furniture. Not to create a home, but the kind of furniture you would put in your home for comfort rather than regimented row-type chairs and desks.

What I'm trying to say is that if you look around at the various forms of current architecture, the one form that is presently known and available that seems particularly appropriate for school design is the estate. That doesn't rule out some special purpose buildings. That doesn't rule out building an auditorium, or any particular single purpose building. But I would say that the need for these is relatively small in a school. You're better off making use of the specialized buildings in the community. They can be shared by everybody, by the community, by the school. You're better off building a really good bona fide theater in the community and giving access to all groups; and if you need more, you build another theater in the community rather than having each school have its own specialized theater. That's a terrible waste of resources and a linearity in the institution which ends up either in having the building not used most of the time or forcing people into the dramatic arts simply to use the facility. Actually, in the present day education, it's more the former than the latter. For example, the average modern school outfits TV multi-media centers and computer centers and so forth, rather than make use of these facilities in the community at large, and most of these facilities sit unused in the schools much of the day. In the few schools where they put up facilities and then insist on their use, it leads to a tremendous regimentation of the whole school in order to justify the outlay.

So I would say that of all the types of structures that are sensible today, a really good campus is one in which you have several large villas, and grounds in between. You can have this in the heart of a city. There are large mansions, and if instead of putting art collections in the Frick building and the Guggenheim home or something like that you put schools in these large buildings, you'd have the same effect in the city. True, you wouldn't have green and trees and outdoors around it, but then you don't in the rest of the city either, so it would be in line with the rest of the city.

I'm not saying that there might not develop in the course of time other styles of architecture that might not be equally well suited to schools, and maybe even better. All I'm saying is that if you look around at the present available architecture, this style stands out as by far the most appropriate one. It has the added feature of being reasonable as far as the expense of constructing it and maintaining it are concerned. The outlay on such a physical plant is a fraction of the outlay of a big modern building. There are lots of reasons for that, but I think the basic reason is that linear institutions tend to waste a tremendous amount of space and equipment because so much is put into providing things that aren't really needed.

Managing the Finances

This brings me to the last major point that I want to discuss about the first year of school: the school's finances. In the first place, the simple reality of the school's finances is worth recounting. A total of some $40,000 in seed money was put up by us to start the school. That was enough to get the school going on July 1, and the intention was that from then on the school would exist primarily on tuition income.

We never wanted the school to be dependent on foundation grants or government grants, because of our constant aspiration to serve as a feasible model in every area for mass public education, and public schools don't depend on grants. This meant that we were determined to show that this kind of school can function at least as efficiently as a public school, and we fully expected to be able to show that it could function on a lower per pupil expenditure than the average public school and produce the kind of education that is compatible with the democratic ethos rather than the kind that isn't, such as the public schools are now producing.

So we had these financial aims before us all the time, and they were an important factor in making us shy away at all times from large foundation grants. It's not that we didn't make some inquiries, and I'm not going so far as to say that we would have rejected a grant; we certainly wouldn't have rejected a grant in a special area, for example a grant to build a library or pay staff salaries in the first year. But we weren't looking for grants and we were convinced that it would be important for us to make it on our own, because this would be an important feature of our ability to convince others all over the country that this was the kind of thing that they too could do.

The first year showed us that we could get through even under the most adverse circumstances, and pay our bills on time and make it. That sounds like a very simple statement, but in fact it covers some heroic efforts that probably will never be adequately appreciated. For example, our decision to refund in full all of the money paid by those who wished to withdraw on or before November 26 meant that we had to have something like $23,000 cash in hand to effect this refund. For a new school in our financial position, it's not to be expected that there would be that kind of money lying around. Yet it's an amazing fact that we were so careful about our expenditures, and so conscientious about not spending money unless we had to, that when the time came to make the refunds, the money was there. I think this is worth special mention. Because most people believe that if you don't have money then you skimp, but if you have money as an institution, then you always find ways to spend it.

There are very few institutions that can maintain a level of expenditures governed by real need rather than a level of expenditure governed by available funds. As soon as people see funds they always concoct needs to spend it on. The fact is that we always operated in the fiscal area just the same as we operated in every other area. We felt that every expenditure had to be made in a responsible way that made sense, that was consistent, that could be justified and accounted for by the person making the expenditure. This was the hallmark of everything we did financially. This meant that our rate of expenditure really was independent of how much income we had, except that when the funds dropped to almost zero we had to forego even some needs. But happily that never happened.

To give an idea how precarious the situation was during the first year, our bank balance during December and January was to my recollection always below $2000. At the end of November we received an anonymous contribution from one of our strongest supporters who had worked for the school for close to a year. The contribution was in the amount of $2000, and was given with the hope that others would emulate it and help bail the school out of its financial straits after the mass refund. But in fact this was the only contribution of any size that was forthcoming, and it kept us going in December and January. Not only that, but it had long-term consequences as well, because although things eased up after the payment of the second installment of tuitions that came in on February 1, we ended our fiscal year in June with less than $2000 unexpended from our budget. Which means that as far as the budget for the year is concerned, that $2000 made the difference of surviving.

In this way, we got through the first year without a deficit and without closing. That's a financial record that I don't think any school can come near. And this was while we were servicing a large number of students, and a good sized physical plant.

Another aspect of the finances of the school was the tuition, and here again the factor of our role as a viable model for public school systems was foremost in our minds. We didn't want the tuition to rise beyond the levels of per-pupil expenditure that were reasonable in the community of Framingham and its environs. Some of these communities had a per-pupil expenditure for the year 1969-70 that was around $1300. Other communities were as low as $600. The average was somewhere around $800, but a great number of communities had per-pupil expenditures of over $900. When we recommended that the tuition for the second year be set at $950, and when the parents accepted this without any demur whatsoever, we had in mind that the thousand dollar mark was a mark that we hoped not to go over. It was our hope that the $950 tuition rate would decrease with time rather than increase, inflation notwithstanding.

There is another side to the financial affairs of the school, in which we broke new ground, and this was one of the great achievements of the year. That had to do with our expenditures on educational materials. A certain part of the budget is always set aside for educational materials, for outfitting the school to serve the learning needs of the students and the needs of a staff of teachers. In an ordinary school all this is spelled out: people decide what ought to be learned and what equipment ought to be used in the learning process, and they go ahead and buy it. The administrative structure makes this decision. It's something that's made in the same authoritarian and arbitrary manner as everything else that's done in ordinary schools.

It was clear to us right from the beginning that we were going to have to break new ground in this area simply because we weren't an authoritarian school. Our ideas in the beginning were a cross between the democratic and self-regulated ideas that the school stood for, and some left-over liberal tidbits that we came with.

Initially, in the summer, the Trustees would have liked us to have an administrative structure for controlling expenditures which would concentrate the actual spending of money in the hands of one or two people so that there wouldn't be any danger of messing up the books, or of error, or of fraud. The staff knew that this was inconsistent with the way the school was envisioned, and inconsistent in particular with the diffusion of responsibility for day to day maintenance of the school among the staff.

So we broke ground immediately by setting up a system of discretionary accounts for staff members, in the amount of $50 apiece for the summer, and then $25 apiece for the fall. The idea was that this money would be available for every staff member to spend as he saw fit on his own needs, and that he could do this completely freely without accounting to anybody; and that it was only if he needed more that he would have to come before the full staff and justify how he spent his money, to see whether more funds ought to be given, whether he knew how to spend money responsibly as far as the institution is concerned, and whether the institution can afford to put more funds under his control.

I should point out that behind this was a clear agreement made at the very outset that the staff was collectively responsible for expenditures on educational materials. There was never any stage in the school where this responsibility wasn't in the hands of the staff collectively. Even before discretionary accounts, every expenditure in educational materials was approved by the staff as a whole, but vote or consensus. This arrangement was given legal authorization when the Trustees voted that the staff would be responsible for expenditures under the category of educational materials. There wasn't much discussion of that vote, and my impression is that it got through the Trustees because there hadn't yet been any problems with staff. The introduction of staff discretionary accounts gave some of this collective responsibility over to individuals.

That still left open the question of how one goes about getting educational materials for student needs; and that's where the progressive leftover came in. We felt that we as staff, in controlling the purse strings, would respond to the needs of the students; they would come to us with requests for money and we would discuss the expenditure and either make it or not make it. We made no allowance for students to exercise responsible control over the money. We made them come to us, and then we took the responsibility for the expenditures. So if an expenditure wasn't a good one, we were the ones who were responsible for the expenditure, not the student.

Even worse than that, when it was a question of outfitting the school initially before July 1, and then during the summer and in the fall, we sat together like a good conscientious staff, either as a group or in subgroups, and thought out what educational materials "ought to be" in a school that's well equipped to meet the needs of children these days. And sure enough, we spent a few thousand dollars equipping the school that way.

That was, without any question, an unequivocal mistake from beginning to end, because it in no way reflected a response to a genuinely expressed need of the students. It didn't even reflect a request from students. We just took the whole matter completely out of the students' hands. The result was predictable: an awful lot of the material that was bought this way was slowly destroyed. It wasn't exactly vandalized, because by and large the attitude of the students towards the equipment in the school and the physical plant was quite responsible – certainly vastly more so than in any other educational institution. But nevertheless the equipment thus purchased was not cared for and rapidly became useless.

The staff's control of funds for educational materials was clearly not right, and proved to be not right in every way. We got into more and more conflicting situations where we would pass questionable judgments over the validity of student requests, and we got ourselves into bigger and bigger holes; it was such a glaringly inconsistent area in the school, because here we weren't judging the students on what they did with their time, and we weren't judging them on what they did with their minds, but we were judging the students all the time on how they wanted to spend money for their education! It just didn't make any sense.

What ultimately developed was a system of student discretionary accounts that was in every way similar to the staff discretionary accounts. In fact, it was established on the same basis for all members of the School Meeting. There was a basic discretionary account for each School Meeting member to spend as he sees fit. He had to be responsible for it only to himself, unless he wanted to spend more.

The staff's responsibility came in making the initial allotment: there was an amount that the Assembly budgeted for educational materials, and the staff had to make a basic decision on how much to give over out of this amount to discretionary accounts and how much to keep in reserve for some expenditures that are non-discretionary – for example, for educational facilities that are needed and requested by all of the school and have to be maintained on an overall basis rather than on an individual basis, like the library. Once the staff made its decision on what should be allotted, from then on the money entered the domain of discretionary accounts. That was a fantastic step forward, because students got the fiscal responsibility that was similar to their educational responsibility. And this last area of internal inconsistency began to fade from the school.

In Conclusion

In summarizing and concluding this book I would say that the first year of the school saw the development of an institution which had a well defined style that was entirely compatible with a democratically based culture. It was a democratically organized school, with a democratically based ethos in which individual rights and individual opportunity were respected, in which individual responsibility was paramount, and in which all matters affecting the community were decided by democratic process. It was a school with its own unique internal legal system and with its own set of traditions.

I'm sure that there will be many, many schools that are based on the democratic ethos. Each will have its own style. The style of The Sudbury Valley School is going to be determined not only by the ethos but also by the set of traditions and laws that will be unique to it, because they developed uniquely in its environment. And it will have its own aesthetic style, which can be summarized in the words "high quality." What typifies the school is the excellence of all of its products, whether it be catalogues, the wording of resolutions, letters, the way it conducts its meeting – everything is characterized by a high degree of excellence. Shoddiness just isn't part of the school.

This brings me, then, to the end of my account. We are on the threshold of great change in American education and in American society. It's a change that has already begun, and has made it possible for The Sudbury Valley School to come into being. It's a change that will be accelerated as a result of the existence and success of the school.

APPENDIX 1

The first draft outline of a proposal for a school
(November 1965)

A Radical Proposal

----- To fulfill the educational needs of the community;

----- To meet the challenge of increasing leisure time for all people;

----- To arouse intellectual curiosity and, through its continued functioning, to promote creativity in all people;

----- To raise the individual to the highest potential of his unique capabilities, and encourage introspection and meditation;

----- To enhance meaningful communication between people;

----- To revive the integral ties that unite all man's intellectual and es-
thetic efforts, and expose the principles that underlie all human activity

By the creation of a Community Education Complex, based on the
values: freedom, mutual respect, and toleration.

I.   Components of the Complex, and their functions

          A.   The School: A single school, accepting transient
                    members from the ages of about 5 to 25 yrs old (called
                    "students") and permanent members (called "faculty").
                    The guiding principle of the school is that every member
                    be free to pursue his own interests entirely, wherever
                    they may lead. Each member may call freely upon
                    any other member for guidance, advice, or reaction;
                    each transient member will be in addition the special
                    responsibility of one permanent member. Permanent
                    members may present public lectures or disputations
                    as they wish (open to the community at large); all
                    members are free to present private lectures or seminars.
                    Facilities are created to supply stimulating surroundings
                    (equipped laboratories with stockrooms; athletic
                    facilities and play areas; wooded areas with trails; arts
                    facilities and library – see ahead), and opportunities

> for private work (study rooms of various sizes) and group sessions (seminar and lecture rooms). There are no required lectures, no required duties, no grades or age groupings (members seek their own companions), no marks or examinations, no departments, no ranks. "Free inquiry" is the motto, and it is <u>meant</u>. A transient member is ready to leave when he feels able to proceed in his interest entirely on his own. If he has produced an independent project before leaving, he takes with him a Ph.D. degree.

[<u>Objections</u>: (1) "Students won't study." Not true. Human beings are naturally curious, and need only to be allowed to indulge their curiosity. No psychologically unimpaired, mentally competent person is free of burning curiosity. Study may not always be orthodox, but the mind will be working always – the more so, the less it is policed. (2) "Students won't learn anything, even if they do study." Not true. That is learned best which is studied most eagerly. Force-fed knowledge is quickly forgotten, as the general ignorance of our largely high-school graduated adult population proves. The only system based on the principle espoused here, at least within a certain broad framework, has been the classical Jewish one (now almost extinct), where the retention rate was phenomenal. (3) "Students won't learn what they should know." Not true. No one can say what everyone should know. The wisdom to decide the intellectual fare of others has not been bestowed on anyone to date. One thing is sure: every student will learn quickly and avidly what he has to know to pursue his interests, if he is given the opportunity to do so. (4) "Faculty will not work." Not true. It will be hard to keep them from working – on what they want! Faculty always tries to get out of work peripheral to its interests, or wasteful of its time and talents. (5) "Faculty will ignore students." One person's interest in another is proportional to the degree of their mutual interests. Faculty will seek young minds to use as foils and sounding boards, or to cultivate as disciples. The faculty member who drives away students will soon find himself in painful loneliness. Today, faculty members drive away students because students are interested in trivial and irritating things – grades, requirements, etc. (6) "Members will be isolated islands." Not true. Meaningful contact and communication will be at a maximum here, since all contact will be grounded in real mutuality, and not in some form of parasitism or imposition. The spectrum of contacts will be the widest possible, as each member seeks out others who share some of his interests, and the overlapping of interests will insure many-branched personal relationships.]

B.   The Library: A fully stocked modern library, complete with catalogued guides, information retrieval service (this is especially important as an aid to independent research), free photocopying service, microfilm reading and copying facilities, and audio-visual departments. Also, numerous reading rooms of various sizes and uniform comfort. Free flow of books, to the public too.

C.   The Communications Center: (1) A full fledged publishing house with ancillary printing equipment (especially offset), equipped to meet all needs of members for publication of lecture material, texts, trade books, monographs, journal articles, popular expositions, and newspapers; this to be set up on a professional basis, to market and distribute materials properly. To be run by and fully integrated with the school, members playing a key role in all operations. Facilities also to be open to community at large, and to people from elsewhere wanting to use them. (2) A radio and TV station, operating limited hours. Programming is not to be simply another sterile repeat of egg-head themes, but worked out in meaningful units giving full play to interests of members involved in planning. Live debates, investigations in depth of issues, experimental uses of medium also to be encourages. Local issues to be part of programming. (3) An arts center. This is to serve not only the legitimate art for art's sake interest of members, but also to be integrates into life of community and work of non-artistic members. Documentaries, performances, etc. relevant to any member's work to be presented, when possible. The idea that the arts are an integral part of life to be stressed, as well as their unique aspects.

All three parts of communications center to be distinguished sharply from present university presses, student radio stations, and student extracurricular (or curricular) arts groups by their integration into the complex, as well as by their professional mode of operation: members will be directly involved in all aspects of these enterprises, giving them a breadth and relevance they do not presently have.

D.   Living quarters: A combination of dormitories at the site of the complex and living quarters in the community to be sought, with the latter preferred.

II.   Relation to the community

The Education Complex must be an integral part of the community in which it is located; a large part of the purpose of the Complex is to educate the public at large to the values underlying the Complex (and thus to convert the community as a whole into such a complex). To this end, close ties with the community are necessary, and these are formed via:

(1)   The school lectures, given by permanent members, which are open to the public. Thus the public is offered not "special" toned-down "adult education" series, but the real thing. The public thus soon finds out that education in the most exciting sense of the term can be an ongoing process for everyone all his life, and finds this out by always hearing people who are excited about what they are saying.

(2)   The library facilities, also open to the public, with perhaps some small charge for special services. The public is thus drawn into the complex via its excellent information service.

(3)   The communications center, which serves the public directly, through books and periodicals (which deal with their problems and are open to their contributions), through radio and TV programs, through movie, drama, dance, and music performances, in which the public too can <u>take part</u>.

(4)   Special additional efforts, to keep close to the community. The library facilities and the talents of members are to be offered to the local government; seminars with local political, business, and religious leaders are to be arranged at their request, or occasionally upon the initiative of members; free public access to the complex is to be maintained to the highest degree possible.

These efforts are aimed at making the entire community an education complex, instead of setting the complex off apart from the affairs of everyday life.

III.   Recruitment

A.   Transient members are to be accepted from the outset at all ages and levels, and from any geographic location. Special efforts should be made to recruit from the local population, and to include a large component from "underprivileged" homes. The latter component will probably do best in the complex (in the beginning, at any rate), in terms of improvement over present situation: whereas now that component is essentially not functioning in school, there is every reason to believe that a genuine attempt to cater to its real interests will open up its full potential in the complex. Under ideal circumstances, there would be no charge to transient members; it may however be essential to collect fees where possible.

B.   Permanent members are to be recruited from anywhere they can be found, at least in the beginning, when the idea of the complex is new and untested. The only criteria should be (1) a proven ability to pursue independent research [with permanent members there is not the luxury, in the beginning, to develop this ability as one goes along]; (2) an understanding of, and sympathy with, the ideals and methods of the complex. Later, both criteria can be relaxed, as the idea of the complex spreads and as the need for modifying the idea grows. Ultimately, recruitment will become local as complex become a regular part of every community. The first complex should attempt to span diverse interests and experience with widely different age groups, so that problems of breadth and inter-member relationships not occupy the center of the stage in the initial phases of the project. Later, with vigor established, the complex should be able to function with almost any spectrum of permanent members. It should be stressed that excellent people to staff the first complex are available in ample numbers. They must be given adequate salaries and housing in addition to tenure.

IV.   Budget

The only way to launch this complex is through a major grant, to be followed after a few years by an endowment campaign and annual fund drive. This should be a private institution, insofar as government has no obvious role in it. Initial funds must be sufficient to get the project on a firm basis. The optimum number of members needs much study, and is also related to the size of the community in which it is established. The location should be somewhere fairly near a large urban center, since the validity of the idea must be tested in the harsh realities of modern urban living, and not in some remote, unrealistic utopian agricultural setting.

November 24-29, 1965   Daniel A. Greenberg
Framingham, Mass.

APPENDIX 2

Blueprint for a new school, as set forth in a draft manuscript entitled "Education in Transition". This description constituted Part III of the manuscript, Chapters 12-22. Part III was called: "A Transition-Period School (A Practical, Prototype Model that Can Be Tested Today)"; the title reflected a line of thought which I no longer consider valid, presented in detail in Part I and II of the manuscript. Many aspects of the school described here likewise stem from a theoretical framework which I have since abandoned or modified.

Part III

A Transition-Period School

(A Practical, Prototype Model that Can Be Tested Today)

Chapter 12

A Bird's-Eye View of the School

1. The detailed blueprint to be presented in the following chapters is for a prototype school located in a suburban, or middle-size town, community. A number of reasons governed this choice of location: (1) This type of community is becoming increasingly important, demographically, on the American scene. (2) It usually presents a good cross-sectional population of all classes, religions, and races. (Even so-called high-class suburban towns often have "underprivileged" sections within town limits.) One therefore avoids the danger of dealing with, and catering to the special tastes of, one limited social group. (3) It still has land available at reasonable prices for developing educational campuses. (4) It is free of the mass of intricate social problems presented by urban centers – problems which would immediately intrude on the school, as they do on every institution, and which would consequently hamper the identification of problems in the prototype that arise from flaws in the school itself. (5) It is not as remote from the realities of American life as is the deep-country setting of so many experimental schools – a setting so idyllic, so isolated, and so distant from the pulse of life that the schools established there are often not designed or appropriate for mass application to the country's public school systems.

The suburban-type community thus presents a blend of realism and isolation especially suitable for testing a prototype model school system. The model is designed to be immediately applied to practice as a public school system in such a community.

2. The School population consists of three major segments: (1) A permanent segment, which has the option and intention of remaining permanently associated with the school. The people making up this segment are referred to as "the permanent members of the school." (2) A long-term segment, which has the option and intention of being associated with the school on a regular, day to day basis for a number of years. The people making up this segment are referred to as "the long-term members of the school." (3) A transient segment, which is associated with the school on a non-permanent and irregular basis. The people making up this segment are referred to as "the public."

These three segments of the school population have rough correlations to the various segments making up the population of present-day schools. The permanent members of the school include what we now call the faculty, administration, and staff of a school. The long-term members include what we now call the student body. The transient population includes what we now call guests and visitors. However, as will become increasingly evident, the new nomenclature involves more than a re-naming of present divisions: it involves a re-evaluation of the functions of various people in the school, and the relationship between the segments of the school population, a re-evaluation necessitated by the school's anticipated role in the transition period.

To give a few examples of what the re-evaluation involves: few distinctions are drawn among permanent members and the school. There are no departments, no special age levels ("elementary school teacher," "college teacher," etc.), no rank, no tenure vs. non-tenure posts, no academic vs. non-academic posts, no special privileges and rights, no special duties. There are, however, distinctions of salary. Similarly, few distinctions are drawn among long-term members of the school. There are no "majors" in the formal sense, no age segregation ("elementary school student," "college student," etc.), no age limitations, no special privileges and rights. There are, however, distinctions between those who must attend school and those who need not. Similarly, few distinctions are drawn among members of the public found in the school. There are no distinguished vs. undistinguished guests, people with vs. people without certain privileges, etc. There are, however, certain limitations on over-all public participation in the school.

The very structure of the school population reflects, then, the freedom of inquiry and freedom of association characteristic of the school, as well as the school's characteristic openness to the community at large.

3. The school population is at any given time engaged in a wide variety of activities, inherently independent of each other.

The core activity is independent individual research, where "research" has its original meaning of "inquiry". The school is society's special haven for inquiry, and exists as we have seen only because society has not quite yet managed to make it possible for inquiry to be omnipresent. Everyone, young and old, permanent or non-permanent, finds himself at the school for the basic purpose of being free to inquire to his heart's content.

As many aids to inquiry as possible are provided in the school. These aids range from facilities for joint inquiry, where several people wish to work together, through libraries, public study rooms, laboratories, private study rooms, arts and crafts centers, to outdoor athletic, hiking, and field-study areas. These aids include as many available stimuli as possible, to cover the broadest possible range of intellectual and spiritual alternatives that can be provided.

In addition, <u>outlets</u> for inquiry are also provided to the greatest extent possible. Opportunities for action, for the realistic testing of hypotheses and theories, for practical innovation, all are plentiful. Work-shops, facilities for group work, theatres, communications facilities, publications, and other such abound. For those who would like to tell others what they have found, the possibility of offering lectures, lecture series or courses is provided. For those who would like to work over their ideas with others, the possibility of organizing seminars is provided.

An outsider looking at the school will see some people studying alone, some at lectures or seminars, some working alone or in groups, some playing, some simply "wasting time" in free thought or free relaxation. An efficient central information system will enable him to see at a glance what activities are going on at what place. The central feature of what he will see is that everyone will be doing what he wants to do, and will therefore be committed to what he is doing.

4. The campus extends over several (of the order of ten) acres, and is arranged to be entirely safe for free pedestrian traffic. It contains much open space, as well as the necessary buildings. Access to campus and buildings is free, to members and to the public at large.

Among the notable special features of the campus are a data-storage and data-retrieval center, conjoint with the library, which includes facilities for cheap photographic reproduction of originals; plentiful and varied rooms for private and small-group study, well-sheltered for sound-proofing; extensive workshops and commercial facilities (many of the type that would now be associated with "vocational" or "business" schools); an arts and communications center; and biological facilities appropriate for field study of animals and plants.

Although many of these features sound prohibitively expensive to people accustomed to thinking in terms of facilities and materials being <u>provided</u> by the community and the staff <u>for</u> students, it will be seen that in the context of the prototype school these features will be available at reasonable expense due to the involved participation of the users in all aspects of acquisition, preparation, and continued maintenance.

5. The school spans the entire educational range, from nursery school through postgraduate studies (and including continuing adult study). In line with the school's protective role for children, attendance is compulsory for all children below some cutoff age (in most communities this age is 16); above that age, attendance is entirely voluntary.

A person leaves the school when he is capable of fending for himself in the world at large. (He is free to return for further study and development at any later time.) Since he has been free to pursue his interests from earliest childhood, he will by the age of adolescence be quite capable of following through any task he may choose; and he will also have gained a certain dexterity and expertise in his central field of interest, not to mention a considerable quantity of peripheral information obtained through long contact with other people deeply committed to their various interests. Eventually, when the prototype school has ceased to be unique, there will be no formal problem in transferring from school to society at large: such transfer will be made according to merit and ability. In the beginning, however, ways will be provided for giving certificates of achievement ("degrees") to those leaving the school, so that these people may be <u>formally</u> compared to people leaving the standard school system of today.

From the beginning, the school will be accredited by formal state authorities to operate on all levels, from elementary through postgraduate. Such accreditation will be based primarily on the excellence and professional acceptability of the permanent members (the "faculty"), and also on the school's adherence to formal state regulations (e.g., as regards attendance, sanitation, etc.).

6. It should be noted that no professional schools are contemplated for the prototype school. In fact, it would be very useful to have prototype professional schools built on the same principles and stressing apprenticeship under close observation and guidance. However, it would seem that there are sufficient questions to be answered about the functioning of a general school without introducing at an early stage the complex problem of professional schools and their accreditation and relation to the profession at large. In addition, there would seem to be no need to maintain professional schools at each general school complex, so that the whole problem is more limited and particularistic in scope.

The above-outlined bird's-eye view is just that – a broad outline with no detail. I shall now proceed to detail each feature, so that the over-view may be converted into a functional blueprint.

CHAPTER 13

The Long-Term Members of the School

1. The long-term members of the school are those who are part of the school population for several years, but not part of the permanent population. Those whose age lies between nursery-school age and the cutoff age attend the school of necessity, because society requires them to attend. Those who are older than the cutoff age attend of their own free will, and are free to remain until they are ready to assume a position in the community at large. There is no upper age limit to long-term members. A person of any age may decide to attend school in order to re-orient or re-train himself, and such a person is welcome to attend and to stay until he feels ready to assume the new role he has projected for himself.

There should be no fear a priori that people will either try to drop out of school "too early" or try to remain in school "too long" ("the perennial student"). Drop-outs are people who want to enter the real world and who feel that school is in no way useful to them as preparation for the roles they want to assume in the real world. In a school where a person's interest is the guide to his pursuits, there is no impetus to premature dropping-out; a person stays until he is ready to leave and do what he wants in the real world, and such a person need not flee from a restrictive school atmosphere, since such an atmosphere does not exist. On the other hand, perennial students are almost always people who have been so crushed by long exposure to school repression that they are incapable to self-motivated action. They have no self-confidence, and are afraid to probe on their own. Such people, therefore, seek to stay within the school as long as possible, in order to continue to be guided by others rather than fend for themselves. Again, this phenomenon will not occur in the prototype school, since there will be no exposure to repression, no breaking of individual will and interest. Healthy people allowed to grow according to their own internal mechanisms, at their own pace, will neither run away nor seek protection. They will use the school as a haven for inquiry until they have found what they want, and then they will eagerly depart for the arena of real life where they can act out and pursue what they have found in school, on the broader and freer stage of real life. To people who have inquired freely and successfully, school becomes confining relative to the world at large, as it must; to people not yet sure of themselves, not yet through with their line of inquiry, school remains a useful place to be.

Anyone from the public at large is welcome in the school as a long-term member. This includes people from all walks of life. The school serves everyone's needs and interests equally, and accords them equal footing. It would be, for example, a grievous error to limit the school to so-called "bright children," and exclude the "underprivileged," on the often-heard grounds that the former <u>are</u> equipped to do "a great deal" on their own, while the latter are not, and therefore require more intensive guidance and care. The whole point of the discussion in Part I and II is that the principles upon which the school is founded are universal human principles that know no distinctions of class or so-called intelligence. To the extent that these principles are correctly formulated, the school must be open to all people equally, and must serve the interests of anyone. Similarly, and for the same reason, the school does not recognize distinctions between "academic" and "non-academic" (e.g. "vocational") interests, and does not adhere to a hierarchy of values as regards study (the "best" being college-oriented study, followed by business-oriented, etc.). All interests of the human mind – and that means all interests of the particular human minds possessed by the members of the school – are a priori equally valid, equally worthy of pursuit by the interested parties; they all have equal ethical status and hence equal intrinsic worth. The school, then, is for anyone and everyone, and is wide enough to serve all comers equally.

2. The school is a prototype of a local school system, and is therefore itself a locally based school. This means that the long-term members are for the most part residents of the locality surrounding the school, and live at home. (Transportation to and from school is provided, as it now is, by means of school buses or a similar arrangement.) The school is not an esoteric boarding school; there is no intention of replac-

ing the home, only of supplementing it. Indeed, it would be inconsistent to design a prototype boarding school, in light of the continuing stability of the home institution in the third phase and the eventual disappearance of the formal school.

There are, then, no dormitories or special facilities for overnight accommodations. To the extent that out-of-towners come to attend the school, these are to be placed in private homes as roomers. This will provide some home atmosphere even for out-of-towners, and avoid the creation of cliques so common on mixed residential and dormitory campuses. But there should be very little inter-city mobility for members below the cutoff age.

For older members, who might want to leave their parents' home and strike out for themselves, or who have families of their own, the same facilities are available as for anyone else in the community: rooms, apartments, and houses. A person ready and willing to assume responsibility for his own personal life should do just that. Dormitory life in this case is totally incongruous: it is a mix of dependence and independence that provides neither. Any college campus today demonstrates this amply. On the one hand, because certain of the students' needs are catered to in the dormitory as they were at home, dormitory students rarely "take care of themselves" at all; hence the squalor, chaos, and irresponsible raucousness of dorm life. On the other hand, despite being away from home, dorm students are not allowed real independence; hence the constant stream of complaint about curfews, social restrictions, etc. Students living away from home in their own apartments (or in apartments jointly with other students) do far better on both counts, as expected.

The long-term members are thus predominantly local residents, in their own or their families' domiciles, with a smattering of out-of-town children living with local families. With this as a basic pattern, the school is structured to serve the functions of a local school system.

3. The spread of ages among the school population will mirror that among the local population, at least until the cutoff age. In smaller communities, the two will be identical, since the school will contain the total local population up to the cutoff age. The more common case

in communities of the type we are discussing is that in which several schools serve the community, and each school has a share of the total population. Roughly speaking, one expects that there will be the same number from each age group up to cutoff age, and then a decrease in each subsequent age grouping until about the age of 25, after which the distribution will be random and small.

As regards absolute numbers, there are simply no guidelines. Until a prototype school is built, one simply has no idea how big a school is optimal, or even whether such a statement is meaningful. Indeed, if it is recalled that in a sense the whole of society in the third phase will be one large "school" of the type being described here, it might even be the case that there is no limit to the size of such a school. Perhaps the largest size compatible with the space available and with the local population size is the best. Much experimentation will have to be done as regards this question.

At any rate, there is certainly a minimum size, though precisely what the minimum size is cannot be foretold. Too small a school – one that is below the "critical mass" for vigorous interaction – will not offer a sufficiently wide range of stimuli or a sufficiently extensive set of colleagues with whom to interact. This is the plight of many experimental schools: they are often too small to provide the atmosphere of ferment and activity necessary for vigor. Based on calculations to be elaborated upon in the next chapter, I would guess that a minimum size is of the order of three thousand long-term members. Assuming that the cutoff age is sixteen, and the starting age is four, this might be distributed as follows: two hundred of each year from four to sixteen (total 2400); one hundred of each year group from sixteen to twenty (total 400); fifty of each year group from twenty to twenty-five (total 250); and perhaps one hundred from all age groups over twenty-five. (These figures total 3150.) It cannot be sufficiently stressed that these are crude approximations, and are presented only for purposes of establishing an order-of-magnitude picture of the smallest feasible school. In any real case there will be wide fluctuations relative to these figures, even where over-all totals are much the same as these. Larger schools are certainly possible, and a prototype starting from the minimum size might gradually expand in order to study the relationship between size and effectiveness.

4. Perhaps the worst misimpression generated by the figures just mentioned is that the school will somehow have formal age-group divisions within it – "classes", "grades", or "divisions". Actually, this will not be the case at all. The long-term members are subject to no associative restrictions. They are free to associate at will. They may stay alone, they may form peer groups to whatever ends they wish (to study, play, or work together), or they may form mixed age groups. Nor is there any stability requires of any group that does form: groups may be short-lived or long-lived, depending only on the will of the members.

The essential features here are mobility, flexibility, and cross-fertilization. Freedom to move among people of different ages is as important to development and growth as is the freedom to move among different areas of thought or different types of activities. In this respect, the school faithfully reproduces an important feature of real life. Children learn by observing their age peers and adults, but more often by observing older children – i.e., people they recognize to be dependent, as they are, but also more experienced than they themselves are. And adults clarify their thoughts and refresh their minds through contact with children – through teaching, through conversation, and often through play.

Furthermore, the flexibility to form and dissolve groups is important in school, as it is in real life. There is no reason to believe that one fixed group will satisfy several purposes – and indeed it usually does not. Different social circles serve different needs, and a person joins now one, now another, now several, as his needs correspond to those of the group.

We can expect to find a wide variety of constellations in the school: groups of the same age, groups of mixed ages, small children tagging after adults (or sitting in on lectures aimed at advanced students), teenagers organizing toddlers' activities, advanced mathematicians teaching small children arithmetic, children of all ages organizing athletic leagues, and so forth. No barriers are places on this heterogeneous group-formation, nor are obstacles placed in the way of those who are loners and wish to be left to their own devices.

One of the features of this free mixing of age groups is a vast increase in teaching activity. The urge to teach, to show others what one has himself learned, to communicate to the world one's discoveries, does not begin to manifest itself in a person when he received a formal teaching diploma. It begins to appear in the infant who has made his first discovery, and never ceases to show itself thereafter. Children and youngsters have this urge at least as much as adults. (Proof, if any is needed, can be found in any children's activity where the participants are allowed to act on this urge. Such activities have no trouble locating leaders, organizers, teachers, etc. from among the children themselves.) In the prototype school, the freedom to mix with all age groups will allow a tremendous outflow of this urge at all age levels. One sees peer groups organizing their own seminars and study groups, writing and performing their own plays, doing their own research; one sees older children offering to show younger children their new-found knowledge, young men doing the same for adolescents, and so on all along the line. The dichotomy between teacher and student disappears. Everyone who has something to show or to say is a teacher, everyone who has something to learn is a student; hence, everyone in the school is both teacher and student, and there is no one incapable of learning from someone else or of teaching someone else. Educational activity in school, as in real life, takes place across the board, at all times and in all circumstances.

5. Since the school does not seek to replace the home, but works instead within the context of home living, every effort must be made – and sustained – to familiarize the families of long-term members with the philosophy and the working of the school. To be sure, insofar as the families are part of the local community, relations between school and community (to be discussed in following chapters) will also encompass relations between school and family. But the latter require additional effort, especially in the prototype school, where so many forms and ideas will be novel.

The home, after all, is and will remain the most influential institution as regards the character-formation of growing children. The school can therefore gain nothing and lose much through the hostility or even indifference of the home. Parents and relatives should be encourages to visit the school, to spend time in it, to see it in its total context, hopefully to do something (by way of study or activity) in it. Since the school is open to the public always, the presence of parents will not appear exceptional, nor will it call forth any of those special activities and tensions so characteristic of staged "parents' days" today. Nor need there be any fear of parental interference, since parents will be bound by the same rules as everyone else, members and public alike (see Chapter 16).

The important point here is that the school views itself as the ally of the home, with the home by far the more influential of the two. As an ally, the school operates openly and honestly, hoping thereby to call forth the kind of willing cooperation from the home that is so necessary to a child's stable character-formation, and indeed to a stable transition from the second to the third phase of a man's history.

CHAPTER 14

The Permanent Members of the School, and the Public

1. The permanent members of the school are those considered necessary to the continued and continuous functioning of the school – those on whom the school depends for its satisfactory functioning. They are permanent in the sense that they are brought into the school community with the initial expectation that they will stay. Thereafter, they may either leave of their own free will (to go elsewhere), or be asked to leave in accordance with regulations that contain a "due process of law" governing removal from permanent membership. In this, then, the school joins the ranks of all progressive organizations, all of which

remove people from their ranks by due process rather than arbitrary whim, and all of which have <u>some</u> process for removal. It should be noted that the school does away with the archaic notion of "tenure," still applied in many colleges and universities (though almost never in nursery, elementary, or high schools), which guarantees teachers their positions regardless of performance, except in cases of malfeasance so gross as almost never to occur (compare impeachment of federal judges, another similarly archaic system). The notion of academic tenure, designed (as was judges' tenure) to counteract the evils of arbitrary removal and the related evils of political manipulation of the educational system, has come to have the appearance of a "divine right of professors to their jobs" in an era where intellectual freedom is widely recognized. At any rate, there can be little argument about the inherent justice of the principle of removal; the argument devolves upon the grounds for removal and the judges who determine when these grounds are met. We shall discuss both questions in Chapter 19.

Permanent members, then, have the <u>expectation</u> of permanence, though no tenure. These members are paid salaries, as service to the school is their life profession. In return for adequate salaries, the members are not expected to receive compensation from other sources for regular services rendered, that would preoccupy them on a regular basis. (Compensation in the form of royalties, fees for occasional consulting, or occasional lectures, is excepted from this.) Permanent members perform all the functions required by the school for its existence: they provide an atmosphere of intellectual stimulation, they assure the administrative functioning of the school, they are <u>responsible</u> for the school and for its activities. The permanent members do, functionally, what senior and junior faculty, administration, clerical and other staffs do in present-day schools, except that the actual way these functions are fulfilled in the prototype school differs entirely from the way they are fulfilled in present-day schools (as will become evident in the course of the following discussion).

Put in a nutshell, the permanent members are those full-time members of the school community who are present of their own free will, who stay on from year to year, who receive salaries, and who bear the immediate responsibility for the school's functioning. By extreme contrast, the public segment of the school population consists of people from the public at large who have occasional and sporadic contact with the school, usually for some specific purpose, and who receive no compensation (except for an occasional honorarium), nor represent a special financial burden on the school.

The public is just that – public. It is for people from all walks of life, from all over the community, who have a reason to come to the school. These people may want to use the library, or others of the school's facilities; they may want to hear a lecture or a course; they may want, singly or in groups, to form study seminars, or work groups, or theatre groups, etc.; they may want to teach. Whatever their desire, <u>they are welcome</u>. Not grudgingly admitted, but <u>welcome</u>. That is the key to the entire enterprise. That is the way the school becomes an integral and interesting part of the community, and prepares the community for eventual merging of the school's activities with those of the community as a whole.

The public has as much to teach as anyone, and wants to learn as much as anyone. The school should be the natural place for the public to turn, for both activities. This means <u>all</u> the public – professionals, religious leaders, politicians, businessmen, workers, everyone. There is here no separation into religious schools, professional forums, political meetings, extension courses, adult education, public lectures, athletic clubs, public libraries, entertainment, concerts, etc., just as there was no separation into vocational vs. academic schools. In the prototype school, as in all transition schools, all these activities are merged into the activities of the school as a whole; all these activities are part and parcel of the school, open to the community as to the members. That is precisely the function the school is created to fulfill, and by being open to everyone the school enters as much as it possibly can into the real life of the community.

Budgetary considerations should not be an obstacle here, as we will see in Chapter 19. After all, the basic support for the school and its activities comes from the community, and to the extent that the community participates in the school and uses school facilities, the community will support these facilities on a level adequate to its needs. The more the public identifies with the school as truly its own, the less the tension between school and community, between the closed world of children and educators versus the "outsider" world of the public at large, that characterizes so much of present-day relations between the schools and the public. With the prototype school, the public school becomes truly the school belonging to the public at large, and as such worthy of public support.

2. The permanent members are not divided into departments, divisions, faculties, or any other such categories (not even academic vs. non-academic categories). They are chosen because they are expected to contribute to the functioning of the school, and because they are willing and eager to do so. The basic criterion of choice is a person's commitment to the school (i.e., as his source of income). Other criteria of choice, such as the ability to translate commitment into effective action, and the way in which the choice is made, are discussed in Chapter 19.

A person is thus not bound by any formal barriers to a particular set of activities, or a particular area of interest. Freedom to pursue one's own genuine interests is therefore characteristic not only of those passing through the school, but of the entire school community. The permanent members provide a continuing model of interest, involvement, and self-fulfillment for the school as a whole, and provision of this model is indeed the permanent members' most important function.

Absence of all barriers to the pursuit of knowledge and to self-fulfillment places, however, a special burden on the initial organizers of the school (as well as on those charged with its maintenance over the years). The stable realization of each person's full potential depends not only on the freedom to probe, but on the availability of a wide range of alternatives among which to probe. The effectiveness of the school therefore depends to a large extent on the breadth of interests permanently represented in the school — that is, on the breadth of interests of the permanent members. To be sure, not everything has to be represented; this is, practically speaking, entirely impossible, and not really necessary, given the existence of books and articles (and, eventually, of other schools where other specialties <u>will</u> be represented, and to which the interested student can turn). But a conscious effort should be maintained to ensure a broad representation of subjects, and hence a variegated atmosphere.

These considerations apply to the selection of permanent members, but some of the edge can be taken off by recalling that the public is represented in the school, and that the public perforce brings with it a breadth of interests of considerable extent. Even if there were no permanent members at all (as is the case in the third stage, when schools are no more), the public would provide a broad range of talent, of interests, and of activities for any interested parties to choose from. Opening the school to the public thus serves the additional purpose of vastly increasing the range of alternatives offered at the school, without increasing the number of permanent members.

3. How many permanent members are necessary? Before actually trying out a prototype school, any answer is pure guesswork. We do not know whether there is an optimum (or maximum) size to the school. Nor do we know the effect of opening the school to the public – a step which increases the range of teaching and the number of learners, both to an unknown extent. Nor do we know the effect of cross-fertilization between different age groups, and the way this cross-fertilization will relate to the work of the permanent members. There is, therefore, no available reasonable "rule of thumb" for the ratio of permanent to long-term members (comparable, for example, to rules of thumb for teacher to student ratios in present-day schools).

We can guess that there is a minimum number, a "critical mass", for the number of permanent members required to sustain a vigorous intellectual atmosphere. It is well-known that too small a group, even if launched with great enthusiasm, eventually languishes. The reason is the same as that requiring a broad front. Too few people simply cannot generate a broad enough spectrum of interests and ideas. But what "too few" means, in absolute numbers, is anyone's guess. No one knows, and no one is likely to know until different numbers have been tried.

The prototype school has to have sufficient permanent members to fulfill the following requirements: (1) there must be at least as many as the critical minimum number for self-sustaining vigorous activity; (2) there must be a broad enough range of interests to provide a sufficient variety of alternatives, as steady fare (i.e., in additional to the interests represented by the transient public); (3) all the functions needed to sustain the school must be taken care of (so that sufficient staff-type help must be available); (4) there must be people at ease with all age groups. All four requirements are vague, as I have already stressed, and there is no way presently known to make them sharp. Note, by the way, that (1) and (2) are quite different in nature. "Self-sustained vigorous activity" in <u>one</u> area may be achievable with a certain number of permanent members (compare research institutes, such as Plato's Academy, or the Rabbinical school at Yavneh, or Bohr's Institute at Copenhagen), but we need <u>many</u> areas in the school. On the other hand, to get vigorous activity in three areas, for example, does not require three times the number necessary for one area, due to overlap and indirect stimulation and cross-fertilization.

I would guess that the prototype school should have about three hundred permanent members to fulfill the listed requirements. Very roughly, this would consist of some 100 accustomed to a university environment, another 100 accustomed to pre-college ages, and another 100 in staff-type work. The crudity of these figures needs no stressing, especially in light of the total absence of age-group divisions in the school. There is every expectation that all permanent members will find themselves working with people in all age groups. It is also necessary to remember that younger children will receive much of their stimulation from older children, and that the entire long-term membership forms within itself a hierarchy of stimulation whose intensity and variety, both clearly considerable, is of unknown extent.

Add to this the purely guessed estimate that a ratio of one permanent to ten long-term members is reasonable, and we arrive at the figure of roughly 3000 long-term members, used in the preceding chapter. Enough has been said to indicate how little there is to guide us in suggesting a proper ratio. The one-to-ten ratio has nothing to recommend it beyond an overall plausible ring to ears accustomed to thinking about schools. It is entirely possible, even probable, that the ratio is quite an over-estimate, and that considerably more long-term members can be accommodated per permanent member due to cross-fertilization and the contribution of the public. If this proves to be the case, the prototype school can gradually be expanded in long-term membership until the proper ratio is found.

4. The permanent members will all live in the locality of the school, and will, together with the public and the long-term members, form the local community which the school serves. It is to be expected that some of the permanent members will be "local products", i.e., former long-term members in the school (or in a nearby school), and that others will be "imports" from other communities. At any rate, the local character of the school is enhanced by the local residence of virtually all members of the school community, as is the case today with most schools.

On the other hand, parochialism and provincialism can best be guarded against by embarking on a regular program of exchange whereby permanent members are allowed regular stays in other communities, and people are brought from other communities to serve as guest members in the school for a year or two. When a sizeable network of such schools will exist, such exchange can be quite widespread, and can take place at little added cost to any particular school. Initially, however, the prototype school will have to subsidize much exchange on its own. Exchange is valuable for all permanent members, regardless of their interests or functions, merely by virtue of these people's permanence, and of the consequent necessity to move them around (or, better, to allow them to move around) a bit to avoid their becoming stale and stagnant.

Relations between the permanent members and the rest of the local community should be warm and natural; in the case of the prototype school, permanent members must make special efforts to communicate with the community and to explain the goals and the workings of the school. In this matter, however, public participation in the school will make the task of promoting good relations between school and community much easier. Because the public is at home in the school – is, indeed, part of the school – there is no need to explain to those "outside" what is going on "inside." Nor will the public feel frustrated at being unable to influence what is going on in their schools. The fact that public and permanent members meet freely and openly as equals <u>in</u> the school makes it likely that they will enjoy meeting freely and openly outside the school, in the homes and elsewhere, and that they will more readily speak the same language and appreciate each other's problems and viewpoints.

CHAPTER 15

Activities Going On In the School

1. In opening, it should be remarked that the traditional separation between academic and non-academic, curricular and extra-curricular activities has no place in the school. There is no approved curriculum (for that matter, no curriculum at all), no single or multi-track system, no a prior reason to prefer any activity over any other for any particular person in the school. Indeed, the only a priori assumption is that any activity undertaken by a person of his own free will is appropriate for him in his quest for self-fulfillment; with this as a priori assumption, the burden is always on those who would curtail or forbid an activity to demonstrate that they have a case for repression.

These remarks are especially directed towards activities which are usually considered a "waste of time", and which are indeed often not even considered to be activities. For example, sheer loafing, relaxing, dreaming, resting; or puttering about with no apparent aim (e.g., in the garden). That such a "waste of time" is universally attested by all creative people to be essential to creativity should be enough to render it respectable once and for all. At any rate, the discussion in Parts I and II makes it amply clear that each member of the school must be accorded the right and privilege of choosing his own way of spending his own time.

2. A large portion of the activity in school is (non-laboratory) research, conducted either by individuals or by groups. A person interested in pursuing a line of inquiry will do just that, until he has reached a satisfactory conclusion.

What are the means available to the individual for research? First, there is the school's information center, comprising a well-catalogued library and whatever other data-storage and data-retrieval system the school has managed to set up, or to associate itself with on a regional scale. The information center provides the researcher with access to other work that has been done in and around his field of interest. Subsidiary equipment, such as a photocopy machine, makes it possible for him to have at hand for constant reference those items which cannot be physically removed from the center.

Second, there is the surrounding proper to research and meditation. Quiet, pleasant areas are available to him where he can work when and how he pleases, without interruption or intrusion. Here too he has the necessary auxiliary aids, such as typewriter facilities, to enable him to proceed.

Third, there are other members of the school who are or have been at one time interested in his field. These people are available for questioning, for leisurely conversation, for critique, and, in cases where they too are engaged in similar research, for possible collaboration (or seminars). In other words, supplementing the written source of information, which is relatively inflexible, and supplementing internal resources, which are relatively limited (indeed, their broadening is the chief impetus to the research), there are also oral sources of information and exchange, having all the flexibility and broadening effect characteristic of philosophical interchange.

Fourth, there is the possibility of hearing a lecture, or a course, in the field of interest. This may happen, if someone else in the school is by chance interested in teaching the subject in question. In such a case, to the benefits of oral interchange are added the benefits of recent contemplation and fresh re-organization of the key ideas in the field. Though this possibility may seem remote, in light of its chance character, it is not quite as unusual as it seemingly ought to be, primarily because often the person setting out on a research project has been stimulated to enter his line of inquiry as a result of the stimulation given by a lecture or course.

Fifth, there is the possibility of actual technical assistance in carrying out the research – for example, assistance in searching the literature, assistance in processing data, assistance in typing, etc. Such assistance often comes from less experienced members (usually younger ones) who volunteer their services in exchange for the benefits of close contact with the person doing the research (benefits such as close observation of research techniques, or of methodology). The older the member doing the research, the more likely he is to obtain such volunteer help, and permanent members are most likely of all.

Sixth, there is the general stimulation provided by colleagues in the school community who, though not specifically interested in this particular area, are by virtue of their natural curiosity and openness ready to discuss the researcher's work with him. This is the kind of stimulation most often found today in academic communities, especially in universities. The lack of pressure on all levels of the prototype school will make this type of exchange characteristic of the whole school.

There is thus no lack of support, assistance, and stimulation available to the person engaging in any line of non-laboratory research. If his interest lags, this will be more out of self-discovery (of the fact that he is not, after all, really interested in the subject) than out of external discouragement – and certainly not out of external repression.

3. There is also laboratory research, and its close kin, field research. Laboratory facilities are available in the basic sciences, equipped (at least to begin with) with the material necessary to maintain ongoing experiments.

There are a number of ways a person can become engaged in laboratory research. If he is experienced, he simply proceeds, guided by experience into the channels proper for commencing a new project. If inexperienced, he can gain experience either by trial and error, with the aid of literature, personal insight, and conversation; or, as is more often the case, by apprenticeship to someone experienced, thereby providing the experienced researcher with technical assistance. Indeed, the only source of assistance available to a researcher is the volunteered help offered by some member of the school: either by an equally experienced member, in which case there is collaboration, or by a less experienced member, in which case there is apprenticeship. (Responsibility for supervising basic safety regulations in the laboratory is shared equally by all permanent members using the laboratory, and also by long-term or public members deemed able to lend a hand.) The problem of how budgetary matters are to be administered is taken up in Chapter 19.

In addition to laboratories, facilities are available for field research. The specific nature of these facilities depends on the members of the school. Small zoological gardens, botanical gardens, geological preserves, aquaria, meteorological stations, experimental farm plots, etc. are all possibilities. Whatever the facilities actually available, they are available to the members (permanent, long-term, and public) just as laboratory facilities are.

Research facilities in the social sciences are also available, though it is not likely that every school can have the necessary computers. At any rate, all the auxiliary facilities are available, with some central computer serving a particular region.

No line is drawn between types of research – "basic" versus "applied" research, for example. Any line of research is a priori acceptable, and the question of utility is not at issue. A person interested in developing a new soap is no less welcome than one studying molecular genetics. As will be seen, the administration of the school will make it unnecessary to draw up theoretical priorities of this sort.

4. Closely allied to laboratory and field research is the work in applied crafts that is going on in the school. Depending, again, on the specific interests of school members, a wide variety of facilities are available for the study and practice of skills. Among the many possibilities are machine shops, automobile repair shops, a food processing plant, a dairy, a garment shop, a computer laboratory, an electronics shop, etc. Although the prototype school has only a few of these, as the number of schools increases the variety available somewhere in the school system

will increase, and eventually cover all known skills. Applied arts, such as design, jewelry work, metal work, etc. are also welcome.

One of the most important features of these activities is that they take place in cooperation with, rather than in competition with, the activities of the community at large. The openness of the school to the public, and the degree to which the public participates in all aspects of the school, makes it natural and necessary that no areas of hostile competition exist between school and public. Toward this end, arrangements are worked out between the school and its potential competition in the community, ensuring in advance that no friction takes place. The exact nature of these arrangements depends critically on the specific issues and parties. The basic principles governing the arrangements are: (1) that the school is intended to benefit the community, and not vice versa; (2) that the various facilities in the school should not exert an undue financial strain on the school – beyond, say, the strain of any other comparable segment. Each specific instance will find its own application of these principles.

Two facilities that are essential to the existence of the school must always be provided. The first is a restaurant facility, which may have to be provided on an outside concession basis, but could profitably be organized as an integral part of the school. There are so many interesting aspects to such a facility – business, accounting, advertising, management, service, cooking – that it could provide a broad spectrum of challenging situations to interested members, either on a permanent or temporary basis.

The second crucial facility is a publishing house, of which only one part, the actual printing establishment, could be let by concession, though that, with its typesetting, photoengraving, offset, printing, cutting, binding, etc., would also be a particularly variegated and exciting activity for the campus proper. The rest of the publishing procedure, however, must be in the hands of members, as it provides the entire school with its most important link to the outside world. The basic principle governing this activity is that members have an a priori right to publish, i.e., to make public, whatever they wish to publish under their names. Towards this end, members are intimately involved with the publishing procedure governing their own work, each member having on his own shoulders the prime responsibility for seeing his work through publication. Author and publisher thus become one, rather than being separate and often hostile entities. That this is essential to the maintenance of a free flow of information between the school and the world can readily be seen. That this is economically feasible – i.e., that it can in fact be done without presenting the school with a financial strain – is my firm conviction, though the specific ways it will be achieved will differ considerably from present publishing practice. The prototype school will have to devote special attention to finding (by testing various alternatives) a way to make the publishing facility a practical reality.

5. Intimately connected with individually-based research and action-type activities outlined so far are teaching activities of various sorts. These virtually all flow from the natural impulse to communicate to others one's own insights – the impulse basic to teaching. (Recall that just as there is no curriculum, so there is no specified course load for a special group called "teachers.")

Any member of the school community – permanent, long-term, or public – is free to teach anything he wishes. He can offer one lecture, a series of lectures, a course, a discussion seminar, or anything else he pleases; and the subject he teaches is <u>entirely</u> up to him, with no reservations. Practically speaking, a person wishing to teach announces (at a place set aside for such announcements) what he is up to, and then proceeds to teach whatever audience chooses to show up. Should no one appear to hear what he was to say, he can try again as often as he wishes to attract an audience.

The tremendous amount of teaching going on at any one time can only be appreciated if we stop to consider what the preceding paragraphs really imply. There is no teaching caste in the school. (Note, in particular, that the permanent members are not "the teachers.") Anyone who has anything to say may say it at will. Young and old, people attending the school and the public at large, all are accorded this right, and all are <u>welcome</u> to exercise it. The religious leader, the professional, the businessman, the laborer, the craftsman, the politician, the housewife – everyone. The school is in the fullest sense of the term the spiritual center of the community. As it <u>must</u> be, since its disappearance in the third phase is dependent on the community's assumption of its role – on the community's ultimately being its own spiritual center.

The school is the forum for all educational activity in the community. Gone is the exclusion of real-life people from the schools, as is the case today. The community re-appears as the only decider of who is competent to teach – and the community decides not by issuing certificates, but by <u>coming to learn</u>.

In such an atmosphere, teaching is solicited as well as offered. A group is free to get together and ask a person to address them – though the person, of course, is free to decline. In such an atmosphere, teaching is a reciprocal process, is learning too. The teacher, faced by an interested rather than a captive audience, is as eager to hear the audience's response as they are eager to hear him. As strong as the urge to communicate is the urge to be understood, to <u>reach</u> the other person.

No subject is excluded from the school. For this reason, there is no need for the community to maintain a battery of auxiliary schools to supplement the regular public school – no need to maintain religious schools, technical school, athletic schools, adult extension schools, etc. Nor is there any need to exclude controversial aspects of real life. The politicians' debate is as much a part of the spiritual life of the community as the minister's sermon or the physicist's lecture; it belongs in the school, side by side with the others.

There are, to be sure, a small number of required courses, dealing primarily with survival: courses in health (human biology) and disease (red cross, principles of medicine) and environmental hazards, among others. I shall discuss in Chapter 19 how the exact content of these courses is determined. They are few, and are taken seriously. Since they are required on grounds of being essential to human survival, every member of the school from the long-term and permanent sector must take them and give evidence of having mastered their contents. (The public sector too is welcome, though there is no way of requiring all members of this sector to participate.)

6. All teaching, then, is done out of conviction and enthusiasm. It is therefore to be expected that the school will be the scene of a great deal of experimentation in new teaching techniques, in light of the universal interest in getting the message across from teacher to pupil. Such experimentation is welcome and is encouraged. Every new method of overcoming mental and physical barriers is of use in advancing human development.

The school invests in experimental equipment, and produces its own. The full range of audio-visual aids, tape recorders, language laboratories, Montessori and Cuisenaire and other special equipment is available, either by purchase, by copy, or on loan. These are not introduced into the school by a committee promoting experimentation; rather, they enter at the request of particular teachers wishing to try them out. If a particular novelty is not asked for by a member, this means the school is not ready for it, and therefore should not have it. It is necessary to have faith that the over-all atmosphere of openness to the world provides adequate guarantee that useful innovations will in due time penetrate the school.

7. A number of activities involve group coordination, at least more so than individually-based and individually-motivated research and skilled work. For example, there are activities in the arts, for which facilities are provided. It is necessary to have a theatre, which any performing group can use for practice and public performance. By "any" I mean outside groups as well as groups formed from within the school. The school is the community's theatre center, and since virtually no community of the size we are referring to has an independent theatre, there is no problem of competition between the school and a local commercial theatre. It is to be expected that a great deal of experimental work will be done, since any playwright who can get together a cast to perform his work has access to the facilities. The theatre, like all those offering services to the public outside the school, is expected to be so organized as to constitute no severe financial burden on the school. There should be no difficulty in this matter, as much of the activity that costs money in a commercial setting is here provided on a volunteer basis.

Similarly, an experimental movie-house is desirable, where experimental, historic, documentary, or educational films can be shown, at the request of members. It would be appropriate too to have facilities for producing experimental films, but this would depend entirely on the inclinations for the members. Again, there is no competition with commercial movie-houses showing recent commercial movies.

Practice rooms and performing rooms exist for musical groups, ranging from soloists through chamber music groups, bands, orchestras, and choral groups. Where possible, the school provides instruments for those who do not have access to their own.

An art gallery is also part of the school, with on-going exhibitions of works done by members, in the community, and by outside artists (on loan). Opportunity is thereby afforded to anyone who produces a piece of art to have it placed on public view, without the need for special "connections".

The school is thus seen to be the natural arts center of the community, and to provide, through its open and free program, the promise of ample artistic activity. There is no reason for small communities to lag in the arts – except the reason of pressure to do other things, and the consequent lack of time to devote to artistic work. In the school, the absence of diverting pressures allows a fertile ground for the leisurely development of all sorts of artistic activities. (In this connection, the outbursts of artistic activity in the ghettoes of the Second World War is a notable example of what can be expected when the pressures of ordinary life – there was no ordinary life left! – are removed.)

8. Other predominantly group activities include athletics, for which facilities are provided, both indoors and outdoors – playing fields, gymnasia, and a pool, at the very least. Members (including the public) are free to organize teams and leagues, and there can be little doubt that individuals will always be found with the initiative and interest to organize team activities.

The school's facilities are also the natural place for the community to hold its public athletic events, such as they are. There is also the likelihood of inter-school athletic competition, though this depends entirely on the will of the members, and may well change from one year to the next.

9. A potentially important group of activities, the presence of which is desirable but entirely dependent on the interests of the members, are those involving communications. These include such things as a local radio station, possibly a UHF television station, a newspaper (daily or weekly), and one or more journalistic periodicals (in addition to whatever scholarly journals may be published). Activities such as these are especially useful in breaking down whatever barriers may exist between the school and the community at large; useful also in bringing members into close contact with the real world outside.

The most important criterion governing these activities is <u>relevance</u>. At no point should restrictions be imposed – e.g., avoidance of controversial issues. On the contrary, the school-based communications activities must be noted for the same openness, freedom, and honesty that characterizes the school as a whole, and that will soon characterize the community as a whole in the third stage. In this sense, the school is showing the community the way toward the future, even as the school is preparing for the community to take over its special functions.

The communications activities enable permanent and long-term members to put to the test of real life the ideas and opinions they have formed in the course of their studies; and enable the public to put to the test of detached critique the ideas and opinions they have formed in the course of the hectic flow of everyday life. To a large extent, this interchange takes place in the school on a face-to-face basis, during the constant confrontation of public with other members in the school proper. But the communications activities allow such an interchange on a broader front, encompassing more people, including many outside the community. For this reason more than any other, such activities can be specially useful in keeping the school from provincialism, parochialism, and isolation, and in providing a steady stream of new ideas, insights, and alternatives flowing into the school.

10. All the activities going on in the school are the kind that will naturally become community-wide activities in the third stage. The prototype transition school, and those to follow, will not maintain activities that "belong in the school, and only in the school." Such esoteric or exclusive activities simply do not exist, and will certainly not exist in the third stage. Anything that belongs in the third stage community belongs in the transition school, and vice versa. This is the main sense in which the transition school serves an important social function in the transition period: the school eases society's transition from second to third stage by providing a model of the third stage. Early experience and familiarity with the model provides society with the insight necessary to adapting the model for global application.

Although the activities have been discussed under separate categories in the various paragraphs of this chapter, these categories have been introduced only for the sake of simplifying the discussion. There are no real categories of division in the school, just as there are no departments. A person is as likely to be involved in one activity as in another, and the same person switches from one activity to another according to his interest. It is therefore no occasion for surprise – indeed, it is more the norm – to find a person now studying physics, later tending the vegetable garden, later seeing through publication of a paper; another person now repairing an automobile, later studying literature, later painting; and so forth. Breaking down interdisciplinary barriers in the school is the first and most important step toward breaking down barriers in the mind.

11. It might well be wondered what the special role of the permanent members is in the school, inasmuch as none of the activities described as going on in the school singles out permanent members in any way. They are clearly not privileged in any way, as regards the daily life of the school. Yet, they are there to stay, and they are supported by the community. Why?

The essential contribution of the permanent member stems from their being permanent: they provide the continuity, they provide the <u>tone</u> of the school, they provide the assurance that the school will go on functioning smoothly. Long-term members and the public come and go; the permanent members remain, and form the backbone of a school tradition, a school character, emerging out of the daily activity in the same way that personal or national traditions and character emerge out of the daily activities of the individual or the nation.

Indeed, the permanent members as a group are responsible for the existence of an unavoidable residual isolation and apartness of school from community; for the character of the school is, in the long run, chiefly determined by these members, and they are only a small subset of the community. True, the community interacts with the school and influences its character, but the existence of a permanent sector in the school guarantees that the character of the school will not automatically reflect the character of the community. Only with the third-stage disappearance of the school as a separate institution will the community's educational facets be organically linked with the life of the community as a whole, with no intervening sub-groups or barriers.

The permanent members are <u>responsible</u> for the school as an ongoing institution. (Again, they go out of existence only in the third stage, when the community as a whole takes over responsibility for education.) They exercise this responsibility in four basic ways: (1) They keep an eye on the school as a whole, and try to spot potential troubles before these become actual. (Responsibility for actual troubles is discussed in Chapter 19.) They are thus not guardians, but scouts. (2) They are accessible to members of the school community. Long-term public members may or may not be available for advice and discussion, but permanent members are in principle always available. (3) They have the primary responsibility for administering the school. (4) They have the primary responsibility for keeping track of the whereabouts of other members. All four of these responsibilities are elaborated on in the following chapters.

CHAPTER 16

Rules and Regulations

1. There will be definite procedures for establishing rules and regulations (see Chapter 19). Therefore, it is not possible to predict or outline in advance what these rules will be, in any of the transition schools; nor is it likely that any two schools will be governed by identical codes, any more than it is likely that any two schools will have the same activities and interests.

My only aim in this chapter is to present some of the issues I think will be basic to the establishment of a code of behavior in the school, and to offer in addition my own views of the directions along which these issues should be resolved.

2. A key question is that of attendance in the school, and responsibility for those attending. Each sector of the school community presents a different problem.

A basic function of the school is to provide a haven for children and young people until they can safely be allowed to fend for themselves in the community. Toward this end, the community requires attendance at the school for all persons up to the cutoff age, and offers to support persons beyond that age if they wish to continue their studies seriously. It is up to the community to decide how much attendance is required up to cutoff age, and beyond cutoff age to qualify for support; in other words, how much attendance is required of long-term members. Judging from present trends, something in the neighborhood of nine months per year of attendance, five days per week is to be expected. The community is responsible for enforcing this attendance rule. Below cutoff age, the community applies its truancy code; above cutoff age, withdrawal of support is sufficient sanction.

The school, like the community, is open all year round, twelve months a year, twenty-four hours a day. For this reason, and because of the free nature of school activities, the community can allow itself considerable flexibility vis-a-vis specific hours or days of required attendance. There seems no a priori reason why <u>any</u> nine months of the year would not be equally valid, and any time of day. Families having odd working hours, or wishing to take vacations at different times of the year, could easily be accommodated, with no inconvenience to school or community.

Permanent members should probably be required to be in attendance about the same length of time each year, with the same flexible option to choose the time of day and the days of the year in which they shall be present. It might be possible also to allow accumulation of vacation time, since the permanent members can be useful all year round, and conversely can be absent at any time with equal effect. In addition, there are provisions for regular paid leaves.

Public members can come and go as they please – which is what their title implies anyway. One wants, however, some idea of how the school facilities are being used, and by whom. It is therefore useful to have some sort of check-in center, preferably automatic, where people entering and leaving are automatically recorded, as well as their probable activities during attendance. A good center of this sort could instantly spot potential log-jams in facilities; also, it could provide the whereabouts of any member upon request.

Such a check-in procedure should apply to anyone on campus, including long-term and permanent members. (It should be a very simple and quick procedure, to minimize annoyance.) In addition, every permanent member is assigned personal responsibility for a certain number (about ten) of the long-term members. This means that outside inquiries about a long-term member can be channeled to the permanent member responsible for him; and also that the long-term member knows that he always has someone to turn to in case of trouble, or in case he needs special assistance in some matter. Note that the responsibility thus assigned to permanent members does not require that they "keep tabs" on their charges, since the purely mechanical act of keeping tabs is performed by the automatic check-in center. Anyway, the campus is safe.

For the youngest long-term members (those around four years of age), and those first entering the school, somewhat more concentrated guidance must be provided, at least until they have gained sufficient confidence and orientation to fend for themselves. In the case of little children, it may be that many months of "weaning" will be necessary. Whatever the need in these instances, the permanent members are responsible for arranging that the need be met adequately.

3. The basic ethical rule of the school community is a modification of the golden rule and the categorical imperative. It is: Do not intrude yourself upon your neighbor. The corollary to this is: Do what you wish with <u>your</u> energy, <u>your</u> time, <u>your</u> possessions – but respect your neighbor's wishes as regards <u>his</u> energy, <u>his</u> time, and <u>his</u> possessions. This is the rule that underlies the educational policies of the school, and it is likewise the rule that underlies interpersonal behavior.

External circumstances must be designed to assist rather than hinder the application of this rule. For example, it would be foolish to locate in close proximity two activities that by nature intrude on one another. (One would not place a study desk in the middle of a football field!) Noisy activities should be isolated, either by distance or by mechanical means (sound-proofing). Machine shops should not be placed near laboratories containing delicate balances. And so forth.

But internal self-regulation is required in addition to external aids, and this self-regulation can be assured by explaining the rational basis for the rule – and by repeating the explanation in various circumstances until behavior compatible with the principle has been completely internalized. It has been the experience of several experimental schools (and individual homes) that this principle is rapidly internalized by all members, provided only that it is explained rather than arbitrarily announced.

The principle makes all violations of privacy matters of mutual consent. Any particular person can choose to isolate himself from the rest of the community as long as he pleases. There is no pressure (at least, none consciously applied) for group participants, for "adjustment", or for any of the other community-oriented, privacy-infringing values. As discussed in Part I and II, the school allows all impulse towards joint action to arise freely from within the individuals making up the group.

The principle also has a corollary the notion of responsibility towards another party when making use of that other party. As long as a person is involved in himself, he may – <u>he should</u> – freely form his own notion of responsibility to himself. But if a person calls on his neighbor's time, or borrows his neighbor's possession, he has a responsibility to honor his neighbor's wishes concerning how the neighbor's time or possessions are to be used. And what is true of a person calling on a second party is equally true of a person calling on a group, or on the community at large. Insofar as the group, or the public, is being used by a person, the user must respect the wishes of those he is using. This applies across the board, to personal borrowing, to responsible use of laboratories, to responsible use of school facilities. There is, I believe, no reason why all this cannot be explained to every member and internalized by every member to the extent that it becomes enforced on a day to day basis through each member's self regulation.

Permanent members have a special problem when it comes to balancing privacy versus accessibility to the public. The permanent members, as we have seen, have a basic responsibility to be accessible to other members of the school. What does this mean in practice? Clearly, it would be an intolerable state of affairs to have each member, or any member, constantly subject to intrusion and imposition. On the other hand, it would be equally intolerable to allow permanent members to close themselves off from everyone else – something we do allow long-term and public members. How the balance will be struck is a matter to be decided by the appropriate administrative channels (see Chapter 19). Here I wish only to point out that in the case of permanent members, <u>some</u> balance must be struck; unfettered application of the basic ethical principle cannot be allowed. This fact is, I believe, completely clear to the permanent members involved, so that considerable discretion can be allowed them in practice.

4. There are two categories of auxiliary rules. The first is the set of rules that follow from the basic principles outlined in Part I and II, and that are therefore inherent in the school situation.

Foremost among these are rules and restrictions protecting the physical survival of members. Every laboratory has its own set of safety instructions. Physical hazards in particular surroundings are identified. Places are put off-bounds, and walled off, with restrictions against entry. Certain equipment is restricted in use to those who have demonstrated competence in handling it. (Compare the automobile.) Those rules govern only essentials, only matters crucial to survival. They are not to be confused with the trivial restrictions that so often appear on the scene, with little reason – for example, the "don't touch this" and "don't handle that" that abounds. Trivial restrictions are absent from the school, as is required by its atmosphere of openness and free access.

Another set of regulations in this category governs the handling of very young children, and has to do with shielding them from external traumas brought on by our technological culture and its impact on young nervous systems not evolutionarily attuned to the culture (see Part I). What precisely this shielding and gradual exposure involves is a matter of continuing discussion and re-evaluation, participated in by members of all ages. The temptation to overprotect must be countered, but at any rate will not be very strong in a situation where completely free exposure is assured at the latest by the age of six. <u>Some</u> protection, <u>some</u> gradual and carefully planned step-wise exposure, must be provided, however.

5. The second category of auxiliary rules is not intrinsic to the school, but has to do with the rules governing behavior in the general community, of which the school is a part. The school is in and of the community, never against the community; the school must therefore be in harmony with prevailing modes of behavior in the community. Under no circumstances can the school be a haven for activity considered criminal or definitely unacceptable by the community.

This means, among other things, that the accepted codes of behavior as regards sex, drugs, liquor, etc. must be honored in the school. This will be easier to achieve in the prototype school, or than it is today in essentially closed campuses. At any rate, problems with accepted norms would receive the same public exposure and reaction in the school as they would in the community at large.

Now, the above in no way implies that the school is a conservative institution, preserver of the status quo. Quite the opposite. The school, by virtue of its extreme openness and its absolute spiritual freedom, is <u>the</u> place in the community where everything new has a hearing, where all arguments, for and against any established or proposed institution, are freely heard. If anything, the school is the spearhead of change, being the spearhead of the free inquiry toward which the whole community is tending. Precisely for this reason, precisely because every idea is freely heard, the school's function is to serve as the focal point for organic change within the community – as the stimulus for experimentation and novelty. And the change so arrived at by the community is change brought about through understanding and conviction, not through blind reaction or violent, emotional upheaval. Therefore, insofar as the school is the symbol of rational progress freely arrived at, the school must be especially firm in eschewing violent, emotional rebellion against community norms, and in repudiating attempts to make it adopt unpopular stances in the face of the community, despite the community, in defiance of the community. Defiant action is a barrier to reasoned change, arousing as it does emotional reactions on all sides. The school, by accepting community norms of behavior, thus opens the door wide to rational re-evaluation of these norms by all parties concerned.

6. How rules and regulations are to be enforced is discussed in Chapter 19. The whole question of sanctions against violators of the public order is a painfully complicated one, and has been struggled with by men from the dawn of humanity. What is to be done with the violator? I shall only set down some general feelings on this question.

It seems reasonable to resort to rehabilitation techniques at first, and as often as possible. Such techniques primarily revolve about the effort to make the violator internalize, through his own insight, the behavior pattern desired, which is presumably dictated by the rest of the community's supposedly valid insight. Much personal effort is required, much discussion, much patient reasoning, and the community must be willing to invest the effort if the enterprise is to succeed. The task will become progressively easier as the third stage is approached, since the third stage presupposes widespread internalization of the kind of behavior being sought here. But in the prototype school, and in all early transition schools, the task will be much harder, since the principles governing the school, while widespread, have not permeated the general consciousness. The fact that they <u>are</u> widespread even now (as has been discussed in Part I and II) is very important for rehabilitation purposes, since one of the strongest persuasions to accepting the norms of the school is that these norms are not arbitrary or esoteric, but are widely found in other (hopefully good) sectors of present community life.

For recalcitrants, although efforts at rehabilitation should never be abandoned, still it may be necessary to protect the rest of the school by applying enforced isolation. (This is the root idea behind the prison in society.) There seems to be no alternative in dealing with a persistent public nuisance to making it impossible for him to continue being a nuisance, even while keeping up attempts to have him internalize a pattern of behavior that will not be a nuisance. It may therefore happen that some members of the community will be persona non grata at the school, at least for a time. How often this extreme sanction has to be applied depends directly on the degree of success the school has.

CHAPTER 17

The Step from School to Real Life

1. Permanent members spend their entire lives in the school. Public members go back and forth freely between school and real-life positions. At what point do long-term members leave school and find themselves a place in the outside world?

To begin with, the question applies only to those who have passed the cutoff age. Willy nilly, those under the cutoff age have no real-life options (except, possibly, for some exposure to the real world during vacations and after school). Also, the question excludes those few long-term members who eventually become permanent members of this or another school. Specifically, then, we are inquiring about the transition of long-term members, who have passed the cutoff age and are not staying permanently in the school, from school to real life.

The factor determining <u>when</u> this transition is made is the person's own feeling of preparedness for full participation in community life. When he feels ready to leave school, he usually is ready; for his feeling is based on self-evaluation vis-a-vis his life goals, and also vis-a-vis the community's standards for a person having these life goals. Suppose a person interested in repairing automobiles feels ready to leave school and join a commercial garage. How has he arrived at this feeling? Usually, two ways: first, by comparing his proficiency with the requirements of the trade, and second, by comparing his proficiency with that required by commercial garages. Having arrived at the feeling that he is ready, he ought to leave; for only by actual exposure can he be sure that he is ready.

Suppose, now, that the decision was based on a misleading feeling. Suppose he was not really ready. Or suppose he was ready for a particular role in life, and, upon actually assuming this role, found out that this role was not really to his taste, so that he now wanted to prepare for another role. In either case, the school is always open to him, always ready to take him back as a long-term member, until he is again ready to leave. There is no point in life too late to return to the school; knowledge of this takes much of the pressure off the decision to leave school in the first place. On the other hand, the natural desire to proceed successfully along a path freely chosen is strong enough to ensure that the possibility of returning to school is no strong inducement to misjudgment or failure in one's chosen line of interest.

2. The long-term member is not entirely isolated in arriving at his decision to leave, even though the decision is entirely his to make.

On the one hand, a number of permanent members have come to know him over the years, and are able to advise him as well as to discus his merits and potentialities with prospective employers. On the other hand, many public members have come to know him through interaction with him in the school, and possibly also outside of school; so that he has some reputation in the community, and some people to whom he can turn for counsel and assistance.

It is important to remember that in the transition school, education is based on personal contact with, in addition to fellow long-term members, permanent and public members too. For this reason, the transition school can never present the spectacle (not at all rare today) of a person ready to leave school without a single member of the school's staff knowing him personally (let alone knowing his thoughts, abilities, and interests). The person leaving a transition school has several people who can speak in an intelligent and informed way on his behalf; who can give not stereotyped three-sentence "letters of recommendation" but extended reports, orally or in writing. Thus, the member leaving school for the outside world has his own talents to show for his schooling, plus informed reports by independent judges. He has, then, considerable assets to launch him on his way.

3. It is possible that even today these assets are sufficient to give a person a fair start. (They certainly will be sufficient when the entire school system has entered the transition phase.) However, for the most part people leaving school today are required to have formal certificates, in addition to the more subjective (and more significant) equipage just mentioned. The prototype school, and also other early transition schools, must be prepared and able to award certificates to leaving long term members – certificates that serve as valid currency on the present academic market.

The need to award certificates (this includes all degrees) raises two problems. First is the problem of receiving official governmental accreditation to award valid degrees. Related to this is the desirable addendum of accreditation from educational associations which considerably enhance the value of the degrees. Governmental accreditation depends on fulfilling certain formal criteria – all of which the school would be fulfilling anyway – and on having competent faculty, i.e., permanent members. Professional association accreditation depends especially on the excellence of the permanent members. The prototype school will certainly have to take pains to gather together an excellent group of permanent members: people having not only excellent moral qualities but also all the trappings of professional excellence. The same holds for all early schools. As the transition-type school system spreads, the requirement for formal trappings will gradually give way, and yield to the requirement for personal excellence – a requirement that will be ever more widely filled as the schools themselves spread and produce a reserve of potential permanent members. The growing transition-type school system is thus seen to be self-reinforcing, and to hasten by its own success the replacement of formal, obsolete requirements.

The second problem attending the award of certificates, after accreditation has been achieved, is how to determine which certificates are to go to which people as they leave school. These decisions are highly subjective – as are all decisions to award degrees (by what objective criteria are the degrees of one school ever compared with those of another?). They must, however, be fair, i.e., conform to the general standards of the community, if they are to be reputed as being valid degrees. The actual mechanism for awarding certificates must be determined by each school independently. It would be reasonable, for example, to have the appropriate certificate determined at the suggestion of those permanent members who personally know the certificate candidate and by vote of the entire permanent membership. The suggestion would be made by subjectively gauging equivalent values on the academic market: person A is the equivalent of a high school graduate and should receive a high school diploma, person B is the equivalent of a college graduate and should receive a B.A., person C has done good professional independent research and should receive a Ph.D., etc. The entire permanent staff could then review the reasoning that led to the suggestion, and approve or disapprove. But there are many other possible procedures. It is likely that the long term members will on the whole do so well in school that they will not be set back if certificate decisions are made with a tendency to lean over backwards in the direction of "high standards". Certainly such a tendency will be of political value to the school.

4. Some people will leave the school and transfer, for one reason or another, to other schools, or to professional schools. In such cases, the procedure for assigning a formal "level" to departing members could be much the same as the procedure for awarding formal certificates.

However, transfers often introduce the additional complication of examinations of various sorts as a prerequisite to transfer. (Note that the long-term member who remains within the school, or remains within the transition-type school system, for his entire education need never undergo these formal examinations.) The school ought certainly to provide members transferring out with all possible assistance to enhance good performance on the tests. This means first of all that all the standard and well-known aids to "cramming" for these tests be available. It means also that the permanent members be ready to actively assist transferring members in their enforced course of study. That all possible assistance should be rendered is dictated not only by the ethics of the situation (i.e., by the obligation not to abandon a charge to hostile forces – the same obligation that requires a shipmaster to provide a gangplank in port, rather than merely throwing departing passengers overboard), but also by prudence, since the school can only be harmed if transferring members are found always to perform poorly in situations still valued by a large segment of society.

5. The step from school to real life is not a grand, irrevocable, one-way step. In the first place, it can be retraced if needs be, as we have seen, and the departing member can return as a long-term member. More important, however, is the fact that the openness of the school to the public at large allows for continued sporadic (or periodically) contact between a former long-term member, now a public member, and the school. The transition school has no alumni; it has instead life-long members, who see the school as the focal point of their life-long, ongoing education. Once the first generation has passed through the school, the relation between school and community will seem natural in its

intimacy, until eventually, with time, the community as a whole will <u>be</u> the school.

CHAPTER 18

The Physical Plant

1. The physical plant should be modest, and adequate to the needs of the school. The exact nature of the plant is determined by the exact list of activities going on in the school. Since the latter is determined only when the interests of the members are known, the former cannot be planned in advance. Still, some of the basic needs are known, and therefore some general idea can be had of the plant needed.

It is not necessary to have elegant new buildings. Any plant, if it is sturdy and physically strong enough to be used, can be transformed into a pleasant work-surrounding. All that is necessary is the determination to effect the transformation. I am convinced that <u>adequacy</u> for the purposes at hand should be the only criterion governing selection of a plant. Only in the event that building funds are freely offered, with the proviso that they can be put to no other use deemed more worthwhile by the community, should extravagant structures be permitted. Comfort, not gaudiness, should be the guide.

2. For individual non-laboratory research, a quiet facility is needed, as near as possible to the library. This facility could contain a few fair-sized reading rooms, and a number of smaller rooms for group work and seminars. Of special importance is a large number of small, private rooms. Of these, some serve as permanent offices for the permanent members, and others as hide-aways for long-term members (and the public, if enough room is available) to use when necessary, though not on permanent assignment. The facility can be housed in one or several

adjacent buildings. One of the buildings contains a stockroom with office supplies available for use.

Central to this area is the information center, with its library and possibly other facilities. It would seem to make sense to locate one of the town's public libraries (or <u>the</u> public library, if there is only one) in the school; that is, to make the school library a public library, since it is open anyway to the public. Free access to all books should be the rule, and with very few exceptions all books should be circulated, with the understanding that they are to be returned on recall. Inter-library loan arrangements are a standard way of making available books not in the library, but to be found in other libraries. Another possible arrangement to augment the collection is through loan of private libraries to the school library. A person could deposit his books in the school library for general use, with the understanding that he has unlimited access (not subject to recall) to his own books. The library contains a free photocopying facility, as well as the standard microcard and microfilm readers and audio-visual equipment. The extent to which sophisticated data-storage equipment is available, on the premises or by cooperation with a regional facility, depends on the resources of the school. Ideally, such a facility should be available, as it would greatly enhance the quality of research at the school, and the usefulness of the school to the community.

These buildings have the standard furnishings – desk, tables, bookshelves, blackboards, filing cabinets, typewriters on loan – none of which need be new.

Not to be forgotten is an outdoor area, a park, with paths, woods, and grass (a few acres is ample) for the kind of leisurely conversation, relaxation, and fresh exposure to the outdoors that is so conducive to mental activity and mental rest. The park could surround these facilities and help isolate them from the more active and noisy facilities in the school.

3. The design of laboratories is a matter of considerable debate. The basic difference is between large-room and small-room design. The former focuses on large floor-areas without wall barriers, where many workbenches are located in one room, albeit comfortably spaced and

each of good size. The advantages of this arrangement are: (1) easy access to large or expensive common equipment; (2) a sense of community, generated by easy access to the work (and mind!) of others. The advantages of the latter design, which focuses on small private laboratories, are: (1) greater peace and quiet; and (2) greater privacy. There is no question that the small-room design tends to produce an atmosphere of isolation, of each person being "an island unto himself." In the school's prevailing atmosphere of exchange and accessibility, large-room laboratories would seem most suitable. On the other hand, it may be that precisely because the school atmosphere is so free, small-room laboratories are a necessary protection of the researcher against too much intrusion. A certain amount of experimentation will certainly be necessary to determine which design is better suited in each school.

Every effort must be made to provide the laboratories with the most modern basic equipment. There is simply no point to building obsolete laboratories in the schools which are to serve as the training centers for future researchers. It would be like training automobile mechanics on 1905 Ford cars.

Field facilities depend on the interest of the members. It may be expected that some sort of model farm will be developed, with vegetable gardens, cow-barns, and chicken-coops, for example, since farms seem to have a universal appeal to young and old alike. Some rudimentary botanical and zoological gardens are also quite likely, there being widespread interest in animals and in raising flowers and plants of various sorts. There is no need to elaborate on this. Several acres of field-type facilities will be a feature of the school, but the exact nature of the facilities varies from school to school.

4. In addition to laboratory and field facilities are the various shops, crafts-centers, and technical centers. Since these tend to be rather noisy, they should be fairly peripheral in location.

Whatever the facility – and the choice depends, again, on the interests of the members – the equipment must be adequate and up-to-date. To the extent that a facility is set up in cooperation with a community commercial facility, the necessity for good equipment will be obvious. But even in more detached enterprises, the school ought not, as a rule, to embark on a new enterprise without the means to equip and supply it according to need, and in line with the best standards.

Another reason these facilities should be on the periphery of the campus is that they demand the most traffic with the outside world. If they were located in an interior position, they would inevitably contribute to a considerable flow of cars and trucks in and out of the school. Located on the periphery, they can have their exterior accesses so placed that they bring no traffic at all onto the campus.

5. It is by now well-known that an arts center should have a great variety of rooms for practice, performance, and exhibition. For example, for music, small soundproofed individual practice and lesson rooms are needed, in addition to middle-sized rooms for chamber groups, and large concert halls for large groups. Similarly, several sizes of theatres are useful to have, including one very large one, which can serve to house public meetings and special events. Art galleries and areas for museum exhibitions, etc., from another sector of the center. These buildings benefit especially from careful acoustical design, for sound isolation from the surroundings on the one hand, and for good sound reproduction and projection inside the halls on the other hand.

Public community events also take place in this area – town meetings, occasional visits by commercial theatres, political meetings and debates, and so forth. All events, of course, are open to the public, whatever the group that puts them on.

Hard by the arts center is the communications area, with its radio, TV, newspaper, or whatever of these happen to be present. It is to be expected, for example, that much of what takes place in the arts center will be appropriate for live or taped coverage. The communications center thus serves an additional important function in making the school a focus for the entire community's cultural life.

6. Finally, athletic facilities are needed. These consist, on the one hand, of fields for various team games – basketball, baseball, football, soccer, etc. – and semi-individual games, such as tennis, badminton,

handball, etc. On the other hand, there are gymnasia, complete with indoor equipment, lockers, and showers. The athletic facilities of the school are those of the community; as such, they may be provided with whatever grandstand and lighting equipment the town wants in its athletic center.

An indoor, year-round pool is a particularly important part of the sports center. The pool should be large enough to accommodate what will doubtless be a large number of users.

7. Teaching facilities are not concentrated in one spot, but are scattered throughout the other facilities, in appropriate number and size. The private research buildings will have several seminar and lecture rooms, none too large, designed for the small to middle-sized groups expected to attend lectures and courses in fairly esoteric subjects. The laboratories need seminar rooms, as do the field facilities. The arts center needs some studios, and several small rooms for private instruction. The shops and crafts needs few teaching rooms, since most teaching takes place <u>in situ</u>. Nevertheless, a few lecture rooms are necessary, for presentations to the interested but uninvolved public. The athletics area too needs small and middle-sized rooms for private and group instruction. Large public lectures, in whatever subject, can be held in the large facilities of the arts center.

Wherever the teaching facilities are located, they should be provided with equipment for teaching with the latest techniques. Thus, not only blackboards, but the full audio-visual range of equipment should be on hand.

8. One of the key considerations in setting up the physical plant is safety. Within school grounds, people of all ages must be free to roam at will without encountering environmental hazards. This means that whatever hazards do, of necessity, exist on campus must be thoroughly isolated from the free flow of human traffic.

For example, it would be best if no vehicular traffic at all were allowed on campus. Where on occasion this rule must be violated, vehicles appearing on campus should proceed slowly and always in company of pedestrian guards to warn off the unwary. If a vehicular artery must traverse the campus, it should be fenced off carefully, with occasional pedestrian overpasses or underpasses.

Similarly, the pool, and dangerous laboratory facilities, and cages for animals, are carefully closed off from casual access. This means that, although these facilities are completely open to the public in principle, they are open in practice only when a responsible member (permanent, or one designated by a permanent member) is in charge, supervising the safety of the users. There can be no exceptions to strict application of safety regulations, especially because the school as a whole is so free.

A possible arrangement of the facilities is shown in the diagram below, which is meant to be schematic rather than representational. Of course, there are as many alternative possibilities as one can conceive.

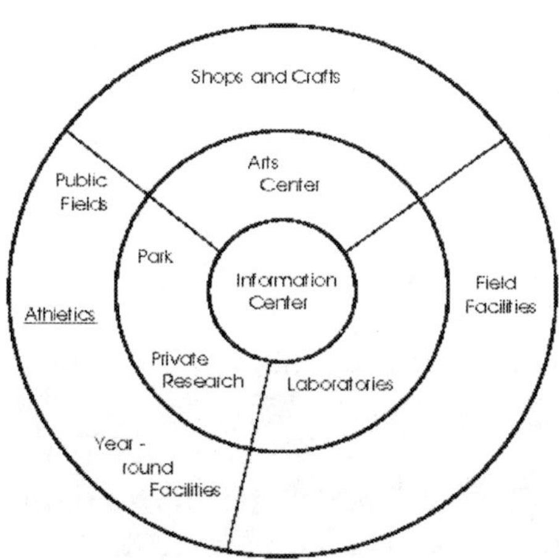

CHAPTER 19

Administration of the School; The Budget

1. The principle underlying all administrative procedures in the school is that of democratic self-government. The people affected by a decision by and large are the ones who make the decision. Just as there is no room in the school for intellectual condescension ("I know better than the other person what he ought to know") so there is no room for administrative condescension ("I know better than the other person how to do what he wants to do"). We must not fear the prospect of introducing freedom and equality into the school, since by now we have had sufficient experience with these "dangerous" concepts in other walks of life, and we have learned that the objections – chaos, anarchy, apathy, nothing will get done – are ill-founded.

A corollary principle is that of responsibility. One of the features of an authoritarian set-up is the absence of responsibility: if someone else takes the burden off you, why should you bother to shoulder it at all? This is a well-known feature of authoritarian governments: the rulers assume the responsibility for everyone else, and the ruled, rather than struggle to get responsibility back into their own hands, often spend their energies complaining that the rulers are not discharging their responsibility adequately and ought to be doing a better job. (From this situation arises a situation that so often seems ironic or downright fraudulent, but in fact is largely true: the rulers are found steeped in self-pity at the immense burden of public service they are carrying.) In our present school system, these features are everywhere in evidence. The administration rules, and in so doing performs all the services for the academic community. This community, in turn, welcoming the service, accepts in principle the idea of being served (and hence of being ruled), and turns its energies to complaining about the quality of the administration, rather than demanding that the administrative responsibilities be given over to them. (Note the widespread contempt for administrators, and for administration. Much like the contempt heaped on public officials "who are not doing their job well" by people who would not deign to come near responsible public office.)

In the transition school, everyone is responsible for himself, intellectually and administratively; no one is served, and no one rules, nor does the school's fortune hinge on one man or on a small group of men.

I shall now proceed to take up <u>seriatim</u> several matters that require administrative attention. I shall not give detailed procedures for coping with these matters, as these procedures cannot be specified by any one person. All I shall do is outline what I consider to be a fair over-all method for administering the school, consistently with the school's principles.

2. The school is a public institution. It is supported by public funds; it is created to serve the public interest; it is populated by the public (i.e., by members of the community). The ultimate control over the school is therefore wielded by the public. There is nothing novel in all this as regards the present public school system (including the state and municipal schools of higher learning). But certain sectors of the academic community still view all this with alarm.

It is the public that provides the funds for the school, and hence decides on the school budget. There is no reason why an annual budget could not be voted upon by a town meeting of all adult voting-age citizens of the town, or of the school district served by the school. (Note that the permanent members would be among those voting and participating.) Furthermore, the community will probably want to appoint a public group to keep an eye on the expenditure of funds during the year, and there is no reason why relations between this group and the school should not be cordial. Some provision for special budgetary town meetings (in the event of an emergency) should be made.

By passing on the budget (and on the taxes to meet the budget), the community exercises effective control over the entire school. There is no need, therefore, to be concerned that certain sectors of internal operations, administered internally, will be beyond the reach of the public. Through the use of fiscal tools the public can reach in and see that its will is obeyed throughout the school.

3. The permanent members are responsible for the smooth continued functioning of the school, so that they must share the day-to-day administrative responsibility for the entire institution. Let us see what this means in detail.

To begin with, every member is responsible for his own work. That means that he, and he alone, has to see to the successful pursuit of his own projects. He receives his annual appropriation (by a mechanism to be discussed shortly) and it is his to spend. No intermediate, no central financial office, no forms in triplicate. He keeps his own books, makes his own orders, as he sees fit. The same holds for groups.

The permanent members are the only ones with fiscal responsibility, and hence with fiscal authority. Long-term and public members who wish to have funds available for certain projects must make arrangements through permanent members. Permanent members are free to delegate responsibility for disbursement of funds – for example, to a long term member carrying out a project on his own – but they are ultimately responsible. Public members unable to find "sponsors" must either find their own private funds, or try to create new permanent members (see ahead).

All books are open. All financial transactions, all use of facilities, are made in the public eye. In this way, the absence of cumbersome accounting and controlling apparatus is compensated for by free public inspection.

Turning now to activities that must take place on a school-wide scale – e.g., certain types of maintenance and procurement – the permanent members as a group are responsible, and may delegate the responsibility to subcommittees. A cardinal feature of subcommittees is their lack of permanence. First of all, membership must be rotating; secondly, these subcommittees are created and disbanded according to need. In no case does the responsibility delegated to subcommittees entail the creation of a separate administrative apparatus. (Note that as many routine maintenance tasks as possible should be carried out by the school community itself. There is, for example, no rule that public areas must be decorated with flower gardens. If the community wants such gardens, there should be members enough to provide them.)

Preparation of a proposed budget is the responsibility of the permanent members. Only part of this can be delegated to a committee. Thus, each member proposes his own budget, and each group and committee does the same. A fiscal committee can be set up to collate the requests, even to make comments, but the budget must be hammered out in a full meeting of the permanent membership (and those not attending or leaving proxies must suffer the consequences of their inaction). Only in this way can budgetary cliques and financial strangleholds be avoided.

Salaries are part of the budget, and a word about this is in order. There is no reason for salaries to be secret – those of all public servants are public. On the other hand, there is no realistic reason for salaries to be uniform, much as uniform salaries contribute to an absence of envy. For the prototype school, and other early transition schools, there will be a need to compete on the market for permanent members, and the school will have to have the latitude of making offers at the going rate. There must be some minimum salary, compatible with decent living. Beyond that, the give and take of salary negotiations will resemble that going on throughout the economy, with the entire permanent membership representing the school, and with both sides free to compromise or part ways.

Once the budget is prepared by the membership at large, it goes to the public for discussion and appropriation. The public can vote item by item, or it can appropriate a fixed sum and send back the budget to the membership with instructions to revise the budget in order to fit the appropriated sum.

4. The permanent membership as a group determines its own composition. Thus, it is the one responsible for filling its own ranks, augmenting its ranks, and removing unwanted members.

Proposals for new appointments can originate anywhere – from members, from outside the community, from any source; they are then judged by the permanent membership as a group. Similarly, proposals to remove a permanent member can emanate from any source, but removal is decided by the group itself. In the case of removal, there must be due process, as spelled out in the school's by-laws. This must include clear-cut charges (violating clear-cut responsibilities) and adequate opportunity for a full, fair hearing.

The role of the public in this matter of appointments and removal is indirect. Thus, the salaries of permanent members appear as one consolidated item in the budget – "salaries". The public can accept or modify this item, but cannot decide how to split it among recipients. This is the chief protection permanent members have against fiscal bills of attainder directed at particular members who happen to be unpopular at the time. On the other hand, there is a limit to how much shielding the permanent membership can provide. The public can withhold all salary appropriations altogether until a certain party is dismissed; the public then risks dismemberment and collapse of the school. It is to be hoped that such locked-horn confrontations will generally be avoided with the aid of good relations between the school and the community at large.

Nor can the public force the permanent members to appoint a particular person to their members, except in one way: if the public feels it would like a certain interest represented, or a certain person hired, it can supply his salary and budget by a supplementary appropriation outside the proposed school budget. In such cases, the person so hired joins the permanent membership with the understanding that his continued presence depends either on continued special public support or on winning over the support of the permanent membership itself.

5. Special attention must be given to the place of grants (foundation or government) in the school. Certain kinds of grants pose no problem: general grants-in-aid for buildings, equipment, or general salary assistance. Such grants are in effect forms of aid to the community in meeting its local school budget.

Private grants are the potential danger, and here past experience must serve as a guide. The present grant system in present colleges and universities has led to the well-known "empire" phenomenon; but not so well-known is the way this happened. Originally, school stipulated that faculty would not be hired on the basis of grants and grant-supported salaries. The rule was made that only such faculty members as would anyway be supported by the school in the absence of a grant would be appointed with a grant. This meant that very few people could get appointments to faculty positions, even with grants. The result was that advanced researchers, many well beyond their doctoral degrees, had to choose between faculty positions at poor schools with poor facilities, and non-faculty positions in the well-provided grant-supported establishment of a professor at a good university. Those that chose the latter path contributed, by their choice, to the building of the empire system, whereby grant funds have come to give one, or a few, faculty members control over a vast army of non-tenured, non-faculty workers. (It's useless to speculate what would have happened had promising Ph.D.'s en masse turned their backs on empires and each struck out on his own in a less lavish initial surrounding.)

Empires are clearly out of line with the transition school philosophy, and can be avoided by returning to the rule that no one is hired to a paid job in the school unless that person is a permanent member, whose salary must be paid by the school in the same way everyone else's salary is paid. Note that this rule can effectively prevent empire building, whereas the similar rule in universities did not, because the latter referred only to tenure positions (i.e., senior faculty) while allowing mass-hiring on a non-tenure basis, whereas the prototype school knows no distinction of rank and requires <u>all</u> hiring to be on an equal level.

Furthermore, equipment empires must also be ruled out. A person receiving money to finance his own research must stipulate in his grant-application that all equipment is available for public use, and is "his" only in the sense that he has a priority claim to its use. Actually, this stipulation is understood to apply to virtually all grants made today.

Within the framework of these qualifications, all grants are welcome, as they are effective ways of making available to the community additional funds to run the school.

6. All educational policies of the school are made by those who are in regular attendance at the school and hence most closely associated with its activities. This means that long-term members and permanent members together, as a group, set educational policies.

In a school where very few specific demands are made (in terms of requirements), there is not much to decide in this area. A constant item on every agenda is the question of required courses – which are necessary, how they should be taught, what changes should be made, how they should be judged, etc. There should be no fear that the long-term members will be irresponsible in deciding these matters; after all, if those who supposedly benefit from the course cannot be made to see the benefit, there is something to be said for a searching re-examination of the whole business. In fact, the opposite tendency will probably prevail: driven by feelings of inadequacy and insecurity, certain long-term members may well wish to introduce several new required courses that would protect them from displaying ignorance on matters considered important by the public at large. ("We should all be given a course in. . .") The problem here will be to convince these people that their best interests are served by informing themselves, rather than relying on others to inform them.

Whatever other educational questions come up – e.g., a survey and critique of the teaching going on in the school – are all properly aired in this forum, and, where decisions are called for, decided here too. This will also be an occasion for evaluation of permanent members' accessibility to long-term members during the year.

7. Matters that have to do with the behavior (and misbehavior) of long-term members are decided by the long-term members themselves. Thus, the general code of behavior for long-term members is drafted by them, revised by them, and implemented by them (just like the permanent members run <u>their</u> own affairs). Self-government is the rule and the practice. In the event long-term members would like to have some external court of appeal, they can make some arrangement with a group of public or permanent members to serve as a review board, but this is entirely up to the group itself to decide.

Complaints about the behavior of long-term members, whatever the origin of these complaints, are turned over to the appropriate channels, as determined by the long-term members.

In matters of criminal activity – i.e., activity considered to be in violation of the laws of the community – the long-term members are subject to the same jurisdiction as are permanent members and everyone else; namely, to the jurisdiction of the community's law-enforcement agencies. In such matters, the school is just another part of the community, and has no special privileges.

8. The entire school is seen to have an administrative structure quite different from that prevailing in present-day schools. Indeed, the school has no administrative structure at all, by current standards. The prospect is therefore that the large sums of money now devoted to administration will find more fruitful uses, and that the usual tensions between administrators and everyone else will simply not exist.

In place of a formal administrative apparatus there are several annual meetings – a public budget meeting, a budget and appointments meeting of permanent members, an educational policies meeting of long-term and permanent members, and a self-government meeting of long-term members – and as many other meetings as the community feels it necessary to hold. In addition, there is the work of several standing committees, all of which are populated on a rotating basis. An important adjunct of the little apparatus that does exist is – as it was in the transition to democratic state government – an efficient and free communications system. This means that there is ample room for notices of all sorts to be posted, and facilities for circulating memoranda, suggestions, petitions, etc. to whomever the sender wants to reach. Good communications, easy to set up and maintain in the relatively small school community, are an effective indicator of the popular will.

9. What can be said of the budget in absolute terms, in dollars and cents? Very little, in view of the vagueness of the other numbers associated with the school. Of the moneys available from public or private grants nothing at all can be said; not even an order-of-magnitude estimate can be given.

As for a reasonable expectation of the degree of public support, the following considerations apply. We can look at the going tuition fees for good private schools, and at the appropriations per student in what are considered good public school systems (all of which, incidentally, are found in suburban communities of the type we are discussing), and get an order-of-magnitude idea of what parents and taxpayers might consider to be reasonable sums. Doing this, and keeping in mind the extreme roughness of these figures, we arrive at something of the order of $500 per long-term member below the age of six, $1000 per long-term member from six to the cutoff age (sixteen), and $1500 per long-term member above the cutoff age. For a prototype school of the size projected in Chapter 13 and 14, this would mean a basic budget of slightly over $3,300,000, or an over all average of slightly over $1050 per long-term member. To this must be added extra funds for maintenance of public facilities hitherto kept up apart from the schools, but now to be part of the transition school – for example, the public library, athletic facilities, public halls, etc. The exact amounts involved are not estimable, since they vary widely from one community to the next, and they depend on which facilities any particular community maintains. There is also additional income from several of the school's special facilities – from the publishing house, restaurant, arts center, communications center, shops and crafts center – all of which contributes to the maintenance of these facilities, and which hopefully makes them self-supporting.

The expenditures are as unknown as the income. In the case of the public and special facilities referred to just above, the expenditures can be taken to be of the same order of magnitude as the appropriations and income. Similarly, private grants can be expected to generate expenditures more or less equal to the amount granted, except that a 15-30% overhead allowance in these grants does yield the school some spare excess income. Expenditures on salaries cannot be estimated, since there is no way of estimating in advance what the salary levels will be. If the average salary lies somewhere between $7000 and $8000 (for a nine month year, paid out over the entire year), expenditures for the 315-odd permanent members will range from $2,200,000 to $2,500,000; but who can tell where the average salary will lie? Comparing salary expenditures with the basic budget figure cited in the preceding paragraph, we find between \$1,100,000 and \$800,000 left over to run the school, exclusive of all income beyond the basic budget.

All that can be seen from such a general discussion is that the school seems to be fiscally feasible even by present educational-budget standards – i.e., it is clear a priori that we are dealing with an institution that does not require some monumental new economic exertion on the part of the community, but that is well within the reach of the community in the United States today.

CHAPTER 20

How the Prototype School is Launched

1. The first step in launching the prototype school is to find a community willing to sponsor the school. Some of the characteristics of such a community can be guessed. It will probably be noted for its civic-mindedness, its readiness to try new ideas, its lack of hotly partisan politics (an indicator of readiness to engage in rational discussion of issues rather than in exchange of epithets). It cannot be a poor community, nor again an exclusive one; it will probably be generally fairly well-to-do and middle class, with a good mix of all economic classes, religions, and races (indicating the presence of a high level of tolerance and readiness to mix openly). It will probably not be noted for its "excellent schools" (such a community would probably tend to be satisfied with its present educational system and not be prepared to try something entirely new) nor again for its "poor schools" (such a community is probably not yet very interested in educational questions). There are a great many towns that fit this description, and any one of them is a likely candidate to support the prototype school. Of course, some entirely different type of community may well come forward to sponsor the school, in which case all guess-work will be useless.

Once the community is located, a place for the school must be found. It would be especially fortunate if some sort of ready-made campus, or at least the beginnings of such a campus, were available. Something in the vicinity of ten or more acres is needed. Occasionally there can be found sites of former institutions (hospitals, rest homes, boarding schools) that can provide a suitable beginning. It would be desirable – and certainly appealing to the sponsoring community – to keep to a minimum the outlay for new buildings and structures. Thus, wherever existing buildings can be used or converted for use, these can represent a substantial saving. (For example, dormitories in former boarding schools have many small rooms, and can provide, at least initially, a practical private research center.) As the school grows, and the community becomes accustomed to it, more can be done in developing the physical plant.

2. Some sort of timetable is necessary for the gradual development of the school from an initially modest size to a size at least of the order of the minimum size discussed in the preceding chapters. The total time from opening until full strength is reached cannot be too long, otherwise the vigorous activity expected upon reaching a "critical mass" will never materialize. On the other hand, haste would be particularly damaging in the prototype school, since here all the forms are new, all experiences are "firsts", and every step has to be measured carefully and tried out gingerly. Perhaps something like a five-year period to get up full steam would be reasonable.

How would such a buildup work in practice? A first group of permanent members would have to be found – say, about one hundred people. Someone would have to be charged with finding the initial group, with the full expectation that during the <u>first year</u> the entire school would go over to the democratic administration described in Chapter 19. (Delay in implementing the transfer of power to the school community would be disastrous, for it would give the impression of "rigging" the whole question at the start. Everyone knows how difficult it is to undo a straitjacket imposed on a newborn organization at its inception.) Thereafter, regular buildups in stages of about fifty each year could bring the permanent sector up to full strength by the fifth year. Similarly, a first group of long-term members would be recruited, in various general age groups (with slight emphasis on the very young, as they should be accommodated as quickly as possible in order to save them the trouble of adjusting into and out of the ordinary school system within a short time). The first group could be about five hundred or so, not too numerous, certainly not at the full final permanent-to-long-term ratio of ten-to-one. The population could then grow by steady increments, a bit more slowly than the permanent staff, since more people are involved. In each succeeding year, we can expect the job of "breaking in" new members to be progressively easier, and to be aided considerably by the presence of a growing body of "old hands". Also, in each succeeding year we can expect greater participation of the public, as the public gets hold of the idea and idea gets hold of them.

Table 1 shows one possible way of building up to full strength, just for purposes of getting an idea of what is involved. The actual rate of buildup may be rather different; at any rate, after the first year, it will be determined by the community at large and the school. Table 2 gives a breakdown of Table 1.

3. A few budgetary considerations can be mentioned concerning the buildup period. Suppose we concentrate only on the basic budget described in Chapter 19. The size of this budget is found from Table 2 to be the following, in successive years: $525,000; $1,050,000; $2,100,000; $3,325,000. On the other hand, if we work with a salary range averaging $7000-$8000 for permanent members, we come up with annual salary expenditures in the following ranges, in successive years (see Table 1): $700,000-$800,000; $1,050,000-$1,200,000; $1,400,000-$1,600,000; $1,750,000-$2,000,000; $2,100,000-$2,400,000; $2,205,000-$2,520,000. Comparing the two sets of figures, we see that only in the fourth year does the budget allotted according to the normal criteria definitely exceed even the salaries, let alone allow for running the school. The cumulative salary deficit for the first three years is in the range $0-$450,000.

Thus, to get the school off the ground and into its normal routine of operation, it is likely that a total of $1,500,000-$2,000,000 will be necessary over and above standard public appropriations. To this must be added whatever capital outlay is necessary to prepare the physical plant – although such capital outlays are expected and provided for in the normal course of operation of the public school system. Some source for the extra allocation must be found – either a special local appropriation, or a grant of some sort from government and/or foundations. The sum required is not large, considering the size of the school which will ultimately be in operation.

4. The prototype school is a model for future transition-period schools, and the first year is a model for future operation of the prototype school. For this reason, special care must be exercised in selecting the first group of permanent and long-term members; in their hands lies the success or failure of the venture at this time, whatever success is ultimately assured the idea. The first group has a double responsibility: the responsibility usually resting on members of the school, and the responsibility to make a go of it now, when the time is ripe, but not overripe, so that we may still act to bring on the future rather than be acted on by a tide that has swept us by.

The first group of permanent members should therefore be homogeneous in one respect: in adherence to the underlying principles of freedom, equality, and uninhibited inquiry that govern the school. The first group of long-term members too may wisely be chosen from among those who, in their own thinking and perhaps also in their homes, have come to respect these principles and to commit their lives to them.

Table 1

1	2	3	4	5	6
Year	Permanent Members	Increase in permanent members	Long-term members	Increase in long-term members	Ratio of 4:2
1	100	---	500	---	5:1
2	150	50	1000	500	6 ⅔:1
3	200	50	1500	500	7 ¼:1
4	250	50	2000	500	8:1
5	300	50	2600	600	8 ⅔:1
6	315	15	3150	550	10:1

Table 2

Analysis of long-term members in Table 1 by rough age groups

1	2	3	4	5	6
Year	Total long-term members	Below age six	Ages 6-16 (cutoff)	Ages 16-20	Above age 20
1	500	100	250	100	50
2	1000	200	500	200	100
3	1500	300	750	300	150
4	2000	400	1000	400	200
5	2600	400	1500	400	300
6	3150	400	2000	400	350

CHAPTER 21

Urban and Country Versions of the School

1. The prototype school described in the preceding chapters has been conceived in a suburban (or middle-sized town) setting, for reasons already stated. Yet, there is no reason why similar transition-period schools, based on the same general principles, should not also be set up in large cities and in rural areas.

Much light will be shed on the urban and rural variants by the actual experience of the prototype school. Having learned to overcome all sorts of problems inherent in the initial, necessarily faulty version, society will be far better equipped to cope with the new set of problems presented by new environments.

Without the experience of the prototype school, I do not wish to attempt a detailed outline of what urban and rural schools might be. I shall limit myself to a few general comments which, by contrast to those already made, may help to highlight some of the special features of the suburban situation.

2. It is immediately obvious that the rural setting allows for much more space in the campus. How much more is desirable is another question. In the first place, there is a limit to the size of a rural school imposed solely by considerations of population density within commuting distance: it would not make sense to build a great big school for ten thousand people where only five thousand can reach the school conveniently. At least, it would not make sense unless a new dimension were added – a dormitory wing, introducing the features of a boarding school for part of the school population.

Another problem is the extent to which the campus can be sprawled out without introducing cross-campus vehicular transportation – and, with that, all the safety problems studiously avoided in the prototype school.

There is also the question of how long the long-term members will want to stay. A rural setting generally produces people who leave school at an earlier age than in urban and suburban situations. This may well change in time, but at present it certainly is the case. Reducing the percentage of older long-term members reduces in turn some of the attraction the school may have for certain potential permanent members, e.g., those who like to work with older children or young adults. This may, or may not, have a bad effect on the composition of the permanent membership. In addition, distance from urban cultural centers and regional information centers may adversely affect the school's appeal to potential permanent members.

Nor is public participation in the school as likely in the rural areas. Distances are greater, it is less convenient to get to and from the school. Rural populations generally have less of a social and cultural life, less of a desire to seek out new experiences. All this will weaken the bond between the school and community, and will tend to preserve the present distance between the two.

These are some of the problems unique to the rural setting, and conveniently avoided in the prototype school.

3. In a city, space is at a premium. The campus immediately shrinks in conception, if it is not to be prohibitive in cost. Field work, athletic facilities, parks, all are severely curtailed or entirely eliminated. Buildings rise upward, with the consequent crowding, the ever-present consciousness of other people on all sides.

Children in a city are early exposed to the shock of the modern technological environment. They are not as sheltered as suburban children; they are more "sophisticated", more "in the know", more jumpy, nervous, even neurotic. They are also more suspicious, less acquainted with freedom, since they have less freedom of action (being more constrained physically) and they are more remote from the sources of power. The city breeds suspicion of the secret workings of a "power structure", a "machine", a remote authority – suspicion by no means unfounded in fact. For these reasons, the city child has a harder time believing in real freedom, believing that there really is not someone sinister behind the scenes pulling strings. The urban school will have to make special exertions to win the confidence of children entering for the first time. Perhaps this will require more permanent members.

The city public will also be less interested in participating in the school. In the first place, there are many "distractions" in the city – a host of cultural, social, and diverting activities, all nearby, all easily accessible. Many of these activities are highly professional, and hence outstrip those of the school in quality. Public participation in the school must therefore be cultivated assiduously, and the main impetus to this participation must be an appeal to the active side of the public – to the side of each person that wants to <u>do</u> something – rather than to the passive side, that wishes to observe and be entertained. In the city, the public will come to the school more in order to put on a show than to watch one. (In the suburbs, both motives will be somewhat more balanced.)

In addition, the public in the city is generally less involved, less "civic-minded", mostly because of the city's bigness and the feeling this generates that nothing any individual does can change the situation. This passivity and apathy has to be countered, by a long patient process of convincing the public that in the school each person can find genuine self-expression – that in the school, he and his wishes and his interests really do count.

These, then, are some of the problems unique to the urban setting, and generally absent in the setting of the prototype school.

4. Nevertheless, the transition-type school is as inevitable in city and country as it is elsewhere. The model of a functioning prototype school in a suburban setting will eventually show the way for all settings, though each will have to overcome its own obstacles in its own way.

CHAPTER 22

Some Final Remarks

1. That society is in transition everyone acknowledges, even though the nature of the transition, and the nature of the initial and final states, is not always clear. I have tried to describe my understanding of what is taking place in the world, and where we are headed. On the basis of the picture I have formed, I have elaborated the consequences for education (in the broadest sense of the term), and have presented a sketch of a prototype school suitable to the transition period we are in.

This prototype school can be set up now in one of a large number of suburban or middle-sized communities in the United States. It should probably also be set up in other communities, and in other countries. I believe that within a fairly short time, of the order of one generation, schools of this type will be the rule everywhere.

2. It is perhaps of some interest to note that many of the specific suggestions I have made for the school have been made by other people writing and talking about education today. To the best of my knowledge, none of the people making suggestions have referred them to the theoretical framework outlined in this book, or to a similar framework.

This should not be surprising. It bears out my feeling that these ideas for education are "in the air" today, and that they are in the air because the natural forces operating in history and in society have put them there. Indeed, if the specific suggestions for new schools were put forth only by the adherents of a particular theory, these suggestions would be highly suspect: being attached to a particular world-view (shared only by a select group), they could scarcely be thought to arise organically from the present nature of things; instead, they would appear to be imposed upon the present situation by a particularist reading of the data. What lends weight to the suggestions presented here is precisely their appearance in all sorts of books, articles, and discussions, in a wide variety of theoretical settings – all of which tends to show that the suggestions themselves are appropriate and organic to the situation, as the situation is viewed from a variety of vantage points.

For this reason, the transition school (as it develops and spreads) will be seen not to be the product of a particular ideology, or a particular society, or a particular educational theory. Rather, the transition school will show itself to be a product of the state of human affairs in the transition period, and as such will be amenable to any ideology, and society, any theory that seeks to give coherence and internal consistency to the phenomena of the present day.

APPENDIX 3

First draft of a prospectus announcing the school
(about February 1967); and final, published draft of
the prospectus (June 1967)

__________ __________ School bases its program on the assumptions that people learn best the things they are most interested in; that they do best the things they learn best; and that society profits most from those citizens who are doing the things they can do best.

Since all people have much they want to learn, and much they are able to teach, __________ __________ School is open to all people of all ages in the community, as students and as teachers. The school is an integral part of the community, taking from the public what the publish wishes to give it, and giving to the public what the public wishes to take from it.

I. THE ORGANIZATION OF THE SCHOOL

<u>The Assembly of Public Members</u>

The school is governed by an Assembly of Public Members. The Public Members are all the parents of the students in the school, all the staff, and other interested citizens of the community, chosen annually by the Assembly. There is no limit to the number of Public Members the school may or wishes to have. The Assembly meets several times a year, and in the interim between meetings governs via duly constituted elected committees. The Moderator of the Assembly for years 1967-1970 is __________.

All fiscal matters are determined by the Assembly. Thus, the Public Members as a group are responsible for setting the tuition fees and all other fees; for specifying salary scales; for appropriating the operating budget; and for determining capital outlays. In short, the people paying for the operation of the school are the ones who determine the school's expenditure of funds.

The Permanent Members

Among the Public Members are the paid staff, who constitute the Permanent Members of the school. They are responsible for the day-to-day functioning of the school in all its details, and for the continuity in the school's operations from year to year.

The Permanent Members are a self-perpetuating and self-regulating group, subject to the will of the Assembly in all fiscal matters, but subject only to the By-Laws of the school in all other matters.

The Student Body

___________ __________ School is coeducational, spanning ages 4-18. The tuition paying students are those who are officially enrolled in the school, for the purpose of obtaining a diploma or certificate of graduation. Insofar as the students are subject to the laws of the Commonwealth of Massachusetts, these laws are properly executed, under the authority of the Permanent Members.

The student body and Permanent Members together form a School Meeting, that convenes weekly and operates democratically. The School Meeting advises in all matters pertaining to the operations of the school, and is responsible for the enforcement of school regulations. It also legislates regulations in those areas specified by the By-Laws.

The ratio of students to Permanent Members is about ten to one.

Visitors

Visitors are always welcome to the school, and free to observe and join in school activities. This freedom is subject only to such restrictions as apply to Public Members and students, except in a few extraordinary situations specified in the By-Laws.

_________ _________ School encourages the public to become part of it, to feel at home on its premises. Although not a public school, it is a school run by and for the people of the community.

II. THE SCHOOL PROGRAM

<u>Formal Studies</u>

A wide variety of lectures, courses, seminars, study groups, and organized tours are presented at all times. Announcements of ongoing and future events are prepared every month, with supplements when needed.

The selection of formal offerings is governed solely by the interests of those who are actually teaching. Any Public Member, student, or visitor may teach whatever he wishes, subject only to administrative regulations governing the use of rooms and materials.

Just as anyone is free to teach as he pleases, so too anyone is free to attend these announced programs as he pleases. There are absolutely no required courses in the school. No attendance is taken, no tests administered, no grades or verbal reports written. However, teachers are obligated to respond to their pupils' requests for assistance in mastering the material under study.

Private Tutoring

Students are free to pursue their own interests, whatever these may be. To the extent that these interests are not satisfied by any ongoing formal course of study, the Permanent Members will provide individual instruction and make every effort to advance each student as far and as rapidly as he desires.

Where possible, Public Members and visitors will also offer individual assistance to students, and will receive individual guidance from Permanent Members.

For students wishing to transfer to other schools, or to prepare for special examinations, preparation will be provided by the school.

Calendar

The school operates throughout the year, and is open five days a week (and on weekends for special events). There are two regular semesters and a summer session. All the standard holidays are observed.

III. THE PERMANENT MEMBERS

Stephen Cooper.

Dennis Flynn.

Daniel Greenberg.

Hanna Greenberg (Mrs. Daniel). Studied at The Hebrew University of Jerusalem, Hunter College of New York (B.A., Biology), Columbia University (Ph.D., Biochemistry). Postdoctoral Research Fellow at Albert Einstein College of Medicine and Massachusetts Institute of Technology.

Margaret (Mrs. Edward) Parra.

Priscilla (Mrs. Richard) Parris.

Sandy Rabison.

IV. TUITION AND FEES

The regular tuition rates per semester for students free to attend a full day (about 8:30 – 5:30) are as follows: Ages 4-6 $500; Ages 6-12, $550; Ages 12-18, $650. For the summer session, the rates are, respectively, $350, $400, and $450.

Arrangements for part-time attendance, as well as fees for meals, snacks, transportation, and special instruction (e.g. regular private music lessons), are made on an individual basis. There is no special charge for books, materials, or ordinary activities and excursions.

Public Members and visitors making use of expendable materials will be asked to cover the direct cost of the materials used.

Especially welcome are young visitors of school age, to participate in the __________ __________ School program after public school hours, during the regular school year. The fees per semester are $150 for ages 6-12, $200 for ages 12-18. These visitors are treated in every way on an equal basis with the school's regular students.

V. ADDITIONAL INFORMATION

The full By-Laws are available to anyone on request. Also available are a full list of the Public Members, together with officers and committee members of the Assembly; complete biographies of all Permanent Members and visiting teachers; and a list of the student body.

Anyone wishing to receive regularly the announcements of the school program and of all special events may place himself on the mailing list by contacting the school office. Copies of school publications circulated to Public Members may be obtained at a nominal cost; and up-to-date catalogue is available on request.

The school welcomes all inquires and suggestions on any aspect of its operation. Feel free to come, to see, and to join.

Announcing

a new school

in the

Framingham-Sudbury area

THE PRINCIPLES OF THE SCHOOL

People are naturally curious; if they are free to follow their curiosity, continued interest and ultimate satisfaction will follow. People become most deeply interested, work hardest, and concentrate most intensely in those areas where their initial involvement has been fostered and given a chance to ripen into mature investigation.

The American economy today is strong and diverse enough to absorb any person devoted to his work, whatever it may be, and committed to its satisfactory execution. The task of the school is therefore not to produce people who will fit in, but to fit out people who will be able to produce something – with skill, enthusiasm, and pleasure, as a natural outgrowth of their initial curiosity.

The interests of people free to follow their curiosity will certainly range over a broad spectrum of areas. In order to accommodate these interests, the school program must be wide-ranging. One way the school can span the variety present in the world today is by enlisting the resources of the entire community, by removing all artificial barriers between the school and its environment – in other words, by making the school one with its community, allowing free interchange between the parents, the students, and the staff.

The school will therefore be open to all people of all ages in the community, as students and as teachers. In this way, the school can benefit from the community's rich experience and practical wisdom, and the community can benefit from the program offered by the school. The school will be an integral part of the community, taking from the public what the public wishes to give it, and giving to the public what the public wishes to take from it.

These, then, are the assumptions underlying the school and its program: that people learn best the things they are most curious about; that they do best the things they have learned best; and that society profits most from those people who are doing the things they can do best.

THE ORGANIZATION OF THE SCHOOL

The school is organized in a way intended to remove the barriers between the school and the community as well as those that tend to separate the various parts of the school itself. All people connected with the school have free access to the school, to the program, and to each other, and all share responsibility for the school's operation.

The Assembly of Public Members

All fiscal matters are determined by an assembly of public members, which consists of the parents of the students in the school, the staff, and other interested citizens of the community who are elected annually. Thus, the people sending their children to the school are among those who determine the school's expenditure of funds. The assembly is responsible, for example, for setting the tuition and other fees, for specifying pay scales, for appropriating the operating budget, and for determining capital outlays.

The assembly meets several times a year, and in the interim between meetings it governs through elected committees.

The Permanent Members

The permanent members (the paid staff) of the school are responsible for its day to day functioning as well as for continuity in the school's operation from year to year. New permanent members are chosen by those currently working in the school.

The permanent members are a self-regulating group, subject to the decisions of the assembly in all fiscal matters, but subject only to the by-laws of the school in all other matters.

The permanent members are not divided into departments, ranks, or academic as opposed to non-academic categories, and are not bound to a particular set of activities or a particular area of interest.

The Student Body

The school is coeducational, with students ranging from the ages of four to eighteen years.

Every week the student body and permanent members meet together to discuss all matters related to the internal operation of the school. The school meeting is responsible for enforcing school regulations, and for legislating regulations in those areas specified by the by-laws – for example, regulations protecting each student and member from interference or distraction during work. The school's affairs are thus the active concern of all the people who are regular participants in its programs.

The ratio of students to permanent members is maintained at about ten to one.

Visitors

Visitors are always welcome at the school, to observe, teach, and join in school activities. This freedom is subject to no restrictions other than those that apply to public members and students, except in a few extraordinary situations specified in the by-laws.

The school encourages the public to become a part of it and to feel at home on its premises. Although not a "public" school, it is a school run by and for the people of the community.

THE PROGRAM OF THE SCHOOL

Formal Studies

Any public member, student, or visitor may teach whatever material he wishes, subject only to school regulations governing the use of rooms and materials. The range of formal offerings thus spans the interests of those who have come to teach. This insures a wide variety of lectures, courses, seminars, study groups, and organized field trips, geared to a variety of age levels and led by people who are enthusiastic about what they are doing. Announcements of new and current activities are prepared periodically at short intervals.

During its first year of operation, the permanent and visiting faculty of the school expect to offer formal instruction in areas including the following: English (Reading and Writing, Composition, Literature, Criticism, Drama), History (Ancient, Medieval, and Modern; American; History of Religion, of Art, of Science, and of Philosophy), Arts (Painting, Ceramics, Sculpture, Music, Performing Arts, Design), Social Science (Government, Sociology, Economics, Anthropology, Psychology), Mathematics (Elementary through Calculus), Natural Science (Botany, Zoology, Ecology, Human Physiology, Health Education, Biochemistry), Exact Science (Chemistry, Physics, Geology, Astronomy), Language (French, Italian, Spanish, German, Russian, Hebrew, Latin, Greek), Education, Law, Philosophy, Religion (the basic tenets of the major world religions), and Physical Education.

For those interested in professional or technical fields, a wide variety of apprenticeship programs are available, in addition to demonstrations and lectures. Opportunities are provided for part-time work in local offices, shops, farms, factories, and laboratories. In addition, programs are arranged on the school premises for training in carpentry, cooking, sewing, and other manual and domestic arts.

There will also be recreational facilities in and near the school for the full range of outdoor activities, including hiking, camping, scout activities, team sports, supervised swimming, ice skating, and free play.

Just as anyone is free to teach according to his interests, so too anyone is free to attend these offerings according to his interests. (Where attendance must be limited, regular students are given priority). The natural curiosity of students, members, and visitors is all that forces them toward the school's activities. All fields – speculative, theoretical, experimental, technical – are considered equally valid as areas of exploration; no field is considered absolutely essential for every student, or for any particular student. There are no required courses in the school. No tests are administered, no grades assigned, no evaluations written. Nevertheless, attendance at the school is compulsory for all students over the age of seven years, in compliance with the laws of the Commonwealth of Massachusetts.

The students are not divided into grade levels, age groups, or classes, but are free to mix as they please and to form their own groups in pursuit of their particular interests. In this way, each student may have, at different times, the advantaged of working alone, with friends of the same age, or with people of different ages.

Private Tutoring

Students are free to pursue their own interests, whatever these may be. To the extent that these interests are not satisfied by any formal course of study, the permanent members make every effort to advance each student as far and as rapidly as he desires, either by providing individual instruction or by seeking outside assistance.

Where possible, public members and visitors also offer individual assistance to students and receive individual guidance from permanent members.

Arrangements are made to give special assistance to students wishing to transfer to other schools or to prepare for special examinations.

Diplomas

The permanent members are responsible for awarding certificates and diplomas to students. A student receives an elementary school, junior high school, or high school diploma, respectively, when, in the opinion of the permanent members, he has achieved a level of competence comparable to the level achieved by graduates in the public schools.

The school maintains close contact with the Admissions Offices of various colleges for the purposes of acquainting them with the school's program and staff.

Calendar

The school operates throughout the year and is open five days a week (and on weekends for special events). There are two regular semesters and a summer session. All the standard holidays are observed, and vacations coincide with those of the public schools.

The proposed opening date of the school is July 1, 1968.

THE PERMANENT MEMBERS OF THE SCHOOL

David Chanoff.
Studied at Johns Hopkins (B.A., English) and Brandeis University (M.A., English). Teaches English at Brandeis University.

Ina Cooper.
Studied at Barnard College (B.A., Physics). Worked with preschoolers, and as a staff member of the Science Curriculum Improvement Study.

Stephen Cooper.
Studied at Columbia College (B.A., Mathematics) and Princeton University (History of Science). Taught in the Peace Corps, in Guinea.

Dennis Flynn.
Studied at Columbia University (B.A., M.A., English). Taught English at the City College of the City University of New York.

Daniel Greenberg.
Studied at Columbia College, The Hebrew University of Jerusalem, Columbia University (M.A., Ph.D., Physics). Taught Physics and History of Science at Barnard College and Columbia University.

Hanna (Mrs. Daniel) Greenberg.
   Studied at The Hebrew University of Jerusalem, Hunter College (B.A., Biology), Columbia University (Ph.D., Biochemistry). Postdoctoral Research Fellow at Albert Einstein College of Medicine and Massachusetts Institute of Technology.

Margaret (Mrs. Edward) Parra.
   High school graduate. Worked with Girl Scouts, and day care of children, especially pre-schoolers. Taught cooking and baking.

Priscilla (Mrs. Richard) Parris.
   High school graduate. Worked with Cub Scouts and day care of pre-schoolers. Wide experience in office administration.

Sandy Rabison.
   Studied at Columbia College (B.A., Government). Taught in the Morningside Gardens Nursery School.

TUITION AND FEES

The assembly sets tuition and other fees annually to provide the funds necessary for the school's operation. The school is in the process of seeking financial support from private and public sources to help defray expenses and make it possible for a broad range of students to attend.

Arrangements for part-time attendance, as well as fees for meals, transportation, and special instruction (e.g., regular private music lessons), will be made on an individual basis. There will be no special charges for books, materials, or ordinary activities and field trips.

Public members and visitors making use of expendable materials will be asked to cover the direct cost of the materials used.

Young visitors of school age are especially welcome to participate in the school program after public school hours, during the regular school year. These visitors are treated on an equal basis with the school's regular students.

ADDITIONAL INFORMATION

The by-laws will be available to anyone on request. Also to be made available are a list of the public members, together with officers and committee members of the assembly; biographies of all permanent members; a list of visiting teachers; and a list of the student body.

Anyone wishing to receive the announcements of the school program and of all special events may place himself on the mailing list by so informing the school office.

The school welcomes all inquires and suggestions on any aspect of its operation. Write to: Priscilla Parris, 29 Charles Street, Natick, Massachusetts 01760.

APPENDIX 4

The original by-laws of the school corporation
(February 1968)

BY-LAWS
THE SUDBURY VALLEY SCHOOL, INC.

ARTICLE I

Name

The name of the corporation shall be THE SUDBURY VAL-
LEY SCHOOL, INC., and it shall be located on Winch Street, Framingham, Middlesex County, Massachusetts, or at such other convenient
place as the members shall from time to time determine.

ARTICLE II

Purposes

The purpose for which this corporation is formed is to establish
and maintain a school for the education of members of the community that is founded upon the principle that learning is best fostered by
self-motivation, self-regulation and self-criticism; provides a curriculum,
determined by the interests of students and teachers, in which equal status shall be given to all pursuits; encourages members of the community
to participate in teaching, learning and other school activities so that
the school may become an integral part of the community; allows the
opportunities and responsibilities of governing the school to be shared
among students, parents, teachers, other employees, and representatives
of the community; and maintains a flexible structure which, while being
free to adhere to valid traditional forms, will be also free to create new
ones.

The corporation shall be empowered to hold, purchase, mortgage and convey real and personal property and to do any and all things
which may be incidental to the foregoing purposes; provided that the
corporation shall not carry on propaganda or otherwise attempt to influence legislation, nor shall it participate in or intervene in (including the
publication or distribution of statements) any political campaign on be-

half of any candidate for public office; and provided further that no part of the net earnings of the corporation shall inure or be payable to or for the benefit of any private member or individual; and provided further that upon dissolution of the corporation its assets shall be distributed to organizations selected by the members which have similar purposes and are exempt from taxation under Section 501 (c) (3) of the Internal Revenue Code of 1954 (or the corresponding provision of any future United States Internal Revenue Law).

ARTICLE III

Membership

The membership of the corporation shall be composed of the following twenty-one years of age or over:
   a)   The parents and each guardian of every full-time student who has attended the school for three months;
   b)   The parents and each guardian of every half-time student below the age of six years who has attended the school for three months;
   c)   Teachers and other employees of the school;
   d)   Public members interested in the school, upon their election as hereinafter provided;
   e)   Trustees upon their election to the office of Trustees if not then a member.

There shall be no limit to the number of members the corporation may have, and the membership shall be known collectively as the School Assembly. The public members of the corporation shall be elected at the fall meeting or at the spring meeting or at any special meeting of the School Assembly and shall be members until the final adjournment of the next following annual spring meeting.

Any member of the corporation shall cease to be a member under the following conditions;
   a)   If membership is as a parent or guardian, upon withdrawal of his child from the school;

b) If membership is as a staff member, upon termination of employment; and

c) If membership is as a public member, upon receipt by the school of his written resignation or final adjournment of the annual spring meeting next following the meeting of their election to membership, except as to the membership of Trustees as hereinafter provided.

ARTICLE IV

Meetings of School Assembly

The members of the corporation shall meet as the School Assembly in the spring and in the fall of each year. These meetings shall be called by the President, and notice thereof stating the place, date and hour of such meeting shall be delivered or mailed to each member by the Secretary at least ten days before such meeting. Unless an alternate date shall be designated by the President, the annual spring meeting shall be held at 8 P.M. on the first Monday of May of each year.

A special meeting of the School Assembly shall be called by the Secretary or, in the case of his death, absence, incapacity or refusal, by any other officer upon written application of a majority of the members of the corporation. A special meeting of the School Assembly may also be called at any time by the President or by majority of the Trustees acting by vote or by written instrument signed by them. Such call shall state the time, place and purposes of the meeting.

Written notice of any special meeting of the School Assembly setting forth the time, place and purposes of such a meeting shall be delivered or mailed to each member of the corporation by the Secretary or, in case of his death, absence, incapacity or refusal, by any other officer of the corporation at least ten days before such meeting.

At any meeting of the School Assembly, a quorum for the election of any Trustee or officer or for the consideration of any question shall consist of ten members of the corporation. When a quorum is present at any meeting, a majority of the votes properly cast for any office or upon any question shall elect to such office or decide such question; except that amendments to the by-laws shall be adopted only by a vote of two-thirds of the votes properly cast.

Each member of the corporation present at a meeting shall have one vote.

ARTICLE V

Powers of the School Assembly

Among the powers of the School Assembly shall be the following:
- a) The determination of policy in educational and fiscal matters;
- b) The determination of tuition, fees and other charges;
- c) The determination of the annual budget of expenditures to be made by the corporation;
- d) The hiring of teachers and other employees and the determination of salary and wage scales;
- e) The awarding of diplomas, certificates and degrees and the determination of the standards related thereto.

The members of the corporation may from time to time elect from their own number such committees as they shall deem necessary or convenient for carrying out their responsibilities; and they may delegate to such committees some or all of their powers, with the exception of those which by law may not be delegated.

ARTICLE VI

Trustees

The corporation shall have a Board of Trustees consisting of not less than seven nor more than twenty-five Trustees, the number to be determined from time to time by the members at any meeting of the School Assembly. The Trustees shall be elected at the annual spring meeting of the corporation to serve for a period of one year or until their successors shall qualify, and in the event of an increase by determination of the members at a special meeting in the number of Trustees, additional Trustees may be elected at such meeting to serve until the next annual spring meeting and until their successors qualify. No Trustee need be a member of the corporation at the time of his election but, if not otherwise a member, shall automatically become a public member upon his election to the office of Trustee and shall retain such membership until his resignation from the office of Trustee or the election and qualification of his successor.

Any vacancy on the Board due to death, incapacity, resignation, removal, refusal to serve or otherwise of a Trustee shall be filled by majority vote of the Board for the unexpired term to which such vacancy relates.

The business of the corporation shall be managed by the Board of Trustees which shall exercise all the powers of the corporation except as otherwise required by law, by the Articles of Organization or by these By-Laws.

Regular meetings of the Trustees may be held at such places and at such times as may be fixed from time to time by the Trustees. Special meetings of the Trustees may be called by two or more Trustees and shall be held at the time and place specified in the call.

Reasonable notice of each special meeting of the Trustees shall be given to each Trustee by the Secretary of the Board or by one of the Trustees calling the meeting. Notice to a Trustee shall in any case be sufficient if mailed at least ninety-six hours before the meeting addressed to the Trustee at his usual or last known business or residence address or if given to him at least forty-eight hours before the meeting in person or by telephone or by handing him a written notice. Notice of a meeting need not be given to any Trustee if a written waiver of notice executed by him before or after the meeting is filed with the records of the meeting or to any Trustee who attends the meeting without protesting prior thereto or at its commencement the lack of notice to him. A notice or a waiver of notice need not specify the purposes of the meeting.

At any meeting of the Trustees a quorum for any election or for the consideration of any question shall consist of five Trustees. When a quorum is present at any meeting the votes of a majority of the Trustees present shall be requisite and sufficient for election to any office and shall decide any questions brought before such meeting, except in the case where a larger vote is required by law or by these By-Laws.

The Trustees may elect from their own number an executive committee or other committees and may by like vote delegate to any such committee some or all of their powers except those which by law may not be delegated.

ARTICLE VII

Officers

The officers of the corporation shall be a President, a Secretary and a Treasurer, each of whom shall be a member of the corporation at the time of his election. Each officer shall be elected at the annual spring meeting of the corporation and shall serve until the next annual spring meeting or until his successor shall qualify. All vacancies in any office shall be filled until the next annual spring meeting by the Board of Trustees.

The Board of Trustees may from time to time provide for or appoint such officers or agents or such committees as they shall determine and fix the duties, powers and terms of service of such agents, officers or committees.

ARTICLE VIII

Duties of Officers

The President shall exercise and maintain general supervision and control over the affairs of the corporation subject to the direction and approval of the Board of Trustees and of the members.

The Secretary shall be the custodian of all records of the corporation not placed in the custody of the Treasurer. He shall record all proceedings of the School Assembly and of the Board of Trustees in separate books to be kept therefore. In the absence of the Secretary from any meeting of the members of the corporation or the Trustees a temporary secretary shall be chosen who shall record the proceedings thereof in the aforesaid book.

The Treasurer shall receive and have custody of the funds of the corporation and shall keep regular books of account. He shall deposit all funds in banks to be designated by the Board of Trustees to the credit of and in the name of the corporation. He shall sign or countersign such instruments as require his signature and give bond for the faithful performance of his duties in such sum and with such sureties as may be required by the Board of Trustees.

The President with the approval of the Board of Trustees shall appoint such committees as shall be deemed necessary or convenient from time to time for the purposes of the corporation.

ARTICLE IX

Resignations

Any Trustee or officer may resign at any time by delivering his resignation in writing to the President or to the Secretary or to a meeting of the Trustees. Such resignation shall take effect at such time as is specified therein, or if no such time is so specified, then upon delivery thereof to the President or the Secretary or to a meeting of the Trustees.

ARTICLE X

The Staff

The Staff shall consist of all employees of the corporation including teachers and shall be chosen by the members of the corporation meeting as the School Assembly. Members of the Staff shall become members of the corporation immediately upon election to the Staff.

Election to the Staff shall be for a term of one year unless sooner terminated by resignation or action of the Board of Trustees. There shall be no tenure for Staff members. Staff members may be removed by vote of the Board of Trustees after such investigation and hearing as the Trustees shall deem necessary or appropriate.

The Staff may from time to time appoint such committees of its members as it shall deem necessary or convenient for the carrying out of its responsibilities.

ARTICLE XI

Amendments

These By-Laws may be amended by a vote of two-thirds of the members of the corporation present and voting at any regular or special meeting of the corporation, provided the notice of such meeting contains a statement of the substance of the proposed amendment.

APPENDIX 5

Draft memoranda on the school's
finances and staff salaries

Some notes on the financial affairs of the school

Prepared by Daniel Greenberg

There are several aspects to the over-all financial picture of The Sudbury Valley School. Many of these were only matters of conjecture when the school was launched, and have now become more firmly established as the result of our experience. Others remain conjectural and will have to await the test of future developments.

In this memoir I am simply trying to outline briefly, with attention only to highlights, the main features of the school's finances as I see them.

1. Perhaps it would be easiest to limit ourselves to consideration of the present physical plant of the school, as it exists today, with no extensive remodeling or additional building. The main building, which is the only all-weather building and the only building approved for general use by students, can probably accommodate the 170 students the authorities will permit us to have. For this full population we will not need more than 12 full time staff members. (It may be worth noting that there is no doubt that the ratio of staff to students will drop steadily as the school expands further).

2. The minimal amount of money required to run the school for a year, <u>exclusive</u> of staff salaries and of mortgage payments, but including everything else, is roughly $23,000. This consists of $5,000 in outlays on curricular materials, and some $18,000 in outlays for fixed expenses that do not vary too greatly from year to year for the main building. It should be stressed that these amounts are minimum requirements and that they certainly cannot be cut appreciably if the school is to function at all.

3. First mortgage payments on the present buildings and grounds come to about $5,000 per year. These are payable to The Framingham Trust Co., which has given a first

mortgage in the principal amount of $56,000 at 7-1/2% annual interest.

4.   When the school is operating at full capacity for the present plant, we should certainly expect to be in a financial position to pay reasonable salaries to its staff. I would consider an <u>average</u> salary, for ten months' service, of $9,000 (including all benefits) to be the least that we would expect to pay. This would mean a total of $108,000 for salaries. Note that the smaller the student body, the greater the relative burden of salaries, because it is impossible simply to scale down the number of staff at a 14-1 student-staff ratio (a school of fifty students cannot run with four full time staff).

5.   The school also has a second mortgage, which I hold, which deserves careful explanation.

In order to get the school going, I agreed to advance the seeding money that would enable us to start. This consisted of some $24,000 as cash down-payment for the campus, and another $16,000 as starting capital. I agreed to lend the entire amount for the first year at 6%, with no provision for repayment during that year, with the understanding that I would in the spring of the first year enter into an agreement with the school corporation for the return of this loan (which will by spring amount to some $43,000 in principal and accrued interest). The loan is secured by a second mortgage, which in fact is clearly not adequate collateral for much more than half of the loaned amount.

I do not think it has to be stressed that the entire philosophy of the school, based as it is on general co-responsibility of all members of the school community for the community's proper functioning, does not harmonize with a situation in which one person has an exceptional financial stake and risk in the school. So long as considerable sums of my money are tied up in the school, I cannot help taking a stance towards the school's affairs that is incompatible with my desire to have a stake and an interest in no way different from that of other members of the staff and the School Assembly. Furthermore, the idea of co-responsibility and participatory democracy is itself in conflict with a financial situation more reminiscent in every respect of that prevailing in proprietary schools.

It is therefore necessary that, now that the first year is drawing to a close, regular arrangements be made by the school to repay this loan. The attached Term Sheet outlines the key features of a draft proposal of an agreement between the school and me that has been prepared for discussion and action by the School Assembly at its Spring meeting. The draft has been drawn up after consultations involving the school's counsel, my counsel, and myself, and has been designed to achieve the following: (1) repayment of the loan over approximately five years, assuming (as I do) that the school will prosper, that our relations will be stable, and that the school will expand at a steady pace, beginning with eighty or more students next year and growing to and beyond full capacity of the present plant; (2) fair safeguards for my funds in the event of future instabilities, of the kind that threatened the existence of the school and my relation to it this past fall; (3) fair safeguard of the school's interests.

According to this proposed agreement, then, the average rate of repayment should be about $10,000 per year.

6. All told, the present school at full capacity of some 170 students and 12 staff would have minimum annual expenditures of $146,000, reflecting a tuition rate of about $860 per student.

On the other hand, consider the situation we might anticipate next year, with, say, eighty students. Fixed expenses <u>including</u> first and second mortgage payments come to some $38,000. We now have eleven staff members. If all eleven choose to return, and if the School Assembly wishes to have them, and even if the staff agrees to work at an <u>average</u> salary of $5,000 for next year, about half-way between the zero salary of this year and the full salary referred to earlier, we would still have some $55,000 of expenses for salaries, or a total of some $93,000 in expenses, reflecting a tuition rate of about $1160 per student. If we repeat the calculation for 90 students, we find a tuition rate of about $1035 per student; for 100 students, a rate of about $930 per student.

7.   Taking all this into consideration, it would seem to me to be most reasonable to raise the tuition to $930 per student next year for full time students ($475 per student for half-time students under six years of age), and to expect this new rate to reflect the following features: (1) the ability of the school to retire its debts in a fair and regular manner; (2) the ability of the school to make reasonably speedy progress towards the desired goal of adequate salaries for staff; and (3) the ability of the school to have sufficient funds to meet its required minimum non-salary expenses, and to exceed the bare minimum as the school grows and finds greater need to spend in certain areas.

It might be worth noting that a tuition rate of $930 per year per student would still be equal to, or below, the current rate of expenditure per pupil in the public schools of the towns in this area, when payments for the physical facilities are included.

8.   As a final note, it may be mentioned that I have said nothing about income from summer tuition, and from other sources, especially from voluntary contributions and grants. I do not believe any of these sources materially affect the situation. Summer tuition rarely exceeds summer expenses, and this, along with other minor sources of funds, can help provide the funds for various activities that are above the minima herein considered – for example, funds to print a catalogue, which we will not be able to do this year (even though we distributed some 5,000 catalogues last year, in 1968). As for major contributions and grants, these are usually earmarked for special goals, and hence cannot serve to improve the general financial picture.

TERM SHEET

The following terms are proposed for a resetting of the financial arrangements between The Sudbury Valley School, Inc., and Mrs. and Mrs. Daniel Greenberg:

1.   <u>Extension of the Debt to the Greenbergs</u>. The existing indebtedness of The Sudbury Valley School to the Greenbergs, which will amount to a total of $42,534.71 as of May 6, 1969, will be extended and rewritten in the manner described below. A new note and second mortgage will be executed as will a Credit Agreement.

2.   <u>Amortization</u>. Payments will be made semi-annually on March 15 and September 15 of each year, commencing September 15, 1968. The amount of each payment will be equal to 13.5% of the total tuition payments received by The Sudbury Valley School since the date of the last payment. However, each such payment shall be not less than an amount equal to accrued interest on the debt to the Greenbergs as of the date thereof, and shall be not more than such accrued interest plus $4,500.00. All payments will be applied first against accrued interest, and second to reduction of principal. It is estimated that this will result in payment of the debt owing the Greenbergs over a period of approximately five years, assuming that The Sudbury Valley School's operations are successful.

3.   <u>Tuition</u>. Paragraph 2 is based on the assumption that tuition will be increased to an annual rate of $930.00, and that it will not be reduced without the prior written consent of the Greenbergs so long as the indebtedness to them has not been repaid in full. If tuition is to be set at less than $930.00, a corresponding adjustment in paragraph 2 is to be effected (specifically, the 13.5% figure is to be adjusted).

4.   <u>Interest</u>. Interest will be increased from 6% to 7-1/2% per annum, the latter figure being the rate of interest payable on the existing first mortgage held by The Framingham Trust Co.

5.   <u>Prepayment</u>. The Sudbury Valley School may prepay the debt to the Greenbergs at the principal amount thereof plus accrued interest at any time.

6.   <u>Acceleration</u>. The entire debt will become immediately due and payable upon involuntary termination of the Greenbergs' employment by The Sudbury Valley School. Should the Greenbergs terminate their employment voluntarily, the entire debt will become due and payable upon the later of (i) the following June 30 or (ii) the sixtieth day following such termination of employment.

7.   <u>Documentation, etc.</u> A Credit Agreement Note, and Mortgage will be prepared by counsel, and may contain other terms and provisions of a customary nature in addition to those outlined above. It is contemplated that the final form of Credit Agreement will be submitted to the trustees and School Assembly of The Sudbury Valley School for their approval.

8.   <u>First Mortgage</u>. The Sudbury Valley School will assume the existing first mortgage on the school property held by The Framingham Trust Co., and will attempt to release Mr. and Mrs. Greenberg from liability thereon.

Memorandum on Staff Salaries for 1969-1970

1.   Based on the economic conditions prevailing at this time, we feel that a full-time staff member at The Sudbury Valley School should receive at the very least an average salary of $9000 (including all benefits) for service during the regular academic year (that is, for ten months' service out of the calendar year). By "average salary" we mean the figure that represents the average of all salaries actually paid, which salaries may differ from one another according to seniority or other criteria mutually agreed upon when detailed terms of employment are concluded.

2.   Our experience at the school so far leads us to conclude that at the main building's full capacity of 170 students we would probably need a full-time staff of twelve persons. This reflects a 14-1 student-staff ratio, which is doubtless far lower than the ratio that will prevail when the school expands further.

3.   It is probably reasonable to assume that next year we will have about one hundred paying students, although there is no way at all to estimate the number in advance. This means that the school would require no fewer than seven full-time staff members, if we use the same 14-1 ratio and extrapolate from this year's experience. In our opinion, it is certainly not possible to operate the school during the year for any number of students, however small, with fewer than seven staff members. At an average salary of $9,000, it is clear that the school's budget for next year must be at least $63,000.

4.   The staff now consists of eleven people, who have worked together effectively and with unity of purpose during this year at no salary. When the time comes this spring to present to the School Assembly candidates for next year's staff, all or most of us may wish to return and continue to work together, even if this means having more than the minimum number of staff members necessary for the school's functioning next year. We have agreed that if the number of us who seek

to return next year and who are elected to greater than that required by the 14-1 student-staff ratio (and greater than seven), we shall somehow come to terms among ourselves to divide equitably the salary figure budgeted by the corporation on the basis of a 14-1 ratio and paragraph 3.

The Staff

Some Notes on The Sudbury Valley School's Financial Future and
Tuition Rates for 1969-1970

1.   The budget of the Sudbury Valley School is prepared in
a somewhat different way from most corporate budgets. Consider the
typical procedure for drawing up a budget. First, an estimate of the
required expenses for the year is prepared. These expenses will include,
among others, all sorts of fixed expenses, outlays for new projects,
outlays for materials, salary expenses, and payments to creditors. Second,
an estimate of the desired surplus, or profit, as the case may be, is
prepared. Third, the income required is estimated, based directly on the
expenses to be covered and the surplus desired. Fourth, the product's
cost to the consumer is set (whether the product be a material object or
services or both), based on estimates of the amount of product that will
be sold, in order to produce the desired income.

There is some flexibility in the procedure, and periodic
readjustments are made before the budget is finally adopted and even
during the budget year. For example, the amount of product sold may
vary considerably from the estimate, causing an increase or decrease in
income, requiring in turn an increase or a decrease in expenditures; or
salaries may be negotiated at a different level than the one projected,
requiring adjustments elsewhere in the budget; and so forth.

But the main feature to note is the close linkage between income
and expenditures: if either of the two varies, the other must vary with
it. Since usually there is little flexibility in the various components of
the structure (unit prices can not generally be changed at will, nor can
salaries, nor credit obligations), there is usually little room for maneuver.

2.   Now, the difference between the usual procedure and the
school's procedure for drawing up a budget lies not in the need for
balanced books (we too must have income equal outlay), but rather in
the degree of flexibility of the various components. The reason for this
flexibility lies at the hart of The Sudbury Valley School's philosophy:
it is, simply, that the first consideration in making up any part of the
budget is fairness. Since fairness is a complex, many-faceted ethical

concept, its application in particular everyday affairs is, and can be expected to be, complex and many-faceted.

3.   Let us illustrate this in some detail for this year's budget, before going on to discuss the future.

As far as income was concerned, a decision had to be reached on the tuition that parents would have to pay to send their children to the school. What is a fair tuition? At the time we in effect set the tuition (November 1967 – though the rate was formally set at the May 6, 1968 meeting of the School Assembly) we felt that some sort of average of the per-pupil expenditure in the public schools of this area would be a reasonable gauge of fairness. This was how the $700 tuition rate was set – based on the 1966-1967 figures. We did not at the time know, nor do we now know, whether this is really a good basis for a fair tuition rate; the fact is that, try as we may, we have not been able to come up with anything better.

When it came to expenses, we had several categories: down-payment for the campus, first mortgage payments (interest plus principal) for the campus, fixed expenses such as heating and utilities, expenses for curricular materials, salaries, and so forth. Now, the basic idea behind the whole first year's operation was this: that it was, first and foremost, fair and proper to get the school going, to put it into actual operation, and thereby to provide an actual model of what we were talking about. All other considerations of fairness were subsidiary to this one. The first year – and the first year only – was seen as the "pilot project" phase of operation, preparatory to future years, which would be seen as the "production", or regular, phase of operation.

This primary consideration had the following concrete consequences: (1) all staff personnel saw it as fair to work the year without any salary or recompense whatsoever; (2) the Greenbergs saw it as fair to assume the full financial responsibility for the school for the first year – signing the first mortgage and loaning all the money (some $40,000) necessary to cover the bills for the first year, over and above money coming in through tuition and some $2500 in contributions.

4.   Now consider the situation for next year. We are still not able to come up with a better criterion for a fair tuition than the prevailing public school average. However, we must bear in mind two things: (1) the projected average for 1969-1970 must be used, which is higher than the 1966-1967 figure; (2) outlays for capital expenditures in the public schools must be included, since our tuition income must cover the costs of our physical plant. Using this criterion, the tuition rate for 1969-1970 should be $950 per full-time student for the regular ten-month school session.

Let us look now at the expenses. All parties agree that the first call goes to making the first mortgage payments to the Framingham Trust Co. (about $5000 for the year). All parties likewise agree that the second call goes to paying fixed expenses of keeping the school going, physically. (These come to a bare minimum of about $23,000). Next, consider the position of the school's only creditors beside the bank, the Greenbergs: fairness certainly dictates that the $40,000 seed money they advanced to get the school going be returned and that an agreement be concluded between them and the school governing this return. It need hardly be added that the unique financial position of the Greenbergs in the school is out of line with the school's basic philosophy of co-responsibility of all members of the school community for the school's affairs. If this philosophy were fully implemented, the Greenbergs would be paid back immediately by joint effort of all corporation members, and thus the Greenbergs' exceptional financial stake in the school (and the exceptional leverage they hold as a result of this stake) would be forthwith eliminated. In the absence of such immediate action, an agreement has been drawn up by counsel for the school and counsel for the Greenbergs, on terms considered by all parties to be fair. The enclosed term sheet outlines this agreement, which will require detailed ratification by the Trustees, the School Assembly, and the Greenbergs before it takes effect this Spring.

Finally, and most important, consider the position of the Staff. On the one hand, if the school wished to pay fair salaries to the present staff, one would have to find a way to ascertain what "fair salaries" would be – and Staff and Assembly must come to mutual agreement on

the criteria for fairness. (This is, of course, the essence of the collective
bargaining process between employers and employees.) We have
not developed such criteria yet, and we shall certainly have to in the
near future. For the sake of discussion, however, say that we took the
"prevailing market value" of the present staff as a criterion for fairness:
if we did that, then the total fair salary budget would probably be in the
vicinity of $110,000.

5.   We are now ready to do some calculations, and reach some
conclusions.

Suppose, as a start, that we agreed on $950 as a fair tuition,
and instituted it. We would have no way of knowing how much our
total income is, until we knew how many students we would have for
next year. At most, the present plant can accommodate 170 students,
so that the highest income we could possibly have in this plant would
be $161,500. Realistically, we might expect far fewer than 170 students
(perhaps 100, perhaps 80, perhaps even fewer), and correspondingly less
income.

Suppose, next, that we decided to pay our fixed expenses and
first and second mortgage expenses. These can be expected to come to
about $38,000, according to the figures cited above. (If we did not pay
these expenses, of course, our very existence would be in jeopardy).

Next, we must see about staff salaries. If the school was full
(170 students), and if the estimate of $110,000 as a fair salary total was
correct, everything would come out just fine. On the other hand, it
is clear that the smaller number of students we in fact expect to have
cannot possibly bring the income required to generate fair salaries.

6.   Under the circumstances, the staff has arrived at the
following decisions for 1969-1970:

    a.   It endorses the tuition rate of $950 for 1969-1970 as a
            fair tuition rate.

    b.   It agrees to make every effort to live with this fair
            tuition rate; in particular, it agrees to make every effort
            to consider as fair recompense for next year whatever

falls to its lots from the income, after the first $38,000
has been used as outlined above.

c.   It will meet to review the situation in May, in light of
the student registration for 1969-1970. If at that time
the staff feels that the money available for salaries is not
adequate by any standard of fairness to them, it will ask
the President to call a Special Meeting of the School
Assembly in early June, and lay the problem before the
Assembly. Presumably, the options open to the Assembly
will be to agree to a tuition surcharge for 1969-1970,
or to raise the additional needed funds through
contributions, or to take more serious action concerning
the entire future of the school.

APPENDIX 6

Report on finances of the school (presented by the Secretary) and on the state of the school (presented by the Staff Chairman), made to the Assembly meeting on December 9, 1968

REPORT ON THE FINANCIAL STATE OF THE SCHOOL
(12/9/68)

We are not in a position to issue a detailed financial statement
tonight for two reasons. First, we have just now engaged Mr. Lambert of
Framingham [who is here this evening] as our accountant, and he is in
the process of setting up our bookkeeping system and preparing our first
financial statement. As soon as this is available, we will distribute it to all
members of the corporation. Second, the crisis the school has just been
through has of course had serious financial repercussions, and we still do
not have the exact figures to define our present financial position.

However, we do have all our books here this evening, and you are
all welcome to examine them. Also, after I have completed this brief
report, our treasurer, Dennis Flynn, will be happy to try to answer any
specific questions that you may have.

We have had to refund some $22,000 in fall tuition payments, and
we have lost roughly the same amount in projected income for the spring
semester.

Originally, the total projected income from tuition, fees, loans, and
contributions for the fiscal year ending June 30, 1969 was $103,000,
including summer and fall money received, and spring money
contracted for. This excludes the actual purchase price of the school
campus, which was $80,000.

After refunds and withdrawals, we are left with a total income,
projected and received, of about $60,000. We have spent about $45,000
of this so far.

It might be of interest to give some idea of the major expenses we
have had to date. Foremost among these are the costs for improving
the safety of the building, and making it not only meet but even
exceed the required safety standards. We have spent $3800 on a fire
detection system tied directly to the Framingham Fire Department and
approved by the New England Insurance Rating Association; $10,000
on remodeling, including a fire-proof boiler room, fire escapes, and fire
doors and exists; and $2800 to rebuild the dam on the pond to protect
us against the danger of a break during storms or floods. In addition,

we have made $4,000 in payments of the first mortgage, held by the Framingham Trust Company; $3600 in legal fees, to cover expenses in setting up the corporation, writing its unique by-laws, taking care of property transactions, and obtaining the tax exemption afforded a non-profit educational institution; $1800 to take care of losses arising from vandalism; $2100 to furnish the empty building we purchased; $1400 to install a new electrical service (the entire building had a total of 100 amps of service when it was bought – less than the average new private home has today!); $2700 to print 5000 catalogues – all of which have been distributed – and 3000 copies of "About the Sudbury Valley School"; and $5500 for instructional materials, of which some $2100 went to our excellent library.

Among our chief remaining expenses are $3000 in mortgage payments; $2300 in premiums for fire, theft, and comprehensive liability insurance; $2300 for heating oil, electricity, water, and phone; $1500 for maintenance contracts, including snow removal, tree care, and pest control; and $3000 for instructional materials.

We are left with about $15,000 available to us until June 30, 1969. Our best projections for now indicate that we will need an additional $4,500 income to meet our expenses.

During the past week, we received a pledge for an anonymous gift of $2,000, which means that our anticipated deficit is now $2,500, an amount that will somehow have to be raised by June.

MEETING OF ASSEMBLY – REPORT OF STAFF CHAIRMAN
(12/9/68)

Two main features of the school:
1. Individual's responsibility for his own private affairs – including learning. Staff is there to help when asked.
2. School community's responsibility for the internal affairs of the school, through School Meeting.

<u>On the first count</u>
1. School is now functioning as it had been conceived, and has been steadily progressing in this direction over last 4 weeks.
2. Many activities and classes going on – individual painting, group purchasing trips, antique hunting, math classes and individual instruction, music lessons and concerts, seminar on the school, production of a play (individuals typing the script and having each participant qualify for all parts), history classes, reading classes, literature, biology, and endless self-instruction and instruction between students.

   A word about classes relative to recent dispute: we were never against classes, but against a particular method of getting things started. ELABORATE
   The "classless" period was basically envisioned as a temporary transition period, to avoid having students fool themselves.
   <u>As a result</u>, when classes are held they are always seriously held, or they stop. This leads to a word about visiting teachers, and why despite our open door, this is a hard school to teach in as a visitor. [NOTE: we are looking for a Russian teacher] ELABORATE
3. Interesting initial observation, runs counter to expectation: children seem to start learning in hardest areas. EXPLAIN

<u>On second area</u>, school mtg:
1. Meeting has emerged from crisis as a much more serious force, and is now taking real steps towards governing the school: e.g., it is taking the problem of decorating the school and displaying serious art work out of the staff's hands.
2. The school meeting is moving toward a regularized procedure through a committee for internal discipline, which handles infractions of school rules by screening them, investigating them, and handling them over to school meeting at large where necessary. This is of course essential in a school where discipline is not a staff problem, but a

school meeting problem. In this respect, must note that trustees have ruled out expulsion or its consideration as proper topics for schl. mtg., but otherwise have reaffirmed their support of this agency as the internal govt. of the school

<u>Final notes</u>
1. School is still open to visitors, and has many every day.
2. Interest continues at a high level among educators and laymen. Visitors do not seem to interfere at all with school affairs as long as they do not come in massive groups.

APPENDIX 7

An open letter to the School Meeting on the administration
of justice in the school (December 1968)

AN OPEN LETTER TO MEMBERS OF THE SCHOOL
MEETING:

There are three elements to the administration of justice in the school: (1) <u>reports</u> of infractions; (2) <u>judgment</u> of alleged offenders; (3) <u>sentencing</u> of those adjudged guilty of an offense. These three elements apply in society at large as well as in the school.

The basic ethical assumption of the school is that <u>every person is capable of making ethical distinctions</u>, of distinguishing right from wrong. Again, the school in this respect does not differ from the rest of society, which holds every sane person responsible for his actions.

From this it follows that every person in the school can be held responsible for his own ethical behavior and is capable of making ethical judgments on the behavior of others. As I understand it, this is the foundation of our concept of the school meeting as a democratic organ of internal government. It is also at the root of the Judaeo-Christian concept of moral law, and the Anglo-Saxon tradition of common law, both of which lie at the base of American jurisprudence.

In intricate social systems, having a long history and a complex structure, the body of laws usually becomes complex. In such cases, specialists are required – lawyers and judges – who know the law and are trained in its interpretation. Specialists are usually <u>not</u> required in simple societies, and they probably will not be needed anywhere when computer programs will be available for the full cataloguing and cross-referencing of laws and decisions. Anyway, I do not foresee a time when The Sudbury Valley School will have such a complex system of rules that the school meeting membership will have to rely on specialists!

It therefore follows that the school meeting as a whole, and every member individually, can perform all three of the judicial functions mentioned in the first paragraph. I can see no alternative to this conclusion, unless we accept the prevalent view in educational circles that some people – for example, "teachers", or "administrators" – are especially suited to judge offenses in schools.

The only question I can see is: How are we in fact to carry out the three judicial functions? Until now, we have allowed the full school meeting to carry out all three steps. This has not produced a functioning, orderly rule of law and order in the school. Among the chief reasons for our failure to date are <u>the inefficiency of our reporting system</u> and <u>the absence of a sentencing system</u>. The school meeting has found itself in the past unable to ascertain the facts of a situation, and unable to decide punishments.

I believe that we must proceed <u>immediately</u> to the establishment of a school meeting subcommittee to prepare reports of infractions, and <u>immediately thereafter</u> to an orderly system of sentences. This should be complete and ready to function no later than upon our return from the new year vacation. Further delays simply mean setbacks in our attempt to create an atmosphere in which every individual's rights, and the group's rights, are respected at all times.

To this end I will propose, off the chair, the following motions at the school meeting on Monday, December 16:

(1) Unanimous consent to suspend the agenda and consider immediately
the school judicial system.

(2) Unanimous consent to withdraw all motions relating to the judicial
system. [Any motions or amendments can be presented in conjunction with (3) below, so there is no danger of cutting off discussion or of curtailing new ideas.]

(3) Consideration of the following motions, in order (explanatory notes are in square brackets);

I. To Establish a Committee on School Affairs [this committee is not the equivalent of a grand jury in society for several reasons: (a) It receives <u>all</u> complaints, while grand juries receive only criminal complaints: (b) It can, and doubtless will, often settle disputes between individuals without recourse to the school meeting. Many complaints arise more from personal conflicts than from offenses against the school community. In such cases, the committee can and should act as an arbitration board, and refer to the school meeting only instances where its efforts have failed; (c) It will not have subpoena powers, and should not, since these are in fact unenforceable in the school.]

A. <u>Purposes</u>
    a. To investigate alleged violations of school meeting resolutions.
    b. To report to the school meeting the results of its investigations.

B. <u>Membership</u>
    a. There shall be ten Committee members, picked by lot as follows: two from the 4-8 yr. age group; two from the 9-13 yr. age group; two from the 14-15 yr. age group; two from the 16-18 yr. age group; two from the staff. Lots shall be drawn by the Chairman of the School Meeting, who will be ineligible to serve on the Committee.
    b. The term of service of each member shall be two months, except as in article d below. [Membership entails hard work, and should not be imposed on anyone for more than two months at a stretch. This is the reason for part c as well.]
    c. No member shall serve two consecutive terms.
    d. Every month five members shall be chosen; except that for the first Committee, five members shall be chosen to two month terms and five members shall be chosen to three month terms.
    e. Any member of the Committee may be impeached by a two-thirds vote of the School Meeting, and the vacancy thereby created filled by lot from the appropriate age group.

C. <u>Procedures</u>
    a. The Committee will meet daily at 12:00 noon in the blackboard room, or at such other regular times and places as the Committee unanimously agrees upon and duly posts on the bulletin board.
    b. Special meetings of the Committee can be called by any two members for purposes clearly stated and at time and place stated in the call. Notice of a special meeting must be delivered orally or in writing to all members of the Committee in attendance on the day of the call.
    c. A quorum shall be five members.

d. Meetings of the Committee may be closed at the request of any complainant, any defendant, or at the request of a majority of the members of the Committee present and voting.

e. The Committee shall use whatever procedures it sees fit to carry out its investigations, provided that it abides at all times with the resolutions of the School Meeting.

f. The Committee shall receive complaints and decide by a majority vote whether to initiate an investigation.

g. The Committee shall report to the School Meeting the result of every investigation. The Committee shall decide for itself its method of presenting reports.

II. To Establish a System of Sentencing Persons Found Guilty of Violating School Regulations

A. For offenses consisting of the violation of school meeting resolutions, the following general order of sentencing will apply:

1. For a first offense, a vote of censure or condemnation by the School Meeting.

2. For a second or higher order offense, a form of reparation, to the school community or to an individual, for the offense committed may be imposed.

3. For a third or higher order offense, a form of deprivation may be imposed on the individual, such deprivation relating to the school's facilities and activities.

4. For a fourth or higher order offense, suspensions for lengths of time up to a week may be imposed.

5. For a fifth or higher order offense, the offender's case may be referred to the trustees for consideration.

B. In cases the School Meeting finds that a person has refused to abide by his sentence, that person may be judged by the School Meeting to be in contempt of the School Meeting, and any sentence up to and including referral to the trustees may be immediately imposed.

C. In all cases of suspension (or referral), a subcommittee of the School Meeting shall meet as soon as possible with the parents of the offender (or trustees), together with the offender, for a conference concerning the offenses and their consequences. This subcommittee shall consist of the Chairman of the School Meeting, the Chairman of the Staff, and a third member elected at the same time, in the same manner, and for the same term as the Chairman of the School Meeting.

[I believe that we cannot fairly impose <u>any</u> punishments unless we have a clear system whereby offenders are aware of the possible punitive consequences of an offense. This is, by the way, an accepted feature of the United States constitutional law.]

> (4) In case these motions, or their equivalents, are not passed by 3:00 PM on Monday, I will move recess until 12:30 PM on Tuesday, and so on, on successive days.

Dan Greenberg

APPENDIX 8

Draft proposal for extending the school beyond the high-school level, presented to the Trustees in June 1969

The Sudbury Valley School
Winch Street
Framingham, Mass. 01701

<u>Center for Postgraduate Studies</u>

1.	The Center for Postgraduate Studies provides people who have completed their high school training with an environment that makes further study and training possible. Through self-study, with such assistance as the staff can offer either directly or by means of apprenticeship programs, under conditions identical to these prevailing in the rest of the school, the Center gives enrolled students the opportunity to reach the highest levels of excellence to which they aspire, in any area they may choose. Students seeking to transfer from the Center to advanced standing in College, to Professional School, or to a University Graduate School, will be provided with whatever help the school can offer.

2.	As the Center grows, the school expects to apply to the Commonwealth of Massachusetts for the right to award degrees on the College and University level. We will seek to grant the various degrees on the basis of achievement in one or more areas of concentration chosen by the student, such achievement to be measured according to standards widely recognized among practitioners in the area concerned.

3.	The Center for Postgraduate Studies enrolls students in the same manner and under the same conditions as the rest of the school, except that students must have either a high school diploma or its equivalent prior to enrolling. Tuition is $2500 per student, and allows the student full use of the school's facilities at all times when the school is open during the academic year July 1-June 30. All costs of the student's education are included in this tuition, including travel expenses and tuition payments to other schools for courses and programs unavailable here.

4.   Students who have reached the age of 21 years by July 1 become members of the School Assembly beginning with the first succeeding Fall meeting of the corporation.